More praise for *360 Degrees of Influence*

"Influence isn't a straight, logical line; it's a crooked path through an audience's values and its perceptions of you. Harrison Monarth offers a GPS of influence, navigating the complex landscape of people's beliefs and expectations—whether your destination is a corner office or a happy relationship."

> **Jay Heinrichs, author of *Thank You for Arguing* and *Word Hero***

"Full of powerful ideas articulately expressed."

> **Chris St. Hilaire, author of 27 *Powers of Persuasion***

"Harrison Monarth walks his talk yet again with savvy, stories, and sincerity. *360 Degrees of Influence* is well-researched and informative."

> **Nicholas Boothman, author of *Convince Them in 90 Seconds or Less***

"Harrison Monarth will teach you many lessons of influence, from careful listening to skillful framing. And as you read his book, you'll find yourself thinking about how to use your influence to help others, as well as yourself."

> **Meir Statman, Ph.D., Glenn Klimek, professor of Finance, Santa Clara University, author of *What Investors Really Want***

"Intentionally increasing your impact is a complex task. Harrison Monarth has clarified the factors that affect your ability to influence: how people form and maintain beliefs, types of resistance and how to handle them, as well as strategies for getting the results you desire. A well-researched and insightful book and a *great read*."

> **Shelle Rose Charvet, author of the international bestseller *Words That Change Minds: Mastering the Language of Influence***

"None of the classic definitions of man from 'symbol-using' to 'rational' animal really capture our essence specifically as well as Harrison Monarth's seeing man as the animal who influences. In *360 Degrees of Influence*, Monarth sees human beings' omnipresent desire to engage in influencing behavior as all-consuming, whether conscious or not. Learning how to do it well can affect practically every human activity, from business success to dealing with bullies. For those of us in the persuasion game, this is a bite of the apple of the definitive human activity that few writers can consume as well as Harrison Monarth."

Richard E. Vatz, Ph.D., professor, Towson University, author of *The Only Persuasive Book of Persuasion*

"Have you ever wished for x-ray vision or the ability to fly? In *360 Degrees of Influence*, Monarth endows us with superpowers far more powerful than those! Step aside, Batman! No longer limited to the sphere of superheroes and CEOs, the extraordinary power of influence is now within everyone's reach. Recent graduates, executive assistants, project managers, and business leaders can all benefit from Monarth's simple steps for 'getting everyone to follow your lead.'"

Marshall Goldsmith, author of the *New York Times* bestsellers, *MOJO* and *What Got You Here Won't Get You There*

"Harrison Monarth's book stands out for its practical and comprehensive coverage of the important topic of influence at work. With useful guidelines on everything from how to most effectively present your ideas to how to manage your boss, Monarth's monograph is must reading for those who need to build their personal brand and sell themselves—which is, of course, everybody."

Jeffrey Pfeffer, Ph.D., professor, Stanford Graduate School of Business, author of *Power: Why Some People Have It—and Others Don't*

"Your ability to influence and persuade others is the single most important skill for success in business and leadership—and this book shows you *how* with simple, powerful, practical, and proven techniques."

Brian Tracy, author of *Full Engagement*

"*360 Degrees of Influence* is going to be one of the year's most sought-after books. Showing you how to persuade others, both smart and pragmatic, Monarth synthesizes cutting-edge science with what happens outside of the laboratory, in the real world. Every influencer needs this book."

Kevin Hogan, Psy.D., author of *The Science of Influence:
How to Get Anyone to Say "Yes" in 8 Minutes or Less*

"Finally! A book about influence that doesn't tell you how to impose your position on others but rather illuminates ways to build authentic relationships that are mutually beneficial. Truly a 21st-century approach to a critical skill."

Lois P. Frankel, Ph.D., author of
Nice Girls Don't Get the Corner Office and
Nice Girls Just Don't Get It

"*360 Degrees of Influence* breaks new ground. Harrison Monarth writes with flair, passion, and insight. Even seasoned professionals will find his advice practical and invaluable."

Harry Mills, managing director of The Mills Group,
author of *Artful Persuasion* and
The StreetSmart Negotiator

360 Degrees

of

Influence

GET EVERYONE TO FOLLOW YOUR LEAD
ON YOUR WAY TO THE TOP

HARRISON MONARTH

New York   Chicago   San Francisco   Lisbon   London   Madrid   Mexico City
Milan   New Delhi   San Juan   Seoul   Singapore   Sydney   Toronto

The **McGraw·Hill** Companies

1 2 3 4 5 6 7 8 9 10 11 12 13 14 15 16 17   QFR/QFR   1 9 8 7 6 5 4 3 2 1

ISBN   978-0-07-177355-3
MHID   0-07-177355-X

e-ISBN 978-0-07-177389-8
e-MHID   0-07-177389-4

This publication is designed to provide accurate and authoritative information in regard to the subject matter covered. It is sold with the understanding that neither the author nor the publisher is engaged in rendering legal, accounting, securities trading, or other professional services. If legal advice or other expert assistance is required, the services of a competent professional person should be sought.

> —*From a Declaration of Principles Jointly Adopted by a Committee of the American Bar Association and a Committee of Publishers and Associations*

Library of Congress Cataloging-in-Publication Data

Monarth, Harrison.
    360 degrees of influence : get everyone to follow your lead on your way to the top / by Harrison Monarth.
        p.   cm.
    ISBN-13: 978-0-07-177355-3 (alk. paper)
    ISBN-10: 0-07-177355-X (alk. paper)
    1. Influence (Psychology)   2. Leadership.   3. Persuasion (Psychology).
I. Title.   II. Title: Three hundred sixty degrees of influence.

BF774.M66   2012
158′4—dc23   2011029213

McGraw-Hill books are available at special quantity discounts to use as premiums and sales promotions or for use in corporate training programs. To contact a representative, please e-mail us at bulksales@mcgraw-hill.com.

This book is printed on acid-free paper.

With love, to my mother,
Roswitha Krems

CONTENTS

Preface   xiii

Acknowledgments   xvii

CHAPTER 1 Swayed, Nudged, and Driven: Influence Is Constant   1

CHAPTER 2 360-Degree Influence Starts with You   25

CHAPTER 3 Breaking Through Resistance: The Major Barriers to Influencing Others   43

CHAPTER 4 Know What Really Motivates People *and* What People Really Care About   59

CHAPTER 5 How Our Decisions Define Our Ability to Influence   73

CHAPTER 6 Setting the Stage: Strategically Influencing People's Decisions   99

CHAPTER 7 Mastering Organizational Politics   119

CHAPTER 8 Influencing Up: Bring Your Bosses Around to Your Way of Thinking   139

CHAPTER 9 Influencing the Opposite Gender for Mutual Success   155

CHAPTER 10 Influencing the Public's Impressions of Your Organization   173

CHAPTER 11 Using Your Words to Influence and Change Minds   195

CHAPTER 12 Managing the Influencing Power of Your
Personal Brand 225

Notes 247

Index 271

PREFACE

Ask anyone what superpowers he or she would want to have—given that were possible—and odds are you won't have to wait long for an answer. The ability to read minds, X-ray vision, lightning speed, or the ability to fly might be some of the responses you'll get.

Ever since Superman was created in 1938, people all over the world have indulged in their fascination with *superheroes*—the term alone produces more than seven million search results on Google—whose images and adventures have anchored themselves in the consciousness of modern society and popular culture. Indeed, hardly a summer passes by without a Batman, Spider-Man, or Iron Man coming to life on the big screen to attract billions of moviegoers across the globe. And it doesn't take Jay Leno to suggest that most people can name five fictional superheroes faster than they can five of the president's cabinet members.

Psychologists have ready explanations for this phenomenon. From our desire for the power to change our world and circumstances to the clear moral codes and specific values of truth and justice the costumed hero stands for and with which we can strongly identify, it all makes sense. Alas, the dream is out of reach for us mortals no matter how many radioactive spiders sink their fangs into our flesh. None of us will turn into Spider-Man.

Yet there is a kind of superpower that beats the combination of all those that the famous caped crusaders might offer, and it's a power anyone can acquire. Practiced by an elite percentage of skilled communicators and with no shortage of "mind reading" involved to understand the needs and beliefs of others going into an exchange, this particular superpower becomes accessible to all who seek to understand and wield this power for themselves.

I speak of the power to influence and change minds whenever we need to, the ability to shape opinions and bring skeptics around to our way of thinking—the holy grail of careers and relationships. Once we have mastered it, we require no leverage to convince others to see things the way we do, we read minds with what social scientists call empathic accuracy, or we learn what others are thinking so we can reach them on a deeper level and successfully pitch our case. This perfectly human power is seated in empathy, the understanding of human needs and goals, and a talent for speaking an empathetic language at the moment when it counts.

While few of us fight supervillains in the course of our work, many of us grew up dealing with bullies—sometimes within our own families—and now, properly degreed and suited, we engage them from the office cubicle to the highest level of upper management. While none of us has the ability to infiltrate minds and control behavior, the power of knowing how others make decisions and lean toward choices can help us influence connected behaviors for mutual good. And while none of us can travel at lightning speed, a powerful influence that emanates from the decisions and choices we make, to the way we communicate and present ourselves, can travel the globe via multimedia while we're asleep, and make others choose our offering.

To be sure, it is no longer enough merely to know a few helpful tricks that will gain you faster access to a photocopier when there's a line waiting for it. Nor is it particularly helpful for you to read about how a certain strategy got an African village of mothers to provide better nutrition for their newborns. Rather, in this book you'll learn how to use the superpowers of influence and presence for the myriad of real-life situations you face each day; when you've practiced and mastered these powers, you may determine your career trajectory and business success. From the ability to negotiate the daily gauntlet of organizational politics, to strategies for making a successful case in a key meeting with senior management, to the ability to craft a narrative that resonates deeply with a key customer, this text will engage you on a personal level with insights into the dynamics of influence you may never have comprehended yet are subjected to on a daily basis. As far as superpowers go, these are far superior and infinitely more useful than being able to leap tall buildings or shoot bolts of energy from your eyeballs.

I sincerely hope that you can find inspiration in these pages, no matter what your profession or background. Influence is a natural human drive, and the ability to achieve it is now in your hands.

ACKNOWLEDGMENTS

My gratitude belongs to Rita Rosenkranz, the most thoughtful and skilled agent an author could ask for. Her high standards paved the way for this book. Much thanks also goes to my longtime senior editor at McGraw-Hill, Donya Dickerson, whose encouragement and enthusiasm helped bring this new book about. I also owe thanks to editors Joe Berkowitz and Nancy Hall, who made sure my writing is as good as it can be.

Thanks to my wonderful colleagues and associates who have contributed research and ideas to this book—among them, Terri Peterson, Ph.D.; Larry Brooks; Joe Walsh; Heather Iarusso, and many others from academia, business, and the professions.

I am grateful to my wife, who is endlessly patient and loving, and to my good friends, who provide the perfect balance to the pressures of multiple deadlines and hectic travel schedules.

Finally, I want to say a heartfelt thank you to the colleagues, experts, and fellow authors who thought well enough of this book to give it their generous endorsements. You see their names and comments on the back cover and in the front of this book. I am indebted to you for your graciousness.

CHAPTER 1

Swayed, Nudged, and Driven: Influence Is Constant

A New Zealand bank helpfully nudges customers to save money on impulse by just pressing a button on their iPhone. Apparently there is an app for that.

School cafeterias across the United States are experimenting with the presentation of healthier food choices—making fruit and vegetables more appealing than the more popular fried food by improving their lighting, positioning, and names (carrots called "X-ray veggies," anyone?)

New York taxicabs have a touchscreen on the back of the front seat suggesting how much passengers should tip the driver upon arriving at a destination. Big, colorful buttons give the option of paying $2, $3, or $4 if the fare is less than $15. If your fare is more than $15, the buttons display percentages from 20 to 25 to 30 percent. Clearly counting on people's laziness or inability to calculate and self-select a fair tip, cabbies are happy to report that gratuities have shot way up, again due in part to these highly suggestive buttons that are tilted toward generosity.

We face tens of thousands of minor and major interactions every day that guide or steer us in one direction or another. While all this

1

influencing and nudging is perhaps becoming more obvious as we get older, it's been a factor from the moment we released our first gut-wrenching screams upon entering this life.

We Are Born to Influence

These days, it's impossible to walk down the street without experiencing the power of influence. Even if the street is completely empty, beckonings, warnings, sales pitches, and opinions fill every conceivable angle of our vision. This exposure to influence begins with our earliest sense of self, at the moment we acknowledge we are not alone and experience desire in some form. For most of us, this begins at birth.

With that first infantile desire emerges a natural instinct as to how to obtain what we want. We cry, we wail, and we adopt this technique long before we learn that we can also get what we want by smiling and laughing. Infants are not able to rationalize, prioritize, or otherwise communicate outside of their own desires, yet they get what they want by opening their cute little mouths and letting it rip.

Just as instinctual is the parental need to notice and respond from a context of providing care and/or learning. The need to nurture is as hardwired as the baby's wailing and brings the earliest hint of nature's intention for us to exert and perceive a full circle of lifelong influence. According to a 1968 study on this interaction, this parent-child exchange is precisely the stuff of attachment, even love. Children and parents begin their journey together through a dance of influence and response, played out on a stage of interaction. From the first frame, verbal and nonverbal clues fill the family room and quickly define a dynamic that will set the tone for an entire childhood.

This first taste of the power of influence begins a process of developing and understanding our inherent powers in that regard.

While social and domestic variables conspire to take this ability to different places and levels, the universal fact is that it is there within us, always available as a power to be reckoned with. Whether that power emerges as harnessing influence to get what we want or succumbing to it and becoming helpless against the desires of others remains an issue not so much of fate as of comprehension.

In other words, some get it and some don't.

A Never-Ending Battle for Rewards and Resources

As natural as it is for us to exert and respond to influence, it is a testament to the power of influence that it takes on so many forms and levels among adults. The constant battle for rewards and the pressures of competition for resources are woven into the fabric of any organization that's populated with goal-oriented professionals. They're a virtual petri dish of human psychology that elevates influence to nothing short of the currency of success.

In trying to cash in this currency, people sometimes overstep ethical and legal boundaries. A recent explosive article in *Rolling Stone* magazine detailed how the U.S. Army may have misused some of its "psychological operations" specialists (or PSYOPs, as they're commonly known) to influence U.S. senators who stopped by for visits. These specialists usually train their sights on hostile foreign organizations and individuals to manipulate various beliefs, value systems, and emotions for strategic gains in conflict situations and territories. In this case, however, the magazine's writer reported that PSYOPs targeted U.S. lawmakers making an appearance in the field, in a calculated effort to sway them toward sanctioning additional troops and other resources. Scandal ensued.

Competition for resources is intrinsic to the evolution of any surviving species, and the ability to adapt it to the prevailing environment has, for the majority of life on earth, defined who lives and who dies. In the human realm, competition is the fuel of pretty much all that is political, economic, and relational. We compete for votes; we vie for jobs and money; we battle for market share; we score the best talent; we strive for prestige, badges of honor, and achievement; and on a global level, we wage war for power, advantage, and the promulgation of our belief systems. The urge to influence is as old as recorded history, and thus it comprises the very essence of human dynamics and evolution.

Winning the Battle with Influence

Whether by carrot or stick or any of the more nuanced forms of influence along the spectrum, everything we desire, negotiate, measure, and reward is the product of our ability to exert influence successfully. As our species has evolved, our brains have literally grown larger, actually tripling in size over the past two million years, according to a study by David Geary, professor of psychological studies at the University of Missouri College of Arts and Science. Natural selection drove this evolution as the complexity of needs became more, well, complex over the centuries. This phenomenon among humans is precisely due to the natural instinct to compete for rewards, because humans do it in a more socially complex and environmentally varied manner than other species, whose brains are largely the same size as they were when giant reptiles roamed the planet. The fastest lion eats; the slowest gazelle gets eaten. But with us, economic and social survival is a much more complex and delicate proposition.

With all our available intellectual square footage, two thousand millennia of evolution, and more rewards than ever up for grabs, our heightened interest in mastering the art of influence is more than understandable. Those who have mastered it are the ones in the corner offices, while the rest of us have to some degree clung to those first pangs of need expressed through crying out and smiling in the hope of getting something in return. That's because, while instinctual, exerting influence at the level at which it becomes

4

effective in a complex economy and culture is as much a learned psychological art as it is a gift of gab.

Our Values Are Targets for Influence

To truly understand the power of influence, one needs to grasp the context from which it springs. According to Shalom H. Schwartz, Ph.D., of the Hebrew University of Jerusalem, *values* are the result of belief systems linked to emotions, and thus they are a strong motivating factor in our daily decision making. These values define the sweet spot for intended influence, because the ultimate goal is to point the decision making of others to the destination of our choice.

According to Dr. Schwartz, our motivations are colored by 10 distinct beliefs that do not distinguish between where we live or who we are in terms of worldview:

1. **Self-direction:** The ability to choose; act on preference; and create, discover, and explore options
2. **Stimulation:** The experience of energy, excitement, and challenge
3. **Hedonism:** Gratification achieved through maximizing pleasure
4. **Achievement:** The channeling of competence toward specific goals that are socially accepted or elicit approval
5. **Power:** Dominance or control, often imbued with prestige and status
6. **Security:** A sense of safety and stability relative to our relationships and ourselves
7. **Conformity:** The avoidance of responses and actions with negative consequences or the risk of disapproval, demonstrated through restraint and denial

8. **Tradition:** Conformity with customs and practices defined by religion, culture, or long-held belief systems that elicit respect and acceptance
9. **Benevolence:** The furtherance of others' well-being, especially those with whom we have personal relationships
10. **Universalism:** A respect and caring for all aspects of nature and other people through appreciation, tolerance, and understanding

The depth of this analysis subordinates the very things that make influence in today's world more challenging than ever: the astounding breadth of human experience and modes of socialization. Never before have we faced this many options with this level of competition for rewards. The scope of potential influence is unprecedented; so much so that we may find it hard to link our desires to our values, at least until we begin to question our motivations and self-knowledge. Self-reflection rather than basic instinct is the basis of an evolved self in an evolved culture, and the art of influence is the beneficiary of this process. Our efforts to change or even sway someone's mind are hindered if we don't comprehend the motivations of our audience or opposition.

Effective influence counts on our understanding of why people resist change even when an idea or opportunity serves their interests. Influence isn't as much about packaging truths for others as it is about presenting those truths in such a way that others think *they* have realized and discovered the ideas for themselves rather than hearing them from us. Among the many factors at the core of resistance is the myriad of belief systems and values that divide our culture into so many subsets and isolated silos of like-minded people. These systems are so powerful that they can conquer logic and evidence, which is why some extremists blow themselves up in the name of their beliefs. This is as true within organizations— and *for* organizations—as it is in any other subgroup. A culture is a hard thing to change and an even harder thing to influence if your intention departs from accepted and well-understood norms.

As leaders, we need to anticipate what it takes to effect change and thus how to shape our efforts to exert influence. A number of esteemed scholars have aligned behind seven basic phases of the cycle of change that influencers need to consider when mounting an effort to move an audience off the status quo. This sequence is as follows:

1. **Business as usual:** The same-as-it-ever-was modality, a frozen state
2. **External threat:** The potential for loss; impending disaster; an ending of sorts; a shift via the introduction of a new element
3. **Denial:** A simple refusal to look at evidence, consider probabilities, and face the truth
4. **Mourning:** The dark and confusing state of letting go of what was
5. **Acceptance:** The final letting go of the past with an open mind to what comes next
6. **Renewal:** The discovery of new realizations, the thrill of new beginnings and forward movement, the sense of vision morphing into reality, the fruition of hope
7. **New structure:** The new becoming the status quo with a sense of stability and permanence

Attached to this values-anchored resistance to change is the presence of emotional inertia, or the simple lack of the energy required to do things differently. Influence is the energy that trumps inertia and whatever subtextual commitment defies the logic of a better path. What appears to be resistance may simply be two opposing emotional forces battling it out. Influential leaders find a way to discover and understand what these conflicting beliefs and forces are.

Employees who demonstrate repeated self-defeating behavior are examples of competing belief systems rather than overt opposition. Take the example of a young man who, in his free time, plays in a rock band and remains close and integral to the social group that embraces him in that area of his life. On the job, he demonstrates good work habits, is well liked and trouble-free, and consistently performs at a level that meets and often exceeds expectations. But he has been passed over for promotion in favor of seemingly lesser performers—it may have something to do with his bloodshot eyes from late-night rehearsals and a sometimes-visible neck tattoo; his performance reviews note that he doesn't quite fit in with the corporate culture and needs to work on integrating with the team. Given time and access, a psychologist might discover that this fellow is having trouble letting go of his underlying identity as a rebel and resists turning into just another one of the "suits" at the office, despite sharing their work ethic and their professional goals. There is potential for reconciliation at both ends of this dynamic, however, if the employee learns of and is given the opportunity to manage his apparent bias against prevailing corporate culture and understand the organization's bias for cultural conformity; the organization itself benefits from self-reflecting stakeholders and leaders who discover that by loosening up their archetypical prototype candidate profile, their influence leads to better forward-looking choices, unencumbered by hidden layers of skewed belief and prejudicial thinking.

A Closer Look at Our "Irrational" Behaviors

While it is perhaps paradoxical, many of us tend to think we know where inexplicable behaviors and belief systems come from. The closer they are to home, the more we think we understand, and as it turns out, it is less likely that we do. That's because an entire grad school year of human psychology could hardly account for what motivates us to act on or resist incoming influence. Again, effective influencers understand this level of complexity and use it to break down barriers more quickly and completely.

The presence of a psychological factor sometimes imbues irrationality with legitimacy. Take, for example, someone who has trouble remembering things. Without acknowledging that anything may be wrong, we assign this behavior to being scatterbrained, overloaded, or unfocused. But the moment we know for certain that a chemical imbalance is in play, the memory issue switches context to something that explains the behavior and elicits a different, more tolerant response. It also provides an opportunity to improve it.

Supposedly rational behavior in modern economic culture stems from decisions and actions that serve the interests and rewards of the decider. But there are ample examples of people who do the exact opposite of what's expected; they resist that which might help them and adopt beliefs and demonstrate behaviors that inevitably come back to bite them in some way. Almost as if this were their intention from square one. Are they masochists in full command of their path, or does something else—an issue of psychological imbalance or neurochemistry—take over at the moment of decision?

The answer is that it could be either or neither. In the growing field of behavioral economics, leading researchers such as Daniel Kahneman, Amos Tversky, Richard Thaler, and *Predictably Irrational* author Dan Ariely have sufficiently debunked the notion that humans are rational at all. Instead of rationality, the effective influencer looks for cues to determine the most likely causal factor for a person's "irrationality" and goes from there.

Sometimes the human voice of unreason that stands in the way of positive decision making is social rather than biochemical. We have to look no further than the community of extremist martyrs to recognize this. Are they all mentally ill? Chemically imbalanced? Or have they been conditioned and programmed to such an extent that their neural pathways run in a direction that aligns with their belief systems and trumps their sense of self and any resident fear? Almost certainly this is the case, and it completely frames the context of any attempt to rationalize with or influence such people.

Whether biological, chemical, or social, if our beliefs are "irrational," so too will be our behaviors. Our brains dictate our choices before they are even on the table, according to a study conducted at the University of Minnesota. A widely cited example is what researchers call the *gambler's fallacy*, which posits that when gamblers believe there is an emerging pattern in an otherwise random deck of cards, they play according to self-proclaimed probability. They believe they're "hot" and will continue to win.

Maybe they will, maybe not. But it's one of the reasons why "the house always wins." Gamblers who see a pattern where randomness is the only thing controlling the cards will follow that pattern right into bankruptcy.

For the more "rational" heads among us, that may be an offbeat example. Everyone knows that gamblers have a problem— one which thankfully doesn't affect you and me. Right?

If you believe that, a quick mental trip to the stock market should sober you up.

Irrationality in the Stock Market

After the economic crash of 2008, behavioral finance was once again a hot topic in the debate about what went wrong. The early research of Amos Tversky and Daniel Kahneman offered some answers. They called it *prospect theory*. Specifically, they learned that investors—all humans really—value gains and losses differently. When it comes to potential losses, our panic may be disproportionately greater than the pleasure we take in the prospect of potential gains. In a nutshell, the idea of losing $100 hits us twice as hard as the idea of gaining $100. In this context, the scholars also discovered that investors—and the rest of us—are much more open to risk to avoid any losses than we are to capture potential gains.

Leavey School of Business's Meir Statman, an expert in behavioral finance, says that people actually grieve after having made bad decisions, including financial ones. For most people, facing the prospect of selling a particular stock is anything but a rational search for clues; rather, it is an emotional exercise tightly connected to the difference in how much we paid for the stock versus how much we can get for it now.

Statman, who studied the cognitive errors and emotions that can influence investor behavior, has a couple of theories:

○ Investors hang on to falling stocks to avoid the painful realization of having made a mistake if they sell it.
○ People are worried about others' judgment in disclosing losses incurred by bad investments, delaying any decision to cut their losses.

Others in the behavioral economics field posit that crowd thinking guides investors' behavior, as it is thought to be safer to follow the crowd—they must know better—than to rely on our own decision making. The result of this is crushingly obvious when a "herd" of investors panics, and everyone sells their shares at once, each spurred on by the behavior of the others.

Another sign of our follow-the-herd behavior crystallizes when hyped-up investors flock to buy an overpriced but highly popular stock, demonstrating the opposite of the rational investment mantra "buy low, sell high." When the stock eventually goes down, investors can rationalize their poor decisions more easily by faulting the herd for the hyperbolic stampede rather than blaming themselves.

Let's look at some other scenarios where we're influenced day in and day out.

Eleven Ways You're Being Influenced Right Now

Don't look now, but you're sitting or standing under a frenzied barrage of high-frequency influence. It is like radio waves from television broadcasts, mobile phones, wireless devices, and spy satellites—they're everywhere, omnipresent, to the extent that we no longer notice. Yet they define our daily lives and provide the means by which we weigh and make choices. So it is with the forces of influence—many of which are born on those very radio waves—that bombard us at every waking moment.

The most obvious inbound influence is, of course, advertising. But not your father's advertising from "All in the Family." Today's advertisers use neuroscience-based techniques straight out of sci-fi movies to hit all the senses and begin the salivation process before you can change the channel. America's favorite fried chicken haunt, KFC, actually enlists aroma dispensers (fried chicken will get you every time) from lunch delivery carts while making deliveries in office parks. According to the company's CEO, this works better than advertising in attracting customers. I believe it, having once advised the owners of an artisan ice-cream shop in Denver to funnel the smell of fresh-baked waffle cones to the shop's surrounding pedestrian areas via a simple piping system. Customers started arriving for a cool treat on cue, like moths to a flame.

Companies spend billions of dollars a year trying to get us to buy their products. In 2009, *Advertising Age* estimated that Procter & Gamble spent $8.68 billion, making it the number-one advertiser in the world. With the development of the relatively new science branch called *neuromarketing*, companies have ratcheted up their persuasive tactics by targeting all of our senses to affect our brain and get us to buy. Here are some examples.

1. Us Versus Them

Apple's brand capitalizes on our brain's natural tendency to want to belong to one group over another. This is what social psychologists call *social identity*: how we value being part of a group, and why and how we identify with people who share similar interests. Apple's ad campaigns over the years, such as the Mac Guy versus the PC Guy, group people into two categories, cool and hip versus dopey and unpopular, without otherwise mentioning any features or product benefits. Mercedes Benz versus Toyota's Prius is another example of marketing geared toward triggering the "need-to-belong" neurons. The former appeals to those who value status and prestige; the Prius campaigns on the other hand tap into their customers' desire to practice environmental responsibility and, perhaps, exhibit under-stated elegance.

2. Feedback Timing

Another form of influence is the phenomenon of asking for, giving, and receiving *feedback*. Studies prove that when feedback is imminent (such as test scores that show up immediately), fear of failure and disappointment is at its highest. Because of this fear, feedback that's just around the corner promotes greater performance and effort. A Canadian study showed that exam scores were 22 percent higher when those being tested knew they were to be graded and evaluated immediately upon completion as opposed to waiting until later for their scores. This becomes a sort of velvet hammer for the influencer, who can leverage the proximity of feedback in her presentation of messages and options.

3. "Enlightning" Influence

One German study proved that the type of background lighting in a room where people are tasting wine favorably influences their perception of the wine's taste and increases their willingness to pay more for it. Red and blue ambient lighting, as opposed to white or green, encouraged tasters of white wine to perceive the wine as sweeter, fruitier, and more expensive. For restaurant owners and others responsible for colors and lighting in a commercial space, the influence of these aspects on the subjective value of a product is something to be considered.

4. No Girlie Men

Cornell researchers conducted a study involving two groups of men in which they pretended to analyze the masculinity of the participants. They fictitiously characterized the men in one of the groups as having weak masculine traits. That group subsequently overcompensated for their perceived lack of manliness and displayed more homophobic tendencies, voiced strong support for the Iraq war, and favored SUVs over other vehicles.

5. Survival of the Prettiest

Voters evaluate the competence of a candidate by his facial appearance. Princeton University research found that those voters most likely to be influenced by appearances are those who watch TV and are less knowledgeable. By manipulating computer models of faces to reflect degrees of competence, the researchers determined that "facial maturity and physical attractiveness" were the main features that made voters perceive a candidate as competent.

6. David 0, Goliath 1

Think the underdog has more motivation to win in an unequal pairing of strength and skill? It's the story we love in the movies. Apparently, it's more of a myth. A recent study found that team members work harder when they're competing against another group that is of lower status or skill than when they're competing against a team of equals. Social psychologists at Ohio State and Cornell universities say their studies contradict the popular notion

14

that underdogs are more highly motivated when they're competing against a higher status group. Robert Lount, coauthor of the study and assistant professor of management and human resources at Ohio State University's Fisher College of Business, said, "We found over and over again, across multiple studies, that people worked about 30 percent harder when their group was competing against a lower-status group. It seems surprising to many people that the high-status team has more motivation, but it really makes sense. The higher-ranked group has more to lose if they don't compare well against a lower-status group. But if you're the lower-status group and lose to your superior rival, nothing has changed—it just reaffirms the way things are."

7. Quick Judge of Character

If the eyes are the window to the soul, then the face is a potential glimpse at a most-wanted poster. New findings published in *Psychological Science* posit that a quick glance at someone's face might be all we need to predict that person's proclivity for anger. Psychologists from Brock University asked volunteers to take a glimpse at photographs of men and then rate how aggressive they were. These were photographs of men whose aggressive tendencies had already been assessed in the lab. Each volunteer stared at the photos for either 2,000 milliseconds or 39 milliseconds. The volunteers' estimation of aggressiveness was fairly accurate. Interestingly, their evaluations also correlated with the one facial feature that prior research had established was an indication of aggressive behavior: the width between the subject's left and right cheeks and the distance from the upper to the midbrow. This is called *facial width-to-height ratio*, and the larger it is, the more aggressive the man tends to be. This suggests that we're influenced by this facial feature, and it might affect our judgment of and interactions with people. The lesson for influencers? Keep your expressions warm, or at least avoid the dreaded furrowed brow, which may not be perceived as threatening but could easily be mistaken for judgment. Both are deal killers.

8. Tactile Tactics

Asking for a raise? Buying a car? Sit in a hard chair. A recent study by several universities discovered that people who sat in hard chairs were tougher negotiators, less flexible and moved less during negotiations. They also perceived the person they were negotiating with as more stable and less emotional. "First impressions are liable to be influenced by the tactile environment, and control over this environment may be especially important for negotiators, pollsters, job seekers, and others interested in interpersonal communication," the authors write in *Science* magazine. "The use of 'tactile tactics' may represent a new frontier in social influence and communication."

9. Heavyweight Champion

The same study aimed to evaluate weight as it relates metaphorically to "seriousness and importance." Participants in the study played recruiters and were given résumés to assess; the papers were attached to either a light or a heavier clipboard. Those participants who viewed résumés attached to a heavier clipboard judged the candidates to be more qualified and serious. In addition, the evaluators gave themselves higher marks for accuracy when holding a heavy clipboard versus a light one.

10. Closing in on Emotional Distance

The next time someone tells you, "I just need some space," you'll know the emotional implications this can have on your relationship. Two Yale University psychologists tested to see if an open, orderly space affects people's emotions differently than a cluttered, closed-in space. (These are the same principles as those of feng shui.) The researchers had subjects draw lines on a graph that primed them to feel either "spatial distance" or "spatial closeness." Here are their results in a nutshell:

Compared to those who were conditioned (primed) for spatial closeness, those who were conditioned for spatial distance via the simple graph exercise were more distant in their emotional reactions to media depictions of embarrassment—meaning they felt more free to enjoy it—and also felt less distressed by fictional depictions of violence. The researchers were somewhat surprised to learn that this simple priming technique also prompted participants to report feeling less of an emotional attachment to family and their hometowns, showing the effect that conditioning for distance can have on our emotions.

11. Primed for Influence

Finally, bringing the way we're influenced full circle, remember the earlier example about investors' irrational decision making when it comes to the stock market? One study found that reading newspaper articles about irrelevant matters involving risk affects people's financial decisions. Researchers at the University of Haifa gave Group A a story about taking risks and reaping large profits and Group B a story about someone who didn't take a risk and avoided significant losses. Both groups were told they were reading the stories to test their memory recall. Both were then given identical information about an unidentified NASDAQ stock. The result? Group A, which had read the story involving successful risk taking, credited the stock with a higher value than did Group B.

Doron Kliger, Ph.D., who carried out the study along with one of his students, commented, "The findings of this research show that risk preferences may be manipulated—while the person making those decisions is unaware of it. An investment advisor

17

who reads reports in the morning news that 'encourage' risk taking might behave entirely differently, on a professional level, than if reading reports on failed risk taking—even if the reports were unrelated to the question at stake. Psychology describes varying human behavior depending on numerous factors. It should not be assumed that financial decision makers are immune to such influences."

The bottom line in all of this is that 360-degree influencers have a bulging tool chest of techniques and psychological instruments at their disposal, without needing a Ph.D. after their name. It's more than charisma or the gift of gab; it's knowledge and strategy that separates professional leaders from those who are better suited to be contributors. Both are critical to the success of any organization and business, but you're reading this book to become the former and to guide the latter to success via your ability to influence in all directions.

Who We Are Makes a Difference in How We Influence

Speaking of the gift of gab, and somewhat contrary to popular opinion, being a trained orator and practiced debater isn't a key requirement to becoming an effective influencer. Research has shown, however, that certain demographics and traits do spawn better influencers.

Women have traditionally proved to be more democratic leaders, who encourage collaboration and involvement at all levels of a team. They also tend to show a more transformational style of leadership (that is, the grooming and growth of subordinates), making them more effective mentors.

On the other side of this politically sensitive coin, women are less likely to adopt aggressive styles when necessary and thus have a narrower field of options when in influencing mode. One study showed that a male presenter has a six times greater likelihood of getting buy-in than a woman presenting the same information. Although unfair, this is great information for female leaders to exploit strategically; they can put a trusted male messenger in front of a group for quicker acceptance of a message. Strategy and psychology beat ego every time when important business goals are at stake.

Some leaders—and this applies equally to both genders—are self-serving in their leadership style to the point of narcissism (which in turn defines their influencing style), putting them in the *bully* category where subordinates and some peers are concerned. Jim Moran, a professor of management at the Florida State University College of Business, found that nearly a third of people polled said their boss was likely to exaggerate accomplishments so he would look good. A little more than a quarter said their boss was a braggart and praise junkie; had an inflated, unrealistic self-image, was self-centered; and, to a slightly lesser extent, did favors only when there was a promise of getting something in return. Unless you own the place, this career strategy won't take you very far.

The studies, while seemingly gender biased, are based on statistical research and are full of exceptions, especially when influencers are dealing from an informed base of techniques rather than relying on their own agendas and psychology.

Getting an Accurate Picture of Your Current Influencing Power

One powerful factor in the science of influencing is assessing where those you need to influence fit in terms of self-image and socialization. Research has shown that people who feel socially excluded are likely to go to extreme measures to change their status in this regard. This stems from a powerful and profound morsel of psychology, one with consequences and barriers that the effective influencer needs to understand.

One experiment showed that people who felt excluded from a group were more likely to buy a product that demonstrated their *belonging* to a group with the intention to "fit in" and be accepted. On a social level, this study also showed that people were more likely to order food they didn't like and even snort cocaine in a back room to ingratiate themselves with people they believed to be insiders in a group from which they felt excluded.

The following information reinforces the need to understand the beliefs of a group you need to influence and align your ideas with those beliefs. Researchers at the universities of Florida and Illinois conducted extensive experiments on how receptive people are to ideas that are contrary to their own and what motivates them (defensively or accurately) to be open or closed to these new ideas. The study combined data from 91 experiments with nearly 8,000 subjects, and the conclusion bears out what we would guess instinctually: people are twice as likely to choose ideas that align with their core beliefs than to consider ideas opposed to their beliefs (67 percent versus 33 percent of respondents). "Certain individuals, those with close-minded personalities, are even more reluctant to expose themselves to differing perspectives," [University of Illinois psychology professor Dolores] Albarracín said. "They will opt for the information that corresponds to their views nearly 75 percent of the time." This is especially true when these choices center on religion, politics, or ethics.

Another study exposed a less obvious but potentially empowering subtlety of influence. Likeability can be a powerful influencing tool; if you want people to like you more so you can have a base from which to exert your influence, then buy a concert ticket instead of an expensive watch. Researchers at the University of Colorado at Boulder discovered that people who spent time, money, and energy on experiences instead of material and esteem-enhancing things were more widely accepted and liked than their more flamboyant counterparts. Professor Leaf Van Boven, lead researcher of the study, noted, "The mistake we can sometimes make is believing that pursuing material possessions will gain us

20

status and admiration while also improving our social relationships. . . . In fact, it seems to have exactly the opposite effect. This is really problematic, because we know that having quality social relationships is one of the best predictors of happiness, health, and well-being."

The past two decades have seen a renaissance in the field of intelligence quotient (IQ) research, breaking down the potential of the brain into the wider spectrum of cognitive, social, and emotional intelligence—and showing a surprisingly low correlation between them. In terms of influence, studies have shown that people with high emotional intelligence are more likely to become student leaders and, later in life, organizational influencers than are their perhaps more academically gifted peers. It certainly isn't news anymore, but there are still large and small organizations that promote subject-matter experts and specialists with high IQs into leadership positions, only to see them fail at inspiring and leading teams. Leaders in a position to promote and employees with a basic understanding of emotional and social intelligence need to recognize that true influence with others isn't related to a three-digit IQ score or expert mastery at spreadsheet manipulation; rather, you need the ability to recognize and regulate your own emotions to manage successful relationships with others.

It is a common perception that people who are trusting by nature are ripe targets for deceitful influencers; that trust too often equates to naïveté. But studies show that people with a high propensity to trust are also more likely to sniff out liars and fraud. Nancy Carter and Mark Weber of the Rotman School of Management at the University of Toronto say that high trusters also form more accurate first impressions that translate to better hiring decisions in the workplace. Forward-looking leaders make certain that people with a high propensity for trust are now being placed in positions that require an adept sense of perception and the ability to make accurate character reads with very little input.

For astute influencers at any level, this means listening to those who have a reputation as trusting individuals in order to stay ahead of the less trustworthy ones.

Your Personal Influencing Arsenal

More information is constantly emerging about our proclivities, decision-making skills, current likes and dislikes, irrationalities, and feelings about something—anything—as we furiously update our profiles on the various social networks. Influencers then become scientists. They're researchers who put the pieces of the puzzle together with the help of books like this and then get to work on incorporating the information into their influencing strategy.

The astute influencer leverages every morsel of information and cultural understanding of how people think and behave in order to optimize messaging and promote buy-in. She also makes use of the most effective channels of influence whenever possible.

Edward M. Hallowell, M.D., an instructor of psychiatry at Harvard Medical School, says that relying on face-to-face meetings is the most effective influencing strategy of all. With the proliferation of digital messaging, the in-person meeting is becoming a lost art; thus, its intended effect as a vehicle of connection and establishing trust is enhanced.

Speaking of trust, using the word itself can send your influencing efforts to a higher level. Regardless of the logic and facts you are using to pitch your position, the moment the word *trust* comes out, the conversation is personalized. It's as if you're staking your reputation on what you're saying, you're invested in both the risk and the outcome, and you're asking the listener to join you rather than to change or forfeit something.

Perhaps more than any other aspects of leadership and career empowerment, the art of influencing others in a 360-degree manner depends on both realms of skill—the ability to craft your thoughts and presentations clearly, strategically, and persuasively, and the ability to apply the proper tools and the power of scientifically proven human psychology to the effort. It all begins and ends with an outward-facing understanding of your audience and shaping your intentions to create a win-win situation that plays into their sense of worthiness, fulfillment, and the better good of all.

In the next chapter, you'll discover that 360-degree influence starts with the self. We'll discuss cognitive intelligence, emotional intelligence, and social intelligence, as well as the need to define your strengths and weaknesses in those areas. You'll also get a better understanding of your personal and social power.

CHAPTER 2

360-Degree Influence
Starts with You

How could someone so smart be so dumb? Plenty of people make us ask this question fairly often. Multimillion-dollar athletes who've built their images as good family men, only to have incriminating voice mails, texts, or videos released to the press. Governors, senators, presidents—powerful people who've worked hard to achieve professional success, only to have it all crumble because of disastrous personal decisions.

And it's not only high-flyers. Perhaps you've called out someone you know—or perhaps they've called you out. "I don't know what I was thinking!" is often the explanation, which roughly translates to "I wasn't thinking."

No one wants to believe that he or she could get caught up in a relationship or scheme that, in hindsight, seems so clearly wrong, but it is not uncommon for intelligent, reasonable people to sabotage themselves by wandering into a thicket of trouble. Even those who don't self-destruct spectacularly and publicly may nonetheless undermine themselves and their careers by not paying attention to their behavior or how that behavior affects others. Brilliant engineers can turn off coworkers with their brusque manner, and canny accountants might dig their own professional graves by not recognizing personal and social boundaries.

And *you* don't want to be the person about whom others say, "He's smart, but . . ." So learn how to be smart in *every* way.

IQ, EQ, and SI: Different Kinds of Intelligence

There is, as I noted in Chapter 1, more than one way to be smart. Some people can crunch through numbers as easily as others punch holes in arguments; some can diagnose a problem and others can fix it. Mechanics, taxi drivers, lawyers, doctors—each field has its own standard of "smart." And then there are those who simply "have a good head on their shoulders" or who have "street smarts" and can improvise on the fly.

Yet even after decades of research into and theories about multiple types of intelligence, the word *intelligence* leads many of us to think of the cognitive kind—a synthesis of analytical ability and memory. Intelligence quotient (IQ) tests are designed to capture cognitive ability, or how well a person is able to reason and draw connections, and a high IQ is a marker of intelligence.

As far back as 1920, E. L. Thorndike advanced the notion that there is more than one kind of intelligence. Scholars John Kihlstrom and Nancy Cantor explain that Thorndike divided intelligence "into three facets, pertaining to the ability to understand and manage ideas (abstract intelligence), concrete objects (mechanical intelligence), and people (social intelligence)." As Kihlstrom and Cantor explain, Thorndike wasn't alone in conceiving of multiple intelligences, but trying to pin down and assess these various intelligences has vexed generations of scholars.

Howard Gardner is widely known for having developed an initial list of seven intelligences: linguistic, logical-mathematical, musical, bodily kinesthetic, spatial, interpersonal, and intrapersonal intelligence. As researcher Mark Smith notes, "The first two have been typically valued in schools; the next three are usually associated with the arts; and the final two are what Howard Gardner called 'personal intelligences.'" Smith observes that Gardner has considered additional forms of intelligence, including spiritual, naturalistic, moral, and existential, but thus far has concluded that there is only sufficient evidence to add naturalistic—or the ability to categorize and make use of one's environment—to his original list of seven.

As with IQ tests, there is some concern as to how these other forms of intelligence may be evaluated or even whether some of them, such as the musical or bodily kinesthetic intelligences, might be better characterized as "talents." Nonetheless, Gardner's work has influenced several fields, particularly education, to cultivate skills beyond those of logic or reading comprehension.

More recently, the concepts of emotional and social intelligence have found a following in the popular literature, most notably in the works of Daniel Goleman. Goleman and his colleagues Richard Boyatzis and Kenneth Rhee say that emotional intelligence (EI) "is observed when a person demonstrates the competencies that constitute self-awareness, self-management, social awareness, and social skills at appropriate times and ways in sufficient frequency to be effective in the situation."

Goleman initially developed the Emotional Competency Inventory (EIC) based on 25 competencies clustered into five main groups: Self-awareness, Self-regulation, Motivation, Empathy, and Social Skills. The EIC was later modified, although the five main clusters remain the same. The difficulty, as Boyatzis, Goleman, and Rhee see it, is in trying to capture a set of abilities unique to emotional intelligence that make both theoretical and empirical sense. In other words, they want to make sure they're talking about and measuring a real phenomenon.

This same difficulty has been confronted by other researchers in EI. In a 2004 article with David Caruso, scholars John Mayer and Peter Salovey laid out the development of their four-branch model of EI, "the ability to (1) perceive emotion, (2) use emotion to facilitate thought, (3) understand emotions, and (4) manage emotion," a schema they used to develop the Mayer-Salovey-Caruso Emotional Intelligence Test (MSCEIT). Earlier models of emotional intelligence were judged by other scholars as deficient in various ways, but the later versions of MSCEIT seem to be both reliable and valid as a test of real-world abilities.

Stéphane Côté and his colleagues, for example, have conducted a number of studies using the MSCEIT and found that both leadership and job performance are positively related to EI. Similarly, Joshua Freedman and Marvin Smith, using the Six Seconds Emotional Intelligence Assessment, concluded, "It appears that athletes who develop greater emotional intelligence are more likely to succeed in life."

And while this theory may be drier than day-old toast, the implications for influence are powerful.

Social intelligence (SI) has had some of the same conceptual and testability problems as EI. While social intelligence has been defined as simply "the ability to get along with others," trying to measure SI has been much more difficult. In their review, Kihlstrom and Cantor trace decades of work in an attempt to construct a good test of SI, work which has often ended in frustration for the researchers involved.

Still, as psychologist Nicholas Humphrey points out, it makes sense from an evolutionary perspective that humans would have developed some kind of capacity to get along with others. Human beings are extraordinarily *social* creatures. The environments to which they have adapted are those of the family, the working group, and the clan. Human interpersonal relationships have a depth, a complexity, and a biological importance that far exceed those of any other animal. Indeed, without the ability to understand, predict, and manipulate the behavior of other members of our own species, we could hardly survive from day to day. Even if we haven't yet figured out a way to test rigorously for SI, it makes sense—as Humphrey suggests—that we must have developed *some* kind of capacity for understanding and getting along with others.

Consultant Karl Albrecht, for example, has created a five-sided rubric of SI based on situational radar (awareness), presence (bearing), authenticity (honesty with self and others), clarity (in verbal expression and ability to persuade), and empathy (connectedness). Behaviors in each of these categories can be assessed as effective or ineffective and can provide clues about a person's level of social intelligence.

Albrecht also distinguishes between toxic and nourishing behaviors. Toxic behaviors contribute to "alienation, conflict, and animosity" and can "cause others to feel devalued, inadequate, angry, frustrated, or guilty." Nourishing behaviors, on the other hand "cause others to feel valued, capable, loved, respected, and appreciated." Needless to say, people with a high SI tend toward nourishing behaviors, whereas those on the low end tend toward the toxic. This makes a kind of intuitive sense, but is there evidence to back it up?

I've already mentioned the work by Côté and his colleagues, but others have studied SI as well. For example, in a 2004 report, the National Scientific Council on the Developing Child argued that "as a person develops into adulthood, these same social skills [of social competence] are essential for the formation of lasting friendships and intimate relationships, effective parenting, the ability to hold a job and work well with others, and for becoming a contributing member of a community." More than that, "emotional well-being and social competence provide a strong foundation for emerging cognitive abilities, and together they are the bricks and mortar that comprise the foundation of human development."

Whatever the difficulties scholars have in pinning down EI and SI, it seems clear that these intelligences *do matter* to personal and professional success. It's clear to anyone with an open mind: there is more than one way to be intelligent; the ability to understand yourself and those around you likely depends not just on cognitive intelligence but also on the emotional and social kinds; and to become an influential leader, you have to harness *all* of those abilities.

There's no one foolproof way to increase your social or emotional intelligence, any more than there's one foolproof way to enhance your cognitive abilities. There is a science to the measurement of intelligence, but the science is incomplete. My book *Executive Presence* outlines a seven-day program that focuses on increasing your social intelligence and discusses this topic in detail.

And there's more that can be done. In fact, a lot of good work has already been done on how to begin to make sense of our social and emotional intelligences. There are several ways to heighten your awareness of EI and SI and to begin to shape these abilities in ways that allow you to see both yourself and others more clearly.

Critical for your noticeable improvement, you have to know your baseline. The website Psychometric Success (http://www.psy chometric-success.com) notes that there are generally three ways to test for EI: self-reporting (the weakest, as it relies on the ability that you are trying to test); interviewing the people around you in a comprehensive 360-degree assessment; and taking tests such as Goleman's EIC, the more recently developed ESCI, which includes social competence; or the MSCEIT. The latter, for example, asks you more than 100 questions based on the four branches Mayer, Salovey, and Caruso identified.

Once you've determined which areas need further development, you can work with a coach or qualified mentor on increasing your competence. While it is possible that a simple identification of lagging behaviors can lead you to change them on your own, to make a substantial leap forward, be prepared to seek out a specialist who can help you hone all the facets of your intelligence.

And while it won't take years of classrooms and Ivy League tuitions to increase your emotional and social competence, just as with learning new technologies, the cultivation of your various intelligences is a lifelong process.

Self-Regulation Can Boost Your Influencing Power

Aristotle believed that the ability of a man—presumably, today he would include women—to use his reason to control his appetites marked him as morally virtuous. It's a shame that he had to miss our current cultural icons of self-indulgence, such as "Jersey Shore's" motley crew of reality millionaires with its poignant mantra of GTL (gym, tan, and laundry) as a lifestyle advertisement. Fast-forward from the virtuous Greek antique 2,300 years ago; it seems as if all understanding of self-mastery has been lost. And aside from our TV misfits, we can also take a virtual walk through YouTube to observe all the ways we let our desires run rampant over our reason. *What is the world coming to?*

Let's not reach for an extra dose of Paxil just yet. One of the reasons we watch the shows and videos we do is precisely because most of us *don't* engage in these behaviors (at least, not once we've fully entered adulthood). We enjoy being appalled by what we recognize as the terrible lack of restraint in these reality stars. How much fun would it be to watch supremely self-disciplined people do their respective things?

If you think about it, though, many of us *do* find pleasure in observing self-disciplined individuals. How many of us watch sporting events or the Olympics; did skier Lindsay Vonn or golfer Jack Nicklaus get to the top by slacking off? Roger Federer is a tremendously gifted tennis player, but his greatness comes from more than

31

just his physical prowess; it's supported by willpower and discipline. Even when he (rarely) loses, we can see that he never gives up.

Such displays of mental toughness can lead us to wonder how we would react if we were in such a high-pressure situation. Do we have what it takes to step up and take control? Do we even know *how* to discipline ourselves, to do what is necessary to get to the top and not break apart once we get there?

Psychology professor Timothy Pychyl says there's no magic involved in self-regulation. He separates this process into two parts: first, the setting of a standard, and second, the monitoring of behavior in light of that standard. A completely automatic self-regulatory system, like a thermostat, allows you to set a temperature; when the temperature deviates too far from that setting, the furnace or air conditioner kicks on to bring it back in line. This process, known as *homeostasis*, is much harder to achieve in non-mechanical beings such as ourselves: we set unreasonable standards; we don't do a good job of monitoring our behavior; or we overcompensate to bring ourselves back in line.

Think about that bestseller you've wanted to write. You finally get around to creating a plan for yourself, pledging to write 20 pages per day. You gather all of the books and subscribe to the periodicals you want to use for research. You get a brand-new, faster computer with an additional monitor so you can view various screens of research at once; Google and LexisNexis are ready to go searching for you. You even splurge on a new ergonomic office chair that'll keep you from turning into a stress-related injury statistic. On day one, you manage to churn out 15 pages but get frustrated because that wonderful concept or story you had in mind is now as elusive as vapor. You toss everything you've done, sending the entire file to the virtual recycle bin. You can start fresh tomorrow, you think. Except there's that show you want to see right after you get home from work, and there's always the weekend. On the first weekend, you actually do really well with your plan—too well.

You go at it for 16 hours straight to make up for lost time, which completely messes you up for Monday morning, when you're so tired that you miss a few key points your boss makes in that very important client meeting at 8:03 A.M.

This scenario applies to everything from professional development to working out to going on a diet, you name it. Most of us have been there in some fashion, becoming frustrated at our seeming inability to stick to the plan or our overcompensation to make the plan work and rendering the process toxic for our mental and physical health.

Was the problem that the plan was too ambitious? Too lax? Or that we didn't do a good enough job of monitoring our available time and effort? In fact, the problem may be with both the plan and the monitoring. Pychyl cites research that found the largest reason for self-regulatory failure is *not paying attention* to the goal-directed activity, and one of the reasons we don't pay attention is that the goal is either unrealistic or insufficiently connected to our interests to make us want to achieve it. Maybe being a bestselling author is farther down on your list of values and priorities than you realized.

That's why self-regulation matters: If you want to advance toward a goal, you have to pay attention both to the goal and to your progress toward it. If you set an unreasonable goal (too hard and you'll lose motivation; too easy and you'll coast) or don't keep your behavior in line with that goal, nothing happens.

Actually, "nothing" is only one possible outcome. In our daily lives, we constantly risk losing credibility for lack of focus, inability to meet deadlines, fiscal irresponsibility, or any other reason closely connected to not being able to self-regulate. Thus, many people find themselves puttering away in the same cubicle they were assigned when they first started at the company. Or worse.

If you are motivated enough to learn the nuances for influencing others, you have to discipline yourself in terms of the goals you set and in monitoring your progress toward those goals.

*Tips to Master Self-Regulation and Boost Your
Influencing Power*

o **Determine exactly what you want to work on.** Be
specific. Maybe you've identified an opportunity for improvement or your boss has given you a gentle nudge. Either way,
you'll have to define the issue in clear language. "I need to
improve my business presentations" is vague and uninspiring.
"I need to structure my presentation content better to make
my message and objective clearer for the audience" is good. "I
need to find more relevant evidence to support the key-points
I'm making" is right on target. Clear thinking and language
are critical to being seen as an influencer.

o **Recruit additional resources.** Whether you're trying to get in
shape or become a more compelling presenter, it's hard and
unnecessary to go it alone. To get off to a good start on a fitness
program, you'll want to speak to a professional—a personal
trainer—on what types of exercises you should do. That way
you aren't spinning your wheels in an area where you have
little expertise. Start with the best information you can get.
As a business presenter, you should first learn what kinds of
organizational flow structures are available so you can arrange
your topics for maximum absorption by the audience. Ask a
coach and watch others who do it well. See if their structures
would work for you. TED is an organization that has many
of today's corporate and cultural leaders present their ideas
on stage, so audience members can learn from the variety of
styles. Influencers keep their eyes and mind open for any tool
and information that will help them reach their goals.

o **Seek feedback everywhere.** Work on your emotional intelligence as you learn about yourself from others' feedback as well
as your own feelings. The more feedback you can gather and
the better your perceptions, the more you can adjust or stay the
course. Drop what doesn't work and keep what does.

○ **Start small.** Trying to completely make over your style and routine all at once can potentially derail your best efforts and motivation. Lasting change rarely occurs overnight. Start small. Incorporate new ideas you learn about. Note the results. Then add some more. Are people more engaged in your presentations now? Do they seem to ask more questions? These are tangible results you can record and build on. Likewise, if getting in shape is your goal, what signs will you look for that signal progress?

○ **Treat your life like a laboratory.** You are experimenting with a new approach, and experimentation means failing is OK. Failure just means that one method isn't working, so you search for another. Always head forward, though. Thomas Edison once said, "Hell, there are no rules here. We're trying to accomplish something." Similarly, not every influencing attempt works, and some take a long time, depending on what you're trying to accomplish. Smart influencers don't give up; they look for other angles.

○ **Allow yourself to focus.** Notice that I said, "allow." Too often we try to force ourselves to focus on one thing and get distracted by another. By giving yourself permission to focus you are also giving yourself permission to ignore detractors and distractions. Empowering yourself has the added benefit of truly feeling free to take action and is part of an astute influencer's core.

○ **Identify any conflicting priorities.** You may be in your own way. When you feel yourself dragging on something or notice you're not making progress, check the priorities for your values. They may be in conflict. One value you might like to move toward is being respected by your peers and bosses for being a more engaging speaker and presenter, but you may also hate being the center of attention and usually avoid it at all costs (which moves you away from the first value). The conflict can hamper any real

35

progress. Identifying these competing forces is the first step in managing them with clear thinking and sound decision making. Checking in on your values and, if necessary, rearranging them in order of priority will help your influencing power by informing the objectives you set when you aim to influence.

- **Check your biases.** Our ingrained beliefs and biases can distort the way we see things and render our reality completely out of sync with that of our equally biased peers. It's best to take a step back, try to see things from others' perspective, and recalibrate your approach to get on the same plane. While it is difficult to recognize our own biases, as many of them are part of our intuitive behavior, influencers who want to succeed can only do so by viewing any option, idea, or proposal from their audience's point of view.

- **Mind your inner dialogue.** Recent research confirms that the way we talk to ourselves has an impact on our behavior. One study with potentially wide-ranging implications on fields like cognitive and developmental psychology, in addition to classroom and work settings, found that asking yourself whether you will complete a task increases your intrinsic motivation more than simply telling yourself you'll finish a project. So in the case of a presenter, the key to better self-regulation might be to ask, "Will I create a stronger opening for this talk next Monday?" For influencers, the hypothetical question "Can I get the client to accept this new proposal?" should be more effective than the statement "I will get the client to accept the new proposal." The science says so.

Ten Skills for Becoming More Influential

Some people are born with the ability to perform. They're gifted physically or intellectually or artistically, and it seems as if they just float to the top.

Don't be fooled by this. However gifted someone may be, he still had to work to achieve a lofty position atop the tennis rankings or the corporate hierarchy. The person may have started with a certain set of talents but had to develop those talents to achieve his goals.

That's good news for the rest of us. Not only does each of us have our own skills and talents, but we too can work to develop them and propel ourselves into positions of influence.

Here are 10 qualities that everyone can develop:

1. **Develop your critical decision-making skills.** Decision-making is among the top leadership competencies for a reason. From the simple choice of where to hold a staff meeting to the strategic options of where to spend marketing dollars, a leader's day is filled with an inexhaustible range of decisions. The outcome of these decisions can affect people from the next cubicle over to a subsidiary halfway across the globe to entire countries.

   Decisiveness is not a trait we're born with; it's a skill that can be learned. Understanding the process of critical decision making allows you to spot weak links in your reasoning and recognize potential biases that can affect a choice for or against something or someone. While we can't control outcomes, it's up to proactive influencers to get a good understanding of the detailed process that leads to outcomes and stack the deck in their favor.

2. **Learn to make a solid argument and take a stand.** You may never address the United Nations Security Council or testify before Congress, but should the opportunity come up, it's helpful to be able to put together a coherent argument. Of course, the ability to argue a perspective is useful in high-stakes conversations, presentations, and question-and-answer sessions with decision makers and anyone else who represents

a certain point of view or asks you to explain yours. To argue means to give reasons; it means to represent your choices over other options and to defend and promote those choices against the arguments of equally adept influencers. Take what you've learned in school and build on with private instruction and by reading books on the subject. You'll find that your ability to think critically and analyze others' arguments will dramatically increase your influence on their choices.

3. **Become a storyteller.** Storytelling has been a premier tool in influencing people across cultures and eras. Influencers tell stories for strategic purposes. From motivating people to act, to teaching, to reducing resistance and changing minds, the power of story can affect people on a deep level. A well-told narrative, presented in person, can influence more effectively than the mere recitation of complex financial or technical facts. Numbers and figures are important, but when it comes to showing their relationship to any issue, large or small, a strategic narrative wrapped around the digits will deliver the message better than anything else. Effective influencers know their message must also be *remembered*, which is why they learn to tell the types of stories that make a lasting impact.

4. **Sharpen your writing.** For astute influencers, the ability to put coherent thought and powerful language on both paper and screen is a critical tool in influencing people's thinking and behavior. Whether it's e-mails to clients and associates or opinionated op-eds in local papers, your ability to take a stand, share an important idea, or weigh in on an issue with a unique perspective in writing is a skill you will use on a daily basis. To make your writing truly effective and sharp, you have to read widely. Explore the great essayists—Christopher Hitchens, William F. Buckley, Hemingway, Arthur Miller, Barbara Kingsolver—and anything else you can get your hands on to sharpen your prose and practice your critical and

analytical thinking. You can't skip the reading for lack of time; you'll need to draw on the styles of other literary works and let them inform your writing to improve its impact. To write good proposals, business reports, or just checking-in-with-you notes, you'll have to suffer despair along the way. It's normal and part of the process. (I've never met an unfrustrated writer.) But think of the effect you can have on your environment and the thoughts of your audience. To write well is to influence.

5. **Increase your emotional and social intelligence.** We discussed this earlier in the chapter and it bears repeating: the ability to know yourself and master your emotions, thinking, and behavior is critical and, as the research confirms, a good indicator of later success in life for children who develop it early. It's also a critical leadership skill. So is the ability to feel empathy and forge relationships with others along the way to success. While experts agree that cognitive intelligence is more or less fixed, the consensus is that EI and SI can be developed and increased. While 360-degree influencers find both EI and SI extremely helpful in working with people, it is no less personally rewarding when relationships with others start developing in more authentic and deeper ways.

6. **Hone your speaking skills.** This is the proverbial no-brainer—the need to be able to influence people via the spoken word. When many of us think of influential people, we think of the great speakers we've heard. When asked whom they admire for their speaking skills, my American clients invariably mention John F. Kennedy, Ronald Reagan, Bill Clinton, Colin Powell, and others who've made an impact on the world. While many influencers operate behind the scenes, it is the ability to speak and persuade that gives powerful leverage to 360-degree influencers.

It isn't just the political heavyweights who have a way with words, delivered in a way that pierces the resistance of people

39

who hear them speak. Every day in organizations and corporations and schools, unnamed and numerous presenters strive to capture the imaginations of workers and executives and students to drive an agenda forward.

While many fear the opportunity to speak in public instead of embracing it, giving in to that panic closes a heavy door to influence. On the other hand, being able to express your thoughts and ideas confidently and compellingly to an audience is a fast-track to success and influence.

7. **Have a basic understanding of economics.** The truth is you can't have an intelligent conversation with your peers and clients if you're stumped when faced with everyday economic topics such as taxes, budget deficits, interest rates, markets, unemployment, whether inflation in China threatens global trade, and the meaning of all these things to the average citizen. You don't need to be an expert on any of these topics, but a basic understanding of their dynamics will let you hold your own in any discourse with your colleagues.

Influence is also about having an opinion that can shape the choices and behaviors of others. Embarrassing holes in specific or everyday knowledge that many of us cover in business or grad school, or the papers if we're so motivated, significantly dampens your 360-degree influencing efforts. With such a knowledge gap, you're forced to steer the conversation carefully away from this vortex and into friendlier waters.

8. **Think like a leader.** Influence is most obvious when it happens at the front of the pack. While 360-degree influence prescribes a method of shaping and influencing choices and behaviors from any position, it is from a recognized position of leadership that you can make the most impact. Most progressive companies develop their high-potential leaders from within. If you're lucky enough to work for a leadership development factory like General Electric, you've got it made, because

everyone else is going to woo you to come on board for them and practice what you've learned. Thankfully, effective leadership is a hot topic, and the development of the necessary skills is taught and practiced at some of the finest companies for which I've consulted. If you don't work for one of the great firms that take leadership development seriously, your company simply doesn't have the resources, or you're just out of school, volunteer to head up something—a community project, a fund-raiser, or anything where you can test your mettle in making difficult decisions, setting strategy, and motivating people toward a goal while keeping an eye on available resources. Volunteering is an excellent start, and it will influence others to pencil you in for a bigger job when the opportunity comes along.

9. **Understand technology.** It's the 21st century, and even five-year-olds know about Twitter, Facebook, and the latest multimedia platforms. There are fundamentals you have to understand to make an impact, if only in your conversations with others. Social media have carved a big foothold in the media landscape, and they're here to stay—and grow. Communicating with clients and customers across the globe is now facilitated by social media platforms that were still in freshman sweats just a few years ago. But they've left the campus and entered the world of big commerce. If you don't have an ongoing online dialogue with your customers or need a 19-year-old to show you the ropes every time you log on to your website's forum, you're behind. Business is online, and customers and recruiters are looking for you to be present. Google yourself right now, and if the search produces 25 other people with your name—but not you—it's time to dive in headfirst. For the majority of people with whom you'll come in contact, your reputation and perceived influence start with what they can find about you on the Internet.

10. (Fill in the blank). This one is all you. Influence isn't all about strategy; it's also about being authentic and original and moving others through your personality. So the final quality you'll develop in yourself is up to you. What do you really want to work on to become more of a person of influence?

A glance at any day's headlines shows you how much that goes on is out of your control. Instead of worrying about what you can't control, however, work on what you can. Work on yourself.

In the next chapter, we'll look at what you can do when you're facing resistance. You'll discover some of the major barriers to influencing others and what tools can help you reach them on a deeper level. We'll also cover some interesting theories and findings on why people cling to stubborn beliefs and persist in holding entrenched views.

CHAPTER 3

Breaking Through Resistance: The Major Barriers to Influencing Others

The 28th president of the United States was certainly not the first leader to observe, "If you want to make enemies, try to change something." Undoubtedly Woodrow Wilson drew this conclusion from extensive firsthand experience in people management, having held a leadership post at Princeton University as its president and the governorship of New Jersey before ascending to the White House. Wilson knew what managers at every organization—from the newly formed start-up to the nonprofit to the multinational conglomerate—learn eventually, sometimes painfully; people typically prefer the status quo and reject the notion of change.

In fact, we have such a strong bias toward keeping things the same, that the late Canadian-American economist John Kenneth Galbraith was once inspired to quip, "Faced with the choice between changing one's mind and proving that there is no need to do so, almost everyone gets busy on the proof."

If you work with people on a daily basis, whether in the cubicle farms or on the real farm, you hardly need a list of examples to back up Galbraith's claim; you have your own. Nonetheless, later in this chapter, you'll find not only a few of the most common expressions of resistance people will throw at you, but also suggestions for how to respond to people who "get busy on the proof." Because respond you must to move things forward, unless you and your bosses find the status quo acceptable.

Why People Cling to Stubborn Beliefs

"I wouldn't have seen it if I hadn't believed it." While this certainly exceeds my intuitive quota of other people's quotations in one chapter, these words from Marshall McLuhan—the renowned rhetorician and communication theorist—are too appropriate to leave out.

So much of what people perceive depends on what they already believe, which makes the task of influencing infinitely more challenging, raising it to the level the military calls psychological operations. It's important to understand why people refuse, resist, or (perhaps more damaging) reluctantly agree to something, only to continuously withhold their best efforts from the task at hand. Better to hear the creaking axle so you can fix it before the wheels come off at 80 miles per hour on an open road.

So here's a primer on why opposing belief systems are the reinforced mental barricades that reason, logic, evidence, or emotional appeals cannot easily pierce. Let's start with evolutionary biology.

Beliefs Have a Biological Survival Function

Notable skeptic and author Michael Shermer discusses this in an article in *Scientific American*:

> I argue that our brains are belief engines: evolved pattern-recognition machines that connect the dots and create meaning out of the patterns that we think we see in nature. Sometimes A really is connected to B; sometimes it is not.

When it is, we have learned something valuable about the environment from which we can make predictions that aid in survival and reproduction. We are the [descendants] of those most successful at finding patterns. This process is called association learning, and it is fundamental to all animal behavior, from the humble Caenorhabditis elegans *(worm) to* Homo sapiens.

Imagine passing a neighbor's yard and seeing, from the corner of your eye, what looks like a snake winding its way through the grass. You instinctively jump back—until the "snake" turns out to be a garden hose on closer inspection. Historically, people who didn't react fast enough when encountering a real snake or mistook it for a harmless stick became unavailable for reproduction and were therefore deselected by evolution. On the flipside, we're here because our own ancestors—evolutionary winners that they were—erred on the side of caution when the wind rustled the grass or a stick looked like a snake and hightailed it out of the "danger zone." Because next time, the wind could be a starved lion, and the branch might be a poisonous reptile. Ultimately, in trying to overcome people's resistance, we could well be gearing up for a battle with their biology.

Shermer continues in *Scientific American* that since "we did not evolve a 'Baloney Detection Network' in the brain to distinguish between true and false patterns, we have no error-detection governor to modulate the pattern-recognition engine." Here he touts the usefulness of "self-correcting mechanisms of replication and peer review" inherent in scientific methods. He also posits that "erroneous cognition is not likely to remove us from the gene pool and would therefore not have been selected against by evolution." In a sense, Shermer is saying that we can't have it both ways when it comes to our beliefs—support the continuation of our survival and offspring on one hand, and know precisely when a false (or useless) belief benefits us on the other. We're already programmed to accept existing beliefs as true, valid, and capable of causing tremendous

45

resistance when someone asks us to change our ways. That's because our capacity to believe makes our life easier. Believing in our unique mental models of how the world works gives us a sense of control without which we'd feel lost.

Like Shermer, psychology professor James Alcock at Canada's York University explores all of the ways we humans are not strictly rational. He calls our brain and nervous system a "belief-generating machine," an engine that "selects information from the environment, shapes it, combines it with information from memory, and produces beliefs that are generally consistent with beliefs already held." He echoes Shermer in saying that unfortunately, this machine does not necessarily come equipped with a truth compass; all that matters is that its beliefs "prove functional for the individual who holds them."

In other words, all that matters is that this engine produces beliefs, not that they are true, fact-based, or even plausible. As long as they make sense to the person and help her make sense of the world, the belief-generating machine is doing its job.

To help distinguish between the different types of reasons for our beliefs, Alcock breaks this engine down into seven (metaphorical) units:

1. The learning unit
2. The critical-thinking unit
3. The yearning unit
4. The input unit
5. The emotional response unit
6. The memory unit
7. The environmental feedback unit

The first, the *learning unit*, is "the key to understanding the belief engine." Learning processes are actually tied into the physical architecture of the brain itself, and these processes are, shall

46

we say, promiscuous. Confirming Shermer's theory, Alcock says that a person learns to associate A with B over and over, whether or not A has anything other than a chance relationship to B. You wear the blue-striped tie to an interview and you're offered the job, so when you interview for a promotion, you dig that same tie out of the back of your closet to wear again. You might "know" the tie has nothing to do with the assessment of your performance, but why take a chance? You'll feel more confident wearing it.

On a more serious note, consider the scenario of a friend who decides not to buckle up just to drive a mile or so to the store, is sideswiped, and ends up with her head smashing into the side window. As a result, you resolve never to drive anywhere without wearing your seat belt. In this case, there is a relationship between the injury and the lack of a safety harness, so even though the chances of getting in an accident are small, it still makes sense to act as if it *could* happen and prepare to mitigate the consequences.

The *critical-thinking unit*, on the other hand, serves as a check on the "magical thinking" produced by the learning unit. This is developed through experience and direct knowledge, and, unlike the learning unit, it can be turned off or suspended. According to Alcock, "We learn to use simple tests of reason to evaluate events around us, but we also learn that certain classes of events are not to be subjected to reason but should be accepted on faith." In other words, we may switch between the critical-thinking mode and an "experiential, intuitive" mode, depending on whether compassion or skepticism seems the more appropriate response. (Con artists, needless to say, try to keep us *out* of the critical-thinking mode.)

The *yearning unit* can save us—not literally, but in the sense of giving us hope, reducing anxiety, or otherwise soothing frayed nerves. We are often at our most vulnerable when neither reason nor logic can give us the answers we so desperately need.

The *input unit* is a kind of one-two vacuum cleaner and sorter of information, helping us to take in and process data bits in ways that make sense to us. As with the learning unit, however, the input unit doesn't distinguish between true and false. It produces patterns in line with previous patterns, and to the extent that we presume rather than question these patterns, cognitive biases (discussed in Chapter 5) may crop up.

The *emotional response unit* often works with the learning unit to reinforce relationships. Recall the friend's car crash. Given how the brain works, it wouldn't be surprising if you thought there was some link between her not wearing her seat belt and the accident itself; that is, it was the *decision* not to buckle up—a tempting of fate—that caused the accident. Again, you know it's not true, but as Alcock tells us, the emotion of the event—your friend being seriously injured—often reinforces the relationship between what happened before and what happened after.

The *memory unit* is just that—a processor of memories. And it is a processor, not a repository: our old memories are reworked as new experiences and perceptions come in, such that the memory itself is less a permanent snapshot of an event than an ever-changing story about that event.

The *environmental feedback unit,* along with the critical-thinking unit, can serve as a reality check on initial or intuitive beliefs. *Can* because, as in the case of conspiracy theorists, any additional information or feedback may serve only to reinforce the belief in conspiracy. Furthermore, because we tend to seek out like-minded individuals or persuade others to share our understandings, it is entirely possible that our beliefs will be reinforced rather than challenged by others.

That our brains are wired for belief helps us to understand why some people persist in holding on to convictions that are irrational and drive us mad in our attempts to influence them with logic, reason, and facts. Logic and facts matter a great deal, but they're not all that matters, and according to Alcock and Shermer, they aren't necessarily the most important drivers of belief.

Beliefs Help Us Make Decisions Amidst Uncertainty

Amos Tversky and Daniel Kahneman—behavioral economists—identified a number of "heuristics" in which we often engage to make decisions amid uncertainty. We'll discuss these heuristics at length in Chapter 5, but I want to note here that these common-sense decision rules or rules of thumb can lead us astray, due in part to persistent perceptual distortions. Tversky and Kahneman traced the persistence of heuristics less to brain structure than to the desire to create certainty out of probability, but their work reinforces the notion that fact is not always enough to overcome fiction.

In fact (no pun intended), we often discount facts that contradict our beliefs. In *Scientific American*, writer Christie Nicholson highlights a recent study on the cultural cognition of risk, in which the researchers Dan Kahan, Hank Jenkins-Smith, and Donald Braman told study subjects about a scientific expert who accepted climate change as real. Subjects who were of the opinion that commerce can be environmentally damaging were ready to accept the scientist as an expert. Those who came into the study believing that economic activity could not hurt the environment, however, were 70 percent less likely to accept that the scientist really was an expert.

Similar results were found when discussing nuclear waste disposal or the safety of carrying concealed weapons in public. The issue was not the dismissal of science per se, but "that people tend to keep a biased score of what experts believe, counting a scientist as an 'expert' only when that scientist agrees with the position they find culturally congenial." So in addition to our neurology and psychology, our social, cultural, economic, and political beliefs may serve to reinforce our biases and block out any countervailing evidence.

The political science research website The Monkey Cage (http://themonkeycage.org), for example, recently posted a number of commentaries on research showing that the partisan divide over the existence and causes of global warming *increased* as respondents' education levels increased—a divide that was not evident when it came to other, less politically controversial subjects. Professor John Sides noted, "One explanation for this is familiar to any reader of John Zaller's *The Nature and Origins of Mass Opinion*: when political elites take contrasting positions on issues, those positions will be reflected in their fellow partisans in the public." In other words, we choose team over evidence or expertise.

Other research points to different kinds of information filters. Yale Law School operates the Cultural Cognition Project in which investigators look at how we think affects what and how we know. One of the key findings of the study states, "Individuals of diverse cultural outlooks—hierarchical and egalitarian, individualistic and communitarian—hold sharply opposed beliefs about a range of societal risks, including those associated with climate change, gun ownership, public health, and national security." Unlike the political scientists, however, these scholars conclude that "differences in these basic values exert substantially more influence over risk perceptions than does any other individual characteristic, including gender, race, socioeconomic status, education, and political ideology and party affiliation."

Whether the cause of our different beliefs is due to political ties, cultural influences, or psychological outlook (or some combination thereof), it is clear that they lead us to read different stories into the same information. And the more important our beliefs are to us, the more likely we are to discount any evidence that might upend them.

As much as we humans may think that we want "the truth, the whole truth, and nothing but the truth," we often choose belief over truth, making 360-degree influence a challenge that deserves all of the attention and resources an influencer can bring to it.

The Foundation for Influence and Changing Minds

Stress causes ulcers—everyone knew that. People on deadlines, those juggling a lot of different commitments, those with high-pressure jobs were all likely to develop peptic ulcers. Calm down, watch the spicy food intake, take something to soothe the stomach—that's what you did to take care of an ulcer. Everybody knew that.

What everybody knew was wrong.

Barry Marshall and his fellow researcher, Robin Warren, didn't set out to prove everybody wrong; in fact, they weren't even initially interested in ulcers. They were interested in bacteria, particularly those that lived in harsh environments. (While it's well-known today that bacteria thrive in all sorts of hostile places, it was not widely known when Marshall and Warren began their investigations in the 1980s.) They were looking at *Helicobacter pylori* and trying to prove that this particular bacterium lived in the stomach.

As Marshall put it, "That led to ulcers via the side door, if you like, because we were trying to find out who had the bacteria—and lo and behold, we noticed that everybody with ulcers had them." The researchers knew within a relatively short period of time that they had found the cause of peptic ulcers, and not only because 90 percent of the patients they treated with antibiotics were cured. Marshall went one step further and swallowed *H. pylori* to give *himself* an ulcer.

Why? "It was a decision point. I had to find out if the bacteria could really affect a healthy person and cause gastritis." He had tried working with piglets but to no avail. "And the skeptics were so determinedly skeptical that I felt like: I'm never going to prove to these guys that the bacteria are harmful. By then everybody knew that 40 percent of the population had the bacteria and did not have ulcers, so that was making life difficult for me. So I took some bacteria off a patient and cooked it up."

Had he not gotten an ulcer, "it really would have been a spanner in the works for the whole theory. I thought, 'If it doesn't work, I'll quiet down about the whole thing; maybe I'll just run away and do some other career for a while because I'm wrong.' But then of course it worked."

Marshall and Warren wrote up the results for publication without making clear that Marshall had experimented on himself. Yet it was precisely the self-experiment that clinched the truth of their theory for their colleagues—Marshall gained credibility with this simple (if painful) demonstration. So how did Marshall and Warren prove everyone else wrong?

The belief that stress caused ulcers was strong, even though there had never been any truly good studies demonstrating causality; it was one of those tropes that was handed down from generation to generation of medical doctors. Add to that the tremendous profits realized by pharmaceutical companies that were selling only marginally effective treatments; these companies made money largely because their antacids only managed the symptoms of the ulcer—which meant, of course, that the medicine needed to be taken repeatedly. As Marshall observed, "If you look at it from a business point of view, it could only do your market harm and lower your share price to find out that you could actually cure people with antibiotics."

Finally, there were the patients themselves, who, along with everyone else, "knew" that stress caused ulcers. Even today, there are people who insist (along with their doctors) that ulcers are a lifestyle issue. Marshall tries to make sense of this nonsensical position: "It's like a religion or something. It's like there's a certain part of your life when you learn things, and then you just stop."

That dynamic affects almost all of us, scientists and laypeople alike. And the problem is made worse because sometimes the "old" knowledge is correct ("wash your hands before eating") or partially correct (stress can makes us feel worse, even if it doesn't cause any specific problem).

So how do you cut through the old wives' tales or bogus advice or, worst of all, common (non)sense? Consider what Marshall and Warren did:

○ First, curiosity drove them to learn, a curiosity that could only be sated by evidence. This evidence led them to the ulcers.

○ Second, they put together that evidence in a manner appropriate to their field. Science generally demands rigorous tests that show not just correlation, but proof of causation. Given that *H. pylori* lives in the guts of far more people than those who get ulcers, how could they prove that the bacteria caused those ulcers, and that the bulk of the evidence showed that people who took antibiotics were cured? Marshall's self-experimentation really drove the point home.

○ Third, they had allies. Marshall points to the gastroenterologist and "thought leader" David Graham at Baylor University, who, while skeptical, was nonetheless willing to consider—and was eventually convinced by—the evidence Marshall and Warren gathered. And then Tachi Yamada (now head of the Gates Foundation's Global Health Program) announced at a scientific conference that it was proven that bacteria caused ulcers and patients should be treated with antibiotics. "It was just like night and day after that," Marshall said. "The whole thing just went ballistic."

Marshall and Warren had a happy ending: the acceptance of their theory and, in 2005, the Nobel Prize in Medicine.

What about the rest of us? How do we convince those around us who think they already know everything they need to know? Ken Broda-Bahm, writing about the influence of scientific testimony on a jury, notes that the mere presentation of the facts is not enough to convince skeptical jurors. "Scientists like to present new knowledge in a revolutionary framework ('this changes everything'), but human learning tends to be more evolutionary." That discovery is so often disruptive can work against you. Therefore, "instead of offering scientific evidence as a challenge to current beliefs, offer it as a supplement."

This advice easily translates to the workplace. How many people do you know who are highly protective of their turf and unwilling to entertain even the thought that someone else might know more than they do? Probably plenty of them! Here's how to gently influence their beliefs. First, instead of outright demolishing their convictions, build off of them; it's much easier to coax people over a bridge than it is to convince them to jump across a chasm.

Second, teach them about the issue before attempting to persuade them. This can work as a kind of priming: by reminding your audience of knowledge they already have and treating them as capable of learning more, you connect their prior knowledge to your "new" facts. Lay the groundwork, then build your story on top of it. In litigation lawyer terms, prepare them to accept your version of events.

Finally, Broda-Bahm states, "The most complete explanation wins." While jurors (and coworkers) are not always impressed with reams of data, lacking those data can certainly hurt your credibility. If you want to persuade others to follow your lead, you have to demonstrate that you have the knowledge to lead, a demonstration that requires you to run down as many objections as possible.

Ten Keys to Overcome Resistance and Start Influencing

Think back to Alcock's seven units of our belief-generating engines. Only one of those units explicitly relies on logic and reason; the rest sort information according to our experiences and preferences. This means that (1) you can't count on everyone understanding a situation in the same way you do, and (2) you can't rely on cold facts to overcome others' resistance to your message.

You have to recognize ahead of time that neither your charm nor your evidence—however necessary—will be sufficient to convince others of the wisdom of your proposals. Instead, you have to be prepared, not just for resistance, but for different forms of resistance, and you must be able to neutralize these concerns at the source right from the start of your influencing attempts. Some forms of resistance will be about the organization, some about the changes themselves, and some about you—not surprising, given that your colleagues will have different attitudes about the company, their own jobs, and you.

Given these different types of concerns, it's important to recognize the source of each. People who don't trust you aren't going to be won over by your credentials or position, but they may be by your willingness to listen to and respond to their concerns in concrete and practical ways. But this tactic won't necessarily work with someone who is afraid that he lacks the ability to implement your changes; that person will need training and feedback to come over to your side.

People may drag their feet or otherwise obstruct your proposals in a lot of ways. To help you on your path toward greater influence, Table 3.1 lists 10 common types of resistance, their likely causes, and how you can overcome them.

Sometimes people resist change just because they can, but most are simply worried about how they're going to fit within any program. Meet those concerns head-on and give people the tools they need to make these changes; they'll convince *themselves* that you know your stuff. Now *that's* influence.

In the next chapter, we'll look at what motivates people; how you can learn the skill of empathic accuracy (realistic mind reading); and how you can become an astute observer of human behavior and communication, including the critical art of listening with all your senses.

TABLE 3.1

TYPE OF RESISTANCE	CAUSE(S)	HOW TO RESPOND
1. *This has nothing to do with anything.*	The resisters either don't see the point or don't see the relevance of your suggestions.	Connect your change to the overall goals of the organization or project, pointing out how it fixes ongoing problems or will improve the current situation.
2. *Been there, done that.*	They see this as nothing new and are skeptical of your efforts.	Ask them to explain the prior innovations and why they failed. Then walk them through your proposal and show them how the two differ. Respect their prior experience and invite questions about your proposal as a way to hook them into seeing the proposal through your eyes.
3. *Another year, another fad.*	They see this as a bandwagon jump with no real content.	Be as specific as possible in your suggestions and tie the changes to particular behaviors or proposed outcomes to demonstrate the real effects of the change.
4. *You don't know what you're talking about.*	They either don't trust you, don't respect you, or both.	Try to get ahead of this possible objection by spending time with the people who will implement the change and soliciting their suggestions on what works and what doesn't. Integrate their insights into your proposal as a way to connect their experiences to your innovation.
5. *What's in it for you?*	They don't trust you.	If the change will improve your own position, don't deny this; honesty can increase trust. Then turn it around and say you understand that everyone has their own concerns. Tell them how your proposal will improve their positions as well. If the improvement is not likely to be apparent for a while, give them a metric by which they can measure progress.
6. *Are you trying to kill us?*	They fear overwork.	Training, training, training: you have to give them the resources to make the change and be responsive to their concerns about their ability to handle the work. Walk them through all changes, give them plenty of feedback, invite questions, and provide a reasonable schedule for when you expect them to be up to speed. This gives them both a standard to reach and time to reach it. By breaking the process down, you remove the fear that stems from uncertainty.

TYPE OF RESISTANCE	CAUSE(S)	HOW TO RESPOND
7. *Too little, too late.*	The problem is so entrenched that no one believes it will ever change.	This is an attitudinal problem and may require organizational or environmental changes to break old patterns of behavior. Court those who are less skeptical, and keep on top of those who insist nothing is happening by pointing to the results of the change. If some people are particularly resistant, you may need to resort to individual discipline to bring people in line or let go of those who are especially disruptive.
8. *This'll never work.*	They don't understand how it will work.	Again, training is key. If applicable, conduct simulations or walk-throughs so they can see exactly what they will need to do differently. By increasing their competence and confidence, you increase their willingness to change.
9. *I don't understand.*	They don't understand, period.	This requires work in advance of and during the change. Not only do you need to walk them through the mechanics of the change during retraining, but you need to prepare them in advance for why the change is necessary. Discuss your goals and how the change will help you progress toward them. In other words, to influence this group, you need to connect their specific tasks to the overall purpose of your organization.
10. *This isn't right for us.*	They see your change as a departure from core values or objectives.	Revisit those goals and values, and connect your innovation to them in a meaningful way. If your organization is expanding beyond its initial mission, then connect that expansion to the motives behind the founding of the organization. In other words, honor both the core values and those who take them seriously by stressing how the change actually puts you in a better position to fulfill those values.

CHAPTER 4

Know What Really Motivates People *and* What People Really Care About

I magine for a moment that you're sitting across from yourself in a comfortably lit office in what will be a high-stakes meeting. Your job is to convince the other You to do things differently—something that may initially be uncomfortable but will ultimately benefit both you and You in the long run.

The advantage you have in this scenario is that you know exactly what buttons you'll have to push to get You to consider the benefits that matter most to You in a proposal. You'll also know precisely what types of resistance You will put up and why. You know what values and beliefs You hold and which ones have priority. You'll know which of them you most need to speak to and honor to motivate You. You will also know which biases to sidestep and which emotions to consider to get You to see things more objectively.

If only.

Now back to reality. Imagine having to do this successfully with people who aren't You—people who have several layers and shades of values and beliefs, memories and associated emotions, not to mention any number of biases that can derail your best efforts at influencing. Their rationalizations and emotions would easily elude analysis from the finest functional magnetic resonance imaging receptors attached to their brain, which is one of the reasons hundreds of leadership and management books like this one are printed every year. Emerging and in-the-trenches leaders need help getting other people to do things they wouldn't necessarily do on their own. Otherwise, who'd need managers and leaders?

Until *Minority Report*–style Precogs (people in the Tom Cruise thriller who predict human behavior) can help us know another person's intentions better than we know our own, we have to rely on the decidedly low-tech strategy of "paying attention." It seems almost too simple an idea—paying attention to others—but as people are complex creatures who send thousands of signals every living second, we influencers have to pay attention to all of those nuances and variables to understand our fellow man and woman a little better.

In the context of paying attention, we learn that the more we perceive and know of another human being, the better equipped we'll be to bring him or her around to our way of thinking. But before that can happen, we need to know what people really care about on an individual basis.

Mind Reading: Mastering the Skill of Empathic Accuracy

If you had to boil the challenge of influence down to one word, it would be *empathy*. Derived from the Greek *pathos* and the German word *Einfühlung*, it is defined as "the ability to identify with and understand somebody else's feeling or difficulties."

The very definition parallels that of reading minds. Common social myth holds that women are better at this than men, but research hasn't sufficiently substantiated that theory. The field here is actually level, at least in one area. While men do just as well with empathy on issues of economics and commerce,

60

research does show that women still rule the empathic roost when it comes to relationships, where keen skills are even more critical to attempts at exerting influence.

Mastering the art of empathy depends on the successful interpretation of both verbal and nonverbal cues that link to the thoughts and feelings of others in a given moment or span of time. Body language, facial expression, content, vocal tone and volume, and how people interact with others on their side of the issue paint a clear picture for astute influencers who have developed the ability to assign meaning instantly to what they see, hear, and perceive.

One Columbia University experiment attempted to measure "empathic accuracy," that is, the ability to perceive correctly what others are experiencing. Researcher Jamil Zaki and his colleagues noted that perceivers were most accurate when they could both see and hear the targets, less accurate when they could hear and not see, and least accurate when they could see but not hear the targets. Clearly vocal cues are terrifically important to the ability to infer what another person is feeling.

No surprise there, perhaps, but it was surprising that those discussing negative experiences tended to be far more expressive than those discussing positive experiences. The researchers suggested that because the expression of negative emotions is less socially acceptable, perceivers are far more likely to pick up these cues and thus to analyze those emotions more accurately. The conclusion was that negative energy and resultant empathy is more easily perceived than positive energy. While this may be obvious, it sharpens the influencer's strategy at both ends of the spectrum. Bottom line—it's easier to sense when you're bombing than when you're nailing it.

One skill that astute influencers practice is that of nonjudgmental *moment awareness*. In essence, this is the sorting out of positive and negative aspects of perception, an analysis that leads to an empathic response. For this to work, we influencers must be self-aware and in the moment to ensure accuracy of perception and to avoid the very human tendency to hear and see what we want to hear and see.

One subtlety involves the *choice* to be empathic, the intention to perceive incoming verbal and nonverbal cues to truly understand how other people feel rather than using those cues and feelings against them. An *agendized* intention risks skewing perception, while the choice to be "in the moment" with someone yields a more accurate read, which is vital to how well we exert influence.

In essence, influencers must turn the skill of empathic accuracy—the key word being *accuracy*—on themselves first. For all parties, the true nugget of raw feeling is always wrapped in context and social coloring, and it is these filters that we seek to understand and strip away in our effort to perceive and empathize accurately. The result can be the recognition of—and invitation to share—common ground, which is the sweet spot of influence.

Listening with All Your Senses

With both verbal and nonverbal cues in play, it can be difficult to discern which are the more illuminating and accurate. According to Allene Grognet and Carol Van Duzer at the Center of Applied Linguistics, *listening* is the realm in which a communicator really exposes his agenda and feelings. Visual prompts have more latitude and variable meaning; everything from bad posture to a sore back is up for interpretative grabs. But vocal tone, volume, and linguistic content are often the more transparent cues of emotion and intention, and the astute influencer listens for them with a keen and empowered ear to discern what's going on behind the curtain of the verbal message itself.

According to the researchers, workplace listening skills are three times more career-critical than speaking skills and four to five times more effective in leading to positive consequences than reading and writing skills. The reason is that more critical information is exchanged in the listening moment than what the eye perceives or the speaker consciously provides. This is valid at all levels of an organization, yet it remains one of the most off-the-map and undertrained of all communications skills.

Effective listening is a process that involves four key elements: the speaker, message content, visualization of the message, and the listener. If the listener is already familiar with the content, comprehension goes up due to an instinctive application of existing context. And listeners who are actively involved in an exchange, versus simply listening in, tend to demonstrate higher comprehension and learning.

The speaker becomes a key variable because her ability to convey nuance, subtext, meaning, and clarity is all over the map, leaving the listener to sort all these variables out. Take conversations between subject matter experts and lay persons, for instance: as experts we don't always use universally comprehensible language; we often communicate in jargon; and when our listeners are left to fill in the blanks, the perceived message can be skewed. Add to this the fact that colloquialisms are almost always a matter of interpretation, one in which the listener applies his own contextual frame of reference to assign meaning. Other paralinguistic signals like pacing, inflection, and volume are also issues, as they can affect a listener's level of concentration. All of these points become a set of subvariables in the key issue of speaker style and competency, and thus they become integral to the listening challenge.

While content is still considered king in most organizations, the king relies on surrounding resources and contextual power—not to mention the occasional court jester—to get things done. So it is with listening, because content is only as meaningful as its interpretation is accurate. Sometimes familiar content comes with the baggage of familiar context, so the listening experience becomes (sometimes dangerously) predictable. It is when content is new and meaningful that listening strategies come into play, especially by the astute influencer. With the use of visual aids such as videos, PowerPoint presentations, graphics, gestures, facial expressions, and body language, the listening strategy broadens and becomes more complex, calling for focus on primary messaging and target results.

At a glance, listening seems like a somewhat passive pursuit. You sit there, you take it all in, you process. But research asserts that effective listening—the kind the astute influencer needs to both master and empower others—is anything but. Strategic listening is actually an *active* endeavor, as the listener immediately interprets, prioritizes, assigns meaning to, and evaluates the context of incoming messages, including nonverbal cues.

In addition to all of the speaker variables to which listeners must attune themselves, they also have their own list of variables that may affect *how* they listen. They must determine a reason to listen, which takes the form of anything from obligation (the boss is talking) to opportunity (What's in it for me?) and even self-service (I need to hear this). Meanwhile, as incoming messages continue, the listener edits and prioritizes, filling in blanks and assigning weight and relevance. Background information and context come into play in this process, coloring the speaker's message according to how information has been received and processed.

It's no simple task and easy to take for granted by the mere fact that even if we aren't doing it strategically, we are still *doing* it each and every time an incoming message knocks. To kick into a strategic listening gear, the Center for Creative Leadership offers six tips for more effective active listening.

Six Steps to Active Listening

First, *pay attention*. This is a choice, a prioritization of the incoming message over all other current stimuli, some of which may be very active behind the curtain of your countenance. When these stimuli are in conflict, they can show up in your body language and expression, thus showing your hand to the speaker. If you, as an influencer, see signs of the listener not being fully present, this is your cue to turn up the heat.

Second, the effective active listener needs to *suspend judgment*. An open mind is the hallmark of a good listener, even when background context—such as opposing beliefs—is already shaking its head from behind that curtain. While judgment is ultimately part of the process, a more effective approach is first to seek to understand fully, a process in which judgment should take a backseat.

Third, *reflection* is a skill effective listeners adopt to keep their background wheels from grinding and offer the presenter an unobstructed path toward her point. This involves nodding your head in the affirmative ("I get it, go on"), paraphrasing what you've heard in your own words ("What I hear you saying is . . ."), and doing so without tipping your hand about your reaction. You are *with* the presenter, and everything from your body language to your locked eyes says you are hanging on every word.

Fourth, *clarification* is the means toward comprehension. Good listeners don't allow a fogged presentation or their own distractions or lack of understanding to create a momentary lapse. Rather, they ask for another take on what they've just heard ("Can you run that last one by me again?") in order to clarify. This is akin to reflection, only now you are throwing up a yellow flag that allows the presenter to rephrase or double back as necessary.

Fifth, *summarizing* key themes is a strategy to make sure you, the listener, are on the same page as the presenter. It doesn't imply endorsement or criticism but rather a satisfactory level of clarity. It is parroting the main message back at the speaker in your own words, indicating your full comprehension. Phrases such as "It's clear your position on this is . . ." allow the speaker to jump back in to make her point in an even stronger and clearer way.

Finally, there is *sharing* what you understand. Prior to this point you've reflected, clarified, and summarized, all without any indication about what response is brewing as a result. When you share immediate feedback, you open the door to a clearer understanding through the presenter's response to yours. If the topic has been even a little foggy in the telling, your response allows the speaker to part the clouds and add more perspective.

An understanding of these tips empowers the astute 360-degree influencer, because objective, empathic listening is the primary pathway to understanding. Whatever the constituency or target of your intentions, you need to approach the moment of presentation having first listened and then prepared using what you've taken away from an active listening process to make sure *your* message and/or response hits all the right notes.

Reading Between the Lines: What People Really Want

While many studies have focused on the variables of effective communications, from both the influencing and the listening side, perhaps no other researcher has plumbed the depths of this niche of social psychology better than Alex Pentland, a professor at MIT. His field is computational social science, organizational engineering, and mobile information systems, which means he's well suited to use technology to gather and analyze data relating to human interaction.

Everything we've discussed thus far points toward a realm of interaction between speaker and listener that plays out behind the curtain of our awareness, if not our intention. We call them nonverbal clues, subtext, and backstory; Pentland posits that this is actually eons of human sociological evolution continuing to influence what we comprehend after seeing and hearing a message.

The product of this social evolution is what he calls "honest signals," which become cues and signs that we astute influencers can observe and leverage to optimize our approach. These are the same signals demonstrated by our earliest ancestors and are seen in upper primates and even other species as a way of sending and receiving messages. Language itself, says Pentland, is a layer of expression that builds in these deeper, more primal, and more honest signals that merely make the process clearer and more accessible. (If you've ever blushed in a moment of embarrassment, then you've called on your ancient communications DNA to express an honest signal.)

Pentland isolates four categories of honest signals:

1. **Mimicry:** The reflexive copying of another's manner of speaking, from tonality to body language and facial expression, even the adoption of speaking patterns and specific uses of colloquialisms and slang (Trading smiles is an example of mimicry.)
2. **Activity:** An indication of focus and interest through excitement and engagement (such as turning down the volume on the TV when someone begins speaking)
3. **Influence:** The greater power of influence held by the person being mimicked or reflected
4. **Consistency:** The smooth and fluid delivery of speech that instills a sense of expertise and confidence; always a key variable in the influencing equation

Using what he calls *reality mining*, Pentland applies technology to the analysis of social data, which, when applied in a strategic manner to basic human patterns, can result in dramatically altered outcomes. It's the anabolic steroid of influencing, enduing those who command these skills with the ability to take control of an exchange while remaining completely in the realm of empathetic listening and the context of striving for win-win outcomes.

As a result of their reality mining studies (in which individual behaviors are tracked, often for a prolonged period of time, in real-life rather than experimental settings), Pentland and his colleagues conclude that as many as 40 percent of decision outcomes may be attributed to honest signals. They further observed that such signaling is crucial to group cohesiveness and productivity: if one member of the group is happy, others are likely to be "infected" by this good mood. Such "mood contagion," Pentland argues, "serves to lower perceptions of risk within groups and to increase bonding."

This is important if you're working within an established group; the various signals help to cement a "common" sense, which in turn may help to move all members toward a common goal. Individuals within the group who wish to move it in a particular direction may present their preferences in an "idea market," while others respond with their own signals and preferences. The group is most likely to choose the option associated with the most positive signals—almost all of it nonverbal.

But what if you're not a member of the group or want to induce people to learn new behaviors? In-group signaling tends toward highly conservative outcomes—not surprising, given that the group seeks to preserve itself. Pentland suggests that the innovator who is a *charismatic connector* is most likely to succeed in persuading others to accept his ideas.

Charisma is, as Pentland admits, tough to define, but certain signals associated with the charismatic individual can be learned. A person who is highly energetic and enthusiastic is far more likely to garner attention, even from those who know little about the speaker's topic. Combine this energy with social connectivity—those who, in a crowd, circulate widely, listen attentively, speak fluidly, and tend to initiate conversations through questions—and these charismatic connectors are highly successful at influencing others.

We're signaling each other all the time. Tune in, and you'll be able to "hear" these signals loud and clear.

Digital Footprints: Social Media Reveal Habits, Preferences, and Behaviors

It shouldn't come as a surprise to anyone living within a stone's throw of modern civilization that we constantly leave "digital footprints" with even the most pedestrian of activities, whether in our social life or our profession. How often have you checked your e-mail today? Your employer will have the count. Texted a friend or retweeted a news item you found interesting? That data is logged by your telecom provider. Updated your Facebook status or managed to sneak in a blog post before lunch? Self-evident. To reinforce the inescapability of leaving your digital DNA behind at every turn, remind yourself where you purchased your last book—on Amazon or the local bookstore. If it's the latter, God bless you for supporting brick-and-mortar bookstores (yes, even the retail giants are dinosaurs). The clerk may have asked for your frequent shopper card, which keeps track of your purchases and rewards you with discounts. Even taxis—at least in New York City—are required to take payment via credit card now, which tells somebody somewhere something about your spending habits. Expedia and its competitors will gladly book your trip online and remind you of any deals for future flights if you sign up for that service. Retrieving your boarding pass at the airport no longer requires a human being, as a kiosk will effortlessly print it out and send you on your way. I'll spare you additional examples that you'll be able to spot for yourself as you go about your daily routines.

So, the "digitalness" of most activities leaves no question as to where we've been, what we did, how long we stayed, what it cost, and so on. And when these data are analyzed, as Pentland did with his honest signals, certain patterns emerge.

If you're in the business, you already know what "sticky" data mean for your influencing efforts. Take your LinkedIn account, for example—if you don't have one, sign up immediately. The more connections you have, the more people know what you have to offer and the more people can approach you for business or career opportunities. I have personally benefited tremendously from connections who have found me on LinkedIn. A nice feature is that you can see who has visited your profile—unless they chose to stay anonymous, which sort of defeats the purpose of networking if you ask me—and where your name has popped up in consideration. One way I have been able to influence fellow LinkedIn users is by posting discussion items I knew to be relevant to various groups from human resources professionals to senior executives in training and development. Their input to my discussion items often started a dialogue that led to the discovery of issues and problems for which I was able to offer potential solutions.

Facebook, too, offers influencers a glimpse into the values, issues, and personal preferences of their clients, target demographics, and constituency, though a fine line separates the smart use and the tragic personal branding mishaps in this forum. As with other social media, from blogs to Twitter to message boards, it is up to the influencer to sniff out the real desires and values of the target. The information is there; you just need to find it.

Googling has become an active verb in our collective lexicon, and most of us do it when we look for clues in making choices for or against something or someone. I personally Google everyone of any significance I meet—often on the spot with my BlackBerry. No, not in front of them; that wouldn't be very socially intelligent. The results of such a search will tell me more than most people are willing to divulge over cream cheese and crackers at a networking event or an initial client meeting. This person went to Harvard's Divinity School and heads up a national charity for homeless mothers who are trying to get back on their feet economically.

That's good to know. That person was a defendant in a lawsuit that alleged embezzlement of state funds. It says so in a digital court document titled *State of New York vs. Cheatum* from a decade ago on Google. Definitely good to know too! Yet another person has a personal website entirely unrelated to her core business of fashion design that educates and encourages people to learn more about animal abuse by big business and what everyone can do to help prevent it.

The Challenges of Transparency

As far as how deeply personal data, or any data, on anyone really helps you be a better influencer, consider this: you can't effectively influence people and make effective choices when you don't have much to go on. To reach people, to motivate them and speak to them on a deeply personal level, you have to know what will move them from a state of inertia or resistance to a certain action. You have to know as much about them as you can.

That includes the good and the bad. In sales and lending, knowing someone's credit score can give you information you need to influence her buying behavior, as well as helping you make better decisions that minimize risk. Instead of steering such a person toward the unaffordable (think mortgage-backed securities crisis blowing up the world's banks in 2008), you can push for a more rational decision. There are virtually thousands of examples of how digital footprints can inform our influencing attempts. All of them have one thing in common. They all give us valuable information and insight into someone's life and allow us to better influence that person to make certain choices over others.

Of course, all of this transparency won't continue to be without resistance and challenge. Issues of privacy are at the forefront of the expansion of social data gathering, driving to the heart of our human and social rights. An entire body of law is forming around this new paradigm, with review boards and benchmarks leading to standards and evolving ethical boundaries. If George Orwell were still around, he might offer a hearty "I told you so," yet the dark side of his prophetic take on the collision of social and economic evolution hasn't quite reached the level of his very literate cynicism.

Thus the challenge of the evolving influencer is defined. We need to be proactive and self-aware to ensure that our influencing strategies and tactics never depart from the principles that make them work: an empathic, win-win context that begins with listening and is applied from the receiving party's point of view. That much won't change with technology, even as that technology delivers an unprecedented depth of data that will allow us to more deeply understand who we are and what works within the dynamics of human exchange.

In the next chapter, we'll discuss how the decisions and choices we make define our ability to influence and learn about some of the most common decision-making traps and how to avoid them.

CHAPTER 5

How Our Decisions Define Our Ability to Influence

The decisions we make—in the worlds of politics and business, in particular—hardly ever affect only us. The benefits of a smart decision and the fallout from bad ones have a potentially wide-ranging impact on the lives of colleagues, peers, families, and communities—the net results from this often being a measure of our personal influence in the aftermath.

To see how this plays out in real life, we might guess—it's hard to know for sure—at the current and future influencing power of two former chief executives from IT giant Hewlett-Packard (HP), Mark Hurd and Carly Fiorina. To put our discussion in a proper context, they are *former* chief executives in part because of what their stakeholders and constituents at HP deemed poor decision making; this earned them a reported collective loss of confidence and, with that, a loss of influence. Let's take a closer look at each case.

After a series of celebrated decisions related to a successful turnaround at the company, former CEO Mark Hurd felt the pressure to step down amid allegations of sexual harassment, as well as admissions that he creatively passed off personal spending as business expenses. Exit influence and Hurd.

His predecessor in the top job at HP, Carly Fiorina, was once considered one of the most powerful women in business. The company's board of directors sacked her in a very public way, in part due to her decision—against board members' advice—to acquire rival Compaq, a merger that was widely derided as a colossal failure. While HP eventually recovered, Fiorina's reputational stock suffered irreparable damage. The prominent business magazine *Portfolio* labeled her one of "The 20 Worst American CEOs of All Time" in 2009 (seven years after her decision to merge Compaq into HP), pointing out, among other things, her excessive self-promotion and busy presence on the speaking circuit while her corporate ship was listing badly. As more tangible evidence of her flawed leadership, the magazine mentioned the significant drop in share value—down to half—while Fiorina was at the HP helm. Incidentally, stock prices jumped nearly 7 percent when her ouster was announced in 2005, according to a CNN Money report at the time.

So while Fiorina's decision making was seen as strategically flawed, her successor's seemed to be more on the ethical periphery. Either way, their decisions led to a very public recognition of loss of confidence and, ultimately, influence.

You don't have to be CEO to have a stake in making good decisions. Sure, for many people working in large organizations it can be easy to avoid making decisions, adeptly deferring problems and forks in the road to another division within the company. If your goal is simply to protect yourself from criticism and consequences of any sort—the good inevitably sacrificed along with the avoidance of the bad—this is not an unreasonable strategy.

If, however, it's potential advancement you seek, you can't hang back and let others shape the agenda, nor can you afford a reputation as someone who won't lock in a decision. Few things drive colleagues crazier than someone who can't or won't make up his or her mind, and few things lead to a loss of respect and influence faster than someone who backs away from important decisions.

Making decisions involves taking responsibility, not just for the decision itself, but also for the *consequences* of that decision. This means you have to think beyond just the decision; consider its implementation and the impact of your choice; and recognize that despite never having perfect information, you nonetheless have to choose. To decide, in short, is to risk.

If that sounds a tad dramatic, maybe you should reflect on why so many people refuse to decide. Ask yourself why you sometimes avoid or dislike making decisions. While the aforementioned inevitable lack of "perfect" or even sufficient information is to blame, the truth is that sometimes people don't want the responsibility that comes with a decision—or more specifically, they don't want to deal with the possibly unpleasant outcomes of a disputed decision.

We 360-degree influencers can't afford such immunity, though. Just look at the people you admire or strive to emulate. Do they waver or equivocate? Do they unload responsibility on someone else?

The fact is leadership and influence are inseparable from challenging decision making, and the more we know about the process, the better equipped we are to bolster our influence in all directions with the making of sound decisions.

We Are Only as Influential as Our Choices Are Smart

As stated previously, vacillating does nothing for your reputation, but being decisively *wrong*—in your public's eyes, at least—doesn't do much for you either. Remember Carly Fiorina?

This is tricky territory. What makes a decision wrong? Is a wrong decision always bad? Is every good decision the "right" one?

In answering these questions, we first need to recognize that making a decision involves two critical steps: (1) the process by which we decide, and (2) the eventual decision itself.

The Decision-Making Process

Most of us have learned over the course of many quandaries that good decision-making processes can lead to bad outcomes, while flawed processes can actually lead to good results. But if we want to increase our chances of making good decisions, we have to put as much emphasis on the "making" as we do on the "decision."

The former Treasury secretary and Wall Street financier Robert Rubin points out that "decisions should not be judged by outcomes but by the quality of the decision making," although, he admits that "outcomes are certainly one useful input in that evaluation." It's important to recognize that "any individual decisions can be badly thought through and yet be successful, or exceedingly well thought through but be unsuccessful." Over time, however, "more thoughtful decision making will lead to better overall results, and more thoughtful decision making can be encouraged by evaluating decisions on how well they were made rather than on outcome."

The management consultant Graham Jeffery, referring to some of our young century's most poignant events, argues that former British prime minister Tony Blair should be judged on the quality of his decisions, not on the outcomes of those decisions, especially when considering his decision to join the United States in its invasion of Iraq: "The quality of the decision to go to war ought to hinge critically on the probability that was assigned to the 'Saddam has WMD?' uncertainty, *at the time the decision was made.*" The preponderance of evidence, Jeffries states, suggested that Saddam Hussein had weapons of mass destruction (WMDs); that he did not was fortunate and ought not to be held against the Blair government.

Others, however, would point to the decision to go to war as an exemplar of flawed decision making, one driven by the *certainty* that Saddam Hussein had WMDs, a certainty that distorted the intelligence gathering and analysis process.

Seymour Hersh interviewed intelligence and foreign-policy officials who despaired of "stovepiping," sending information to higher authorities before it had been vetted for reliability. One intelligence agent told Hersh that he left the CIA when he thought information was being misused by Bush administration officials: "They didn't like the intelligence they were getting, and so they brought in people to write the stuff. They were so crazed and so far out and so difficult to reason with—to the point of being bizarre. Dogmatic, as if they were on a mission from God." Such single-mindedness meant that "if it [information] doesn't fit their theory, they don't want to accept it."

I bring up this example, not to refight the battle over Iraq, but to emphasize that the decision-making process can be overwhelmed by urgency and that the desire for an outcome can be so great as to warp the structure and integrity of that process. Certainty at the outset of the process can make a sham of decision making itself, subordinating it to the preordained outcome and deforming analysis into wish fulfillment. Rubin cautions against such certainty, asserting that we live in a world of probabilities, not proven absolutes: "Rejecting the idea of certainties and needing to make the best judgments possible about probabilities should drive you restlessly and rigorously to analyze and question whatever is before you—and to treat assertions as launching pads for analysis, not as accepted truths—in pursuit of better understanding."

Key to this sensibility is the recognition that *there is no perfect information*. David Weinberger, writing in the *Harvard Business Review*, notes that the phrase "garbage in/garbage out" may make sense when applied to computers, but in the complex and contradictory real world, human managers have to be able to sift through and make decisions based on, well, garbage. The issue, then, is less about garbage in than it is on asking, "Which inputs will keep you from putting garbage out?"

Another, more sanitary, way of putting this is that the problem is often less a *lack of* information than one of *too much* information. Says Weinberger, "The fact is that making an informed decision means not just saying yea or nay but evaluating your sources and deciding which to trust." Again, focus not just on the end point but on the analysis that leads to that point.

The Decision Itself

Too often, we look only at the decision point, which means we may misjudge the abilities of the decision maker based solely on our assessment of the decision itself. Economics professor Dan Ariely observes, "Our focus on outcomes is understandable. When a company loses money, people demand that heads roll. . . . Moreover, measuring outcomes is relatively easy to do; decision making–based reward systems will be more complex."

According to an informal survey Ariely conducted with numerous corporate board members, he learned that most boards don't think a good CEO is necessarily that much better than a mediocre one as far as added stock value is concerned—a mere 10 percent on average, according to the respondents. Ariely interprets this as an understanding among board members that final results aren't always within a leader's control.

Business professors David Garvin and Michael Roberto agree that decisions should be understood as part of a process: "Our research shows that the difference between leaders who make good decisions and those who make bad ones is striking. The former recognize that all decisions are processes, and they explicitly design and manage them as such. The latter persevere in the fantasy that decisions are events they alone control."

Unfortunately, the powerful desire to believe we are in control (particularly the higher up the corporate ladder we are) means we don't question ourselves or our assumptions, and this gives us a greater illusion of infallibility. Conversely, in a low-ranking position, we may question our decision-making abilities, especially if our decisions are out of sync with the majority of those made by our superiors.

The fundamental error here is that we confuse the status or position of the decision maker with the quality of the decision-making process. If we have evidence—based on our title, say, or the size of our investment portfolio—that we're competent and smart, and if choices we've made in the past have turned out well for us, we may not consider the ways we came to those decisions and assume that we are particularly prescient or wise. We think a choice is good because *we* made it, not because of the rigor of the analysis prior to the choice.

You may be smart—very smart. But don't outsmart yourself into believing in a kind of decisional alchemy, that every choice you make must be right because it came from you. As we'll discuss next, and as we learn daily from the headlines, smart people do make dumb decisions more often than we'd like to believe.

Why Smart People Often Make Dumb Decisions

Having just met a client for lunch in the world-famous Lipstick building in New York City, I couldn't help but reflect on the address's most infamous former tenant. Bernie Madoff scammed a lot of smart people; "ponzied" them right out of billions of dollars. He promised regular high returns, and even though some other very smart people—including those in an oversight role—questioned the reliability of his numbers, most of those involved with him happily accepted the promised returns. To echo a question I asked earlier in the book, how could these smart people have been so dumb?

The *New York Times* business columnist Joe Nocera wondered about this too: "A lot of rich, smart people who should have known better handed over their fortunes to someone who turned out to be a crook." Nocera is clear in his condemnation of Madoff's crimes ("He was—is—the worst of the worst"), but these crimes could not have occurred without a certain kind of "magical thinking" on the part of his victims. Behavioral economists refer to this magical thinking as one of the cognitive traps that can lead typically smart people to make dumb decisions. Magical thinking is what we engage in when we believe that we can influence events with our minds—or certain rituals we perform—alone.

My own father believes that he can control traffic lights with his mind when he needs to. What gave him that idea? Every time he was in a rush to get somewhere, he would try to get the lights to turn green just as he was approaching them so he didn't have to slow down or stop on his way to an appointment. And since light changes have sometimes worked out for him that way, he got reinforcement from this "evidence" that he has the power to manipulate traffic controls with his thoughts. Never mind the thousands of times he had to stop at a light when it was inconvenient, because that evidence does not conform to his beliefs in his magic powers. But, in his defense, who doesn't know someone who wears a "lucky" pair of socks to his golf game, firmly believing it can give him an edge for the win?

There are thousands of examples of how we make questionable decisions based on erroneous beliefs, and even otherwise prudent investors can fall victim to the likes of a Madoff. This is not to say the victims are to blame; Madoff broke the law and stole people's money. But it is striking to note how little thought went into the decision to hand over hundreds of thousands—even millions—of dollars to a man who was notoriously secretive about his operations.

Elie Wiesel, whose foundation lost more than $15 million, spoke on a panel arranged by *Portfolio* about his involvement with Madoff: "I remember that it was a myth that he created around him. That everything was so special, so unique, that it had to be secret. . . . It was like a mystical mythology that nobody could understand. Just as the myth of exclusivity, he gave the impression that maybe a hundred people belonged to his club. Now we know thousands of them were cheated by him."

A number of commentators on the Madoff scheme have noted that the "exclusivity" was seen as a marker of reliability, but as Nocera observes, "Just about anybody who actually took the time to kick the tires of Mr. Madoff's operation tended to run in the other direction." Instead of due diligence, these investors (and in some cases, their financial advisers) trusted this man to take care of them.

Jim Chanos, another member of the *Portfolio* panel, cited the quote "the greater the mania, the higher the intellect that succumbs to it." In some sense, it is precisely because people are smart that they get pulled into dubious schemes. Chanos further observed, "As the financial juices get flowing, as they certainly were a few years ago, we begin to suspend belief in what normally would be a situation where one would equate risk with reward and would be skeptical of anything that appears too good to be true. When everybody's making money, it's very easy to set that aside."

Too good to be true—that phrase should be enough to set off anyone's warning bells. But, as Chanos notes, people too often want to get while the getting is good, so much so that anyone who *doesn't* jump in is seen as the fool.

Nocera used the term *seduction* to describe Madoff's approach to his victims; Chanos reminds us that we are often all too willing to be seduced, to forget that what goes up might come down. Warren Buffet concurs, observing that "people don't get smarter about things as basic as greed."

That's the problem, of course. We think we can outsmart everyone else and end up outsmarting ourselves.

The Most Common Decision-Making Traps and How to Avoid Them

Leaders live and die—and careers thrive or stall—based on the decisions made along the way to the corner office. An entire book could be filled with the cognitive traps that derail our decision-making processes, but for practicality's sake, we'll focus on those most relevant for business-related decision making. Any of these can torpedo and sink your ability to influence faster than you can shout, "Incoming!" But forewarned is forearmed, as they say, which makes the following a list both to remember and to use when important decisions are the order of the day.

Five Important Decision-Making Traps

John Hammond, Ralph Keeney, and Howard Raiffa, authors of *Smart Choices: A Practical Guide to Making Better Decisions,* singled out the following traps:

1. Anchoring
2. Status quo
3. Sunk costs
4. Confirming evidence
5. Framing

Anchoring. This is a common trap and often present in negotiations. As Hammond and his colleagues define it, "When considering a decision, the mind gives disproportionate weight to the first information it receives. Initial impressions, estimates, or data anchor subsequent thoughts and judgments." Anchors serve as a baseline for present and future considerations. While this is not always unreasonable, since past experience can provide information, unthinking reliance on the anchor can lead to skewed forecasts or, as when someone starts with a high bid, to overpayment, even if the end price is lower than the high bid.

The main way to avoid anchoring bias is to recognize that it can affect critical thinking and, especially, perspective in negotiations. Think through an issue and try to gain as much information from as many different perspectives as possible; be aware of your own preconceptions as well as those of your advisers, who may have their own anchors. On the other hand, you may also be able to use anchors in negotiations, such as when you start with that high bid.

Status Quo. We can be misled by our preference for the status quo, even if we didn't have much to do with creating it. We get used to what we have very quickly and just as quickly become unwilling to part with it. One way to counter this bias is to treat the status quo as just another alternative and to ask if you would choose your current situation if you weren't already in it. Recognize, too, that the status quo has its own drawbacks, and that while it might once have been optimal, the time may have come for an adjustment.

Sunk Costs. With sunk costs, we try to recover what is, in fact, irrecoverable and thus center decisions on recovery rather than on moving forward. It can be difficult to admit that something or someone is a lost cause (especially if we were the ones who advocated for the project or person), but a willingness to reconsider our initial decision as well as our own reluctance to move on can help us avoid "throwing good money after bad." This bias can show up in a situation as innocuous as waiting on hold for a customer service representative on the phone. Even if the help we need is not necessarily mission-critical at the time, the fact that we may have already "invested" or "sunk" 20 minutes or more of our valuable time is often enough to make us continue holding for a payoff instead of hanging up and conceding to a clear and unrecoverable loss of time.

Confirming Evidence. An example that will show up in history and economics classes the world over is the aforementioned need of Bush administration officials to find evidence of WMDs in Iraq at the beginning of the Gulf War. This represented an extreme form of confirming evidence trap—that is, the officials' willingness to seize on any information that supported their case and to discount anything that countered it. That you might have a strong inclination toward a particular outcome or interpretation isn't bad in itself, but a willingness to question yourself or, better yet, have someone you respect play devil's advocate or dissenter can force you off of your bias.

Framing. As we'll discuss in Chapter 11, framing is a powerful influencing device and can help you present your argument in its most favorable light. This said, recognize that anyone can make use of frames to slant, spin, and otherwise present information in a way that influences your decisions to their maximum benefit. Neutralize the framing effect by questioning what is left out and how your understanding of an issue would change if it were framed differently.

Hammond and his colleagues also looked at estimating and forecasting traps that encompass overconfidence, prudence ("just to be safe" adjustments), and recallability (when big, rare events overshadow smaller, ordinary events). They noted that in these traps, as well as all others, awareness that such biases may exist is the first step in countering them.

Other Biases and Illusions

Psychologists Stephen Garcia, Hyunjin Song, and Abraham Tesser have identified the social comparison bias. Pioneers in the field of cognitive biases, Amos Tversky and Daniel Kahneman consider the variations of biases that include representativeness and availability. Psychology professor Suzanne Thompson considers the illusion of control, while management professor Dan Lovallo, working with Kahneman, notes the distorting affects of managerial optimism.

The Social Comparison Bias. This bias is an insidious one and may be activated during hiring and promotion considerations: someone who is seen as a threat to those making the decision may lose out to another candidate who allows higher-ups to retain their status. Garcia and his colleagues note that there is no quick fix for this bias other than to recognize that it may be operating on, and impeding the future progress of, your group.

Representativeness and Availability. These separate biases can lead us to connect (or fail to connect) sets of information and to rely on information that we can easily recall or is familiar to us. In some cases, such connections are simply heuristics, or useful guides for making sense of uncertainty, but when we forget they are simply rough guides, we may miss other information that can affect our judgment.

Illusion of Control and Optimism. All of the preceding biases can feed into both illusions of control and managerial optimism. Personal involvement, familiarity, the desire for a specific outcome, and past success may, as Thompson points out, lead us to an illusory belief in our control over the situation. This "control heuristic" contains two elements: (1) an intention to achieve a particular end, and (2) a perceived link between our actions and the outcome. She notes that, as a heuristic, this can lead to accurate assessments, but it "can also lead to overestimations of control because intention and connection can occur in situations in which a person has little or no control."

Think of our earlier example of magical thinking, or that of a baseball player on a hitting streak who wears the same mismatched socks to every game, or even the childhood rhyme "Step on a crack, break your mother's back." We may engage in harmless superstitions, but we need to be aware of the drawbacks of these and similar illusions of control.

Ironically, recent research suggests that people who are mildly depressed may have a more accurate understanding of the limits of control, perhaps because they concentrate on failure rather than success. This isn't to suggest—in the spirit of controlling this illusion—that we are better off feeling rotten about ourselves, but instead that we might want to reflect on the universal fact that we haven't always gotten what we wanted.

Lovallo and Kahneman explain that both biases and organizational pressures can also lead to overly optimistic estimates of outcomes. They note that illusions of control come into play, especially when outcomes are favorable, which in turn may lead to undue optimism in forecasting outcomes. "Executives and entrepreneurs," they write, "seem to be highly susceptible to these biases."

How do we counter the ingrained bias toward optimism? Kahneman and associates advocate in favor of the *outside view,* or *reference-class forecasting.* Reference-class forecasting is designed to eliminate various common biases in decision making through cultivation of an "outside view." The process involves gathering information outside of your own point of view or project—in particular, finding cases similar to your project, gathering as much information as possible about the variables and outcomes of those cases, and comparing this information to your situation to try to determine the chances of your project's success.

Lovello and Kahneman offer five steps to help you take the outside view:

1. Select a reference class.
2. Assess a distribution of outcomes.
3. Make a prediction of your place on that distribution.
4. Assess the reliability of your prediction.
5. Correct your initial prediction.

Each step requires a fair amount of thought (how to determine the appropriate reference class, for example), but the idea is to give you perspective on your project in terms of outside information.

When to Listen to Intuition and When Not To

Everyone has at times wavered between different options, uncertain of how to decide. It's not uncommon for someone to advise you to "go with your gut" or perform a "gut check"—that is, to follow subconscious cues to reach a judgment.

Popular books like Malcolm Gladwell's *Blink* have focused our attention on the powers of the subconscious, working its mysterious ways in a manner more honest or accurate than the conscious mind. And frankly, we've likely all had those moments when something "seemed off" and we avoided a bad situation, or when we "just clicked" with someone who later became a valued associate, great friend, or life partner.

But just as our rationality has its biases, so too does our "subrationality" have its own quirks. Intuition may lead us astray just as surely as conscious analysis, but we may end up excusing or discounting errors resulting from the former precisely because it is not rational. And while most of us can admit (however unhappily) that we analyzed a situation incorrectly, how many of us are willing to admit that our intuition is flawed, especially if deciding on a "blink" is supposed to be so effective?

The psychologist Barry Dunn studied the notion that we ought to listen to our bodies when making decisions amid uncertainty. He noted that an awareness of their physiological state may lead some people to master a skill more quickly. In others, however, such awareness leads them astray and actually impedes their learning process. As he told Keri Chiodo, "What happens in our bodies really does appear to influence what goes on in our minds. We should be careful about following these gut instincts, however, as sometimes they help and sometimes they hinder our decision making."

Scientist Andrew McAfee is similarly dubious about the metaphorical version of the gut check. He notes that intuition is a skill that must be cultivated over the long term, that it only works in highly specific situations, and that cognitive biases such as anchoring—relying too much on a particular characteristic or morsel of information when we make decisions—are as likely to distort intuition as they do conscious analysis.

But if intuition takes a long time to construct, is it really intuition? In other words, what we call "intuition" may simply be knowledge gained through experience. We "just know" something, not because our tummies are talking to us, but because we've seen a similar phenomenon often enough to be able to identify the issue or solution in a flash (which we may then call a "flash of insight").

Jeff Stibel, chairman and CEO of Dun & Bradstreet Credibility Corp. and blogger for *Harvard Business Review,* distinguishes between intuition as instant pattern recognition and *forethought,* which requires an omnivorous attention to detail and continual analysis. Forethought, as Stibel defines it, requires conscious preparation, whereas intuition simply calls on unmediated experiences. But this definition seems too either-or, not least because intuition may also arise (in that flash of insight) as a result of reflection on experience or in the kind of "mindless" knowledge accrued through repetition and habituation; all we need to bring intuition forth are certain cues in our environment.

Such an understanding of intuition is quite different from that actual, physical gut check; still, just as our gut may mislead us, so too may our intuition, and for all of the reasons McAfee mentions. The psychology professor William Grove and his colleagues evaluated the outcomes of mechanical (using actuarial tables, statistical models, and computer algorithms) versus clinical (relying on oneself to put together the relevant data) medical judgments and concluded that, in almost every case, reliance on mechanical processes led to more accurate diagnoses. This conclusion concurs with an earlier study by Professor Lewis Goldberg, in which computer models led to better outcomes than individual judgments.

Skilled Intuition

Should we, then, run all of our decisions through a computer before acting? Not only is this impossible—actuarial tables and statistical models are not available for every contingency—it may not be necessary. Gary Klein, who advocates in favor of *naturalistic decision making* (NDM), and Daniel Kahneman, who takes the more skeptical *heuristics and biases* (HB) approach to decision processes, collaborated on a paper and discovered, to their mutual surprise, how much they agreed with one another.

Their agreement centered on their shared understanding of skilled intuition as something that can be learned (as opposed to some kind of mystical force). People who are able to practice skilled intuition operates in an environment that provides cues which they, in turn, are trained or have sufficient experience to recognize. Kahneman was willing to recognize that in some situations NDM can lead to effective judgments, whereas Klein accepted that not all environments (especially those involving high levels of uncertainty) may allow for the deployment of skilled intuition. They did state that scholars in the HB tradition are still more likely to focus on the errors of intuitive judgments, and those working the NDM line may be averse to considerations of bias, but anyone concerned with decision making has to take the *full* measure of intuition.

So when should you rely on intuition? Klein and Kahneman note that it works well when you have long experience or training in a specific field and when you work in a "high-validity" environment—that is, one in which "there are stable relationships between objectively identifiable cues and subsequent events or between cues and the outcomes of possible actions." Medicine and firefighting, for example, operate in high-validity environments, whereas unpredictable areas such as individual stock forecasting or long-term political phenomena are unfavorable to intuition. Just as important is your opportunity to develop your skill over a long period in your operating environment, one that provides both good cues and good feedback. Chance, as Louis Pasteur observed, favors the prepared mind.

Unfortunately, people who work in low-validity, high-uncertainty environments (such as finance) may misattribute chance good outcomes to their own intuitive skills. And those with expertise in one field may be similarly overconfident when applying their skills to another field or even another area within their own. A skilled forensic accountant, for example, may not be the right person to work out complex tax issues, as the expertise doesn't easily transfer or apply. Similarly, in the area of leadership, the genius of a respected propulsion engineer—that's a bona fide rocket scientist—may fall short in leading and motivating a team in spite of a can-do attitude, regardless of his or her demonstrated excellence in launching shuttles into orbit.

There are also situations in which the mechanical process is clearly superior to human intuition, especially in crunching through mounds of data in a timely and consistent manner. When the computer Watson competed against—and bested—two former "Jeopardy" champions, a number of commentators wondered if this was the beginning of the end for humans. Was our uniquely human ability to make the "leaps" across the data mounds now shared by computers that could both crunch and leap?

I like the observation of one of pundit Andrew Sullivan's readers. That person saw Watson not as a competitor to or adversary of humans, but as a highly efficacious adjunct to human analysts, like the computer in the "Star Trek" series. The computer, this reader noted, could scan resources outside of the Starfleet officer's ken, which in turn freed that officer up to focus on asking the right questions: "As long as a person is trained on *how* to ask the questions, the Computer can pull answers from all available sources and suggest multiple related items that might never have been considered before." As that reader noted, "The potential is extraordinary, right?"

The Reasons for Indecision

You've been looking for a new job and have interviewed for a couple of positions. A start-up offers you a position doing the same work you're currently doing but for considerably more money. Another firm gives you the chance to go in a new direction, one you've been thinking about for a while, for slightly less than what you're currently earning but with the prospect of regular salary increases. And then, seemingly out of the blue, your boss tells you that the company is considering a new venture and implies that you would be the perfect person to head up this project; you'd get more authority, more responsibility, and more money—if the new project is approved. What do you do?

If you're a black-and-white thinker, chances are you'll reach a decision pretty quickly. You'll have figured out what matters most to you and not worry that you might make the wrong decision. If you've already decided to leave, your boss's suggestion is unlikely to persuade you to stay, and if you know that what really matters isn't the money but the chance to blaze a new path, your decision is easy.

If, on the other hand, you're a more ambivalent sort, all of these variables—money, continuity, opportunity, and uncertainty—may lead you into a thicket of indecision. You like your current job but had been feeling stale, so this new opportunity could be just what you want; on the other hand, nothing has been promised, and it might be good to make a clean break and try something new. As for the job with the start-up, the money would certainly be nice, and doing the work you're already doing would make the transition easier; then again, it *is* a start-up, and what if it flames out in a year? Then what? And that other job? Wouldn't it be nice to try something new, something you've always wanted? But what if the idea of that new direction is better than the reality? And even though the salary cut isn't the most important thing, money does matter. . . .

Sound like anyone you know?

Shirley Wang at the *Wall Street Journal* interviewed a number of psychologists about ambivalence, and they noted that it isn't always bad. People may be more thoughtful about decisions and more likely to consider multiple viewpoints in making decisions, which can be a benefit in collaborative situations.

So what do you do when you find yourself agonizing over the options? Wang cites Professor Richard Boyatzis's suggestion to cut down the number of details and try to focus on a few key variables. Black-and-white thinkers, for example, *don't* weigh all variables equally; instead, they give clear priority to those that matter most to them.

The social psychologist Frenk van Harreveld offers another tactic. If, after careful consideration, he is still unable to figure out the best option, he flips a coin, and if his immediate reaction when the coin lands on heads is negative, then he knows what he should do.

Both tactics share an underlying premise: the need for clarity in the ordering of your preferences, which is to say, clarity in self-understanding. Do you regret roads not taken or fear losing what you have? Think a year or two down the road: Where do you want to be? What if the job you choose does not go well? What will make you happier: the money or the chance to stretch yourself? What do you want?

What do you want? Focus on that central question. If your only response is "I don't know," then you need to figure out how you reacted to big decisions you made in the past and what made you more or less happy. If you have to make a decision in the course of your job, then you still need to determine what the central issue or skill is that needs to be addressed and make sure that drives your decision.

Finally, if you are the type to worry about the unforeseen consequences of any decision, it might help to recognize that there are *always* unforeseen consequences, and it's unreasonable to expect yourself to know everything. Draw a line around what you can control and minimize the amount of time you worry about what you can't.

How to Consistently Make Better Decisions with Fewer Regrets

It's hard not to worry about the consequences of your decisions, especially when a lot rides on them. The last section delved into the importance of identifying all the pieces of the particular puzzle you are trying to solve and ranking those that are more and less important. If this leads to a clear set of preferences, great, but what if your list contains variables of equal—and apparently incommensurable—worth?

John Hammond, Ralph Keeney, and Howard Raiffa have come up with a process they call *even swaps*, which can help you make trade-offs among different kinds of values: "In essence, the even-swap method is a form of bartering; it forces you to think about the value of one objective in terms of another." Let's return to our hypothetical job offer example. Hammond and his colleagues suggest that you create a "consequences table" in which you list the objectives you seek down the left side of the table and the different job opportunities across the top; you then fill it in as shown in Table 5.1.

Such a layout, Hammond and his fellow professors explain, allows you to see exactly what is at stake with each position: "It gives you a clear framework for making trade-offs. Moreover, it imposes an important discipline, forcing you to define all alternatives, all objectives, and all relevant consequences at the outset of the decision process."

TABLE 5.1

	CURRENT JOB	JOB OFFER 1	JOB OFFER 2
Compensation	$80,000/year	$95,000/year	$75,000/year
Responsibility level	Midmanager	Manager	Manager
Reliability	Company is large and solid	Start-up	Company is small and solid
Job skills	Use current skills	Use current skills	Develop new skills
Enjoyment	Okay, a bit bored	Likely will become bored	Have long wanted to do this
Advancement opportunities	Possibility of moving into new area	Possibility of taking on additional management responsibilities	Possibility of leadership participation as company branches out

The next step is to rank each company in each category—job offer 1 ranks first in salary, for example, while job offer 3 ranks first in enjoyment. If one job clearly ranks below the others in all categories, that job is "dominated" and may be eliminated. (The creation of a secondary dominance table can be particularly helpful when you have a large number of options and/or a long list of variables.)

What if no option is clearly dominated, that is, the rankings yield no clear winners or losers? That's where even swaps come into play. According to the authors, "The even-swap method provides a way to adjust the values of different alternatives' consequences in order to render them equivalent and thus irrelevant." In other words, the objective is to eliminate objectives.

This is relatively easy to do when you're dealing with numeric values—if all the jobs offered the same salary, then salary could be eliminated as a consideration—but you can also apply it to things like titles or, in this case, responsibility level. You might calculate that to be a midmanager in a large firm is equivalent to being a manager in a small firm and so eliminate that as an objective.

Or you could temporarily expand or create a side consequences table in which you assign a number ranking to the importance of enjoyment; job skills; and—knowing that you worry about regretting whatever decision you make—potential regret, in which you figure out what kinds of regrets you can live with and what you can't. You then plug these rankings back into your original table and use them, if they're equal, to eliminate objectives; if they're not equal, clarify what matters more and less. The key, as Hammond and his colleagues observe, is that "no matter how subjective a trade-off, you never want to be guided by whim—you must think carefully about the value of each consequence to you."

Ten Decision-Making Tools You Can Use Immediately

It should be clear by now that we humans do not always think as clearly as we should in making decisions. So what can we do to ensure that we do make good decisions?

1. **Focus on the process, not (primarily) the outcome.** You might get good outcomes just by leaping to a conclusion. But considering that outcomes are largely outside of your control, it makes good sense to use a solid decision-making process that can offer a better chance for delivering good results.

2. **Be skeptical.** Critical thinking is underrated, and testing the validity of assumptions and evidence means you'll be in a better position to defend your decisions than those who merely believe or take the word of pseudoexperts.

3. **List the relevant variables.** Tom Davenport, President's Chair in Information Technology and Management at Babson College, cautions, "Without some inventory, all decisions will

be treated as equal—which probably means that decisions won't be addressed at all."

4. **Sort the relevant information.** After making your lists (and checking them twice), draw up consequences tables, and scrutinize your objectives; do anything that forces you to separate out the significant variables from background noise.

5. **Eliminate irrelevant information.** One part of the process of making a consequences table is to engage in even swaps, that is, to determine what is similar enough across your various options that it can effectively be excluded from consideration. In some situations, you might simply want to go through your lists and eliminate those items that are less important to you.

6. **Question the relevant information.** Part of this is making sure that you do, in fact, have all the necessary information, but you must also make sure the information is reliable.

7. **Question the process.** Setting up a process is important, but remember that the decision rules you set up are a means to an end, not the end itself. As the management consultant John Baldoni suggests to avoid groupthink, ask, "What did we miss? What if we did the opposite? What happens if we're wrong?"

8. **Perform a gut check.** As an adjunct, this is good policy. You already know your gut can (metaphorically speaking) lead you astray, and while you wouldn't want to base your decisions solely on your emotions, I agree with Frenk van Harreveld, who said that sometimes your immediate reaction to a possible outcome can clue you in to your real feelings about the decision.

9. **Cultivate the outside view.** Use the tools of reference-class forecasting; seek out and collect information about projects similar to yours and examine their successes and failures. Use the data you find to get a more realistic picture of the potential outcomes for your project before letting the overconfi-

dence bias sweep you off your (rational) feet and inform your decision making completely.

10. **Say no.** Decision making is not always about saying, "Proceed." Nobody likes to stop after sinking considerable costs into a project, but sometimes the best decision is to stop, in spite what has already been invested. Cutting your losses can be an effective part of the decision-making process.

Each of these strategies can help you cut through the biases that can cloud your thinking and give you ways to make hard decisions with clarity and without—or with far less—regret.

In the next chapter, we'll look at how you can strategically influence the choices and decisions people make, how to know what perceptions you're creating, and how to better understand how people's values and beliefs affect their decision making in order to improve your success in becoming a 360-degree influencer.

CHAPTER 6

Setting the Stage: Strategically Influencing People's Decisions

Now that you've got all of *your* decision making figured out, how do you go about influencing the decisions of others? It would be nice if the best way were by basing arguments on solid evidence that met all the central demands of the issue or problem at hand. Yes, it would be nice to tell you that reason and evidence matter more than anything—but you've probably figured out that that would be untrue.

Reason and evidence do matter a great deal and having them on your side via diligent research and preparation can make influencing easier. But if you don't consider all of the other variables at play in the decision-making process, you are likely to be pushed aside in favor of someone who has—and has pitched her argument in a way designed to appeal to the people with the final word.

Perception Shapes Thinking and Behavior

Have you ever been passed over for a promotion and wondered why? Have you ever been in the final phase of a series of job interviews only to lose out to the other candidate who, in your opinion, would make a better runner-up? Have you ever been rejected by someone you thought the world of or not picked for a team you wanted to be part of?

If you answered yes to any of these questions, you're not alone. It's the fate of most people in most endeavors and venues in life, since there are always necessarily more candidates than open slots. But still, it's annoying. And particularly if it becomes some sort of pattern.

Unfortunately, asking why you weren't picked often produces polite evasions of the truth. Something along the lines of, "It's not you; it's me." Recruiters will rarely tell you the truth about why they were swayed to the other side at the last minute. Did you come across as too brash or not confident enough in your last interview? Did they feel you were lacking the chutzpah necessary to lead a team of senior associates? Or was it the way you hesitated over their question about the hypothetical scenario involving one of their prospective clients? Maybe you're too soft-spoken; your previous boss liked your calm and collected demeanor, but your potential immediate supervisor felt you lacked enthusiasm and energy.

Who knows? All they said was, "We've decided to go another route." Then they wished you good luck in the future.

Fact is, few people tell us the truth about how we really come across, how we're perceived and judged for suitability on all levels. Recruiters refrain for legal reasons and because they have no reason to hurt the feelings of someone who's about to become a stranger again. Friends and peers want to maintain a good relationship with you, so they hold back on the constructive stuff for fear of sinking your morale and gravitate to those they have more in common with, leaving you out of the proverbial and very real loop at work and elsewhere.

Time for some analysis then. Reflect on how people typically approach you. Do they come to you when there's a problem they need solved? When they need specific information on someone or something? To just chat, gossip, and kick back and relax? Do they trust you to complain about a boss or colleagues? Are you often asked to collaborate on a project, or do people politely shrug off your offers of help?

Depending on the interactions you have and to what degree and purpose others seek out your company, expertise, help, or input, you are somewhere along the continuum of likeable, contributing, valuable resource, influential. It's important to know where.

Having an unbiased view of how others perceive you is an absolute must in any quest for leadership. You can't lead, guide, teach, and inspire if you don't have an accurate picture of your level of influence with others. You have to know whether people see you as competent but intimidating. Whether they don't take you seriously or take you way too seriously. Whether they feel they can trust you or that you're someone who hogs all the credit. The list of variables is inexhaustible, just like the range of human judgment with all of its nuances and shades of gray.

High-potentials and executives on the fast track are given all kinds of tests to help them see the blind spots in their communication and leadership styles. From 360-degree multirater feedback to Myers-Briggs Type Indicator to DiSC and our colors on the Personality Dimensions scale, there's no shortage of assessment tools to tell us where we fall short or hit the mark on leadership.

A colleague of mine teaches at a local college and confided that women she observed often have it rough in the classroom and struggle to be taken seriously. "I never really had that problem," she said. "Probably because it never occurred to me not to speak up." She was quick to add that while she runs a "pretty casual" classroom, "I make very clear at the outset that I don't tolerate any disrespect, either toward me or toward their fellow classmates." She also invites her students to challenge her interpretations, both because she thinks it important for the students themselves to speak up and take a stand and also because it "sends the signal that I'm not going to be thrown off my game."

This colleague is aware that every semester she has to establish herself with a new class of students, which she finds gives her an advantage over other leaders: if things didn't go as planned the previous semester, she gets the chance to start over. It could be a long semester, though, if minds and hearts don't align.

Not everyone gets that chance of a do-over every 18 weeks. Professor Jeffrey Pfeffer considers perception so important that he's suggested, if you've made a bad impression at your current workplace, "it's a waste of precious time to fight that uphill battle. Why make heroic efforts to dig out of a hole when the same energy spent elsewhere could make you a star?" I would argue, however, that just as corporations can alter their public image and consumers' perceptions, so can you. Plus, it strikes me as somewhat of a defeatist attitude to assume that you have but one chance, and if you blow that, it's the corporate D-list for you from that point forward.

You can begin to get a sense of what your colleagues think of you by making note of how they relate to you and, when appropriate, asking them directly what they think of you as a colleague. (If you ask them to be "brutally honest," make sure you can handle such honesty. You do yourself no favors if you ask for feedback and then immediately contest it.) If you listen, really listen, to what comes your way and apply what fits to change unhelpful behaviors, you might also gain a few allies in your attempt to reposition yourself.

Allies matter. I'm fully on board with Pfeffer and a number of his colleagues, who suggest that having others singing your praises is, in fact, far more effective than warbling your own ode to yourself: "People whose praises are sung by others are perceived as more likeable, and this likeability leads, in turn, to a greater willingness to do favors or expend extra effort on behalf of that individual." Similarly, endorsements of competence by others increase perceptions of your competence.

Engage your colleagues. By helping you improve your image, they may become invested in you and, as a result, help you succeed.

Values and Beliefs Affect Decision Making

We've discussed in earlier chapters how cognitive biases may undermine rationality in decision making, and here I want to draw your focus to the values and beliefs that often unconsciously guide our choices. One person's belief can be another person's irrational bias: the outspoken skeptic Michael Shermer considers all beliefs in the supernatural to be irrational, but telling people they're irrational is unlikely to earn you any fans or make any real progress as far as influencing them is concerned.

Instead, consider the notion of "thick" rationality. Given that each of us has our own set of beliefs, values, preferences, and desires, it would make sense to recognize that such beliefs, values, and so on are likely to affect how and what we decide. If "thin" rationality is simply the ability to rank your preferences in order and then choose your top preference (the basic structure of rational decision making), then thick rationality takes into account the how and what we may *build into* those preference-ordering structures.

Culture, for example, has an enormous influence on decision making. While it's important to recognize that generalizations can go too far and lead to a kind of restrictive stereotyping, it's just as important to recognize that our norms and behaviors are shaped by our environment.

The marketing professor Lars Perner stresses that most cultural attitudes and behaviors exist along a continuum, and he points to the Dutch researcher Gert Hofstede's four dimensions of cultural differences as one way to try to understand a culture's dynamics:

1. **Individualism versus collectivism:** Where is the locus of responsibility, in the individual or in the group?
2. **Power distance:** To what degree do those with less power expect and accept the notion that others have more power?

3. **Masculinity versus femininity:** Is there competition or harmony between the sexes?
4. **Uncertainty avoidance:** To what degree does a culture condition its members to be either uneasy or comfortable with ambiguity?

To put the notion of cultural impact in perspective, think of the vast differences in culture at some of the top U.S. universities—the ultraliberal University of California at Berkeley versus the conservative U.S. Military Academy at West Point. Or the Midwest's conservative Notre Dame, with its front-and-center football prowess, versus the East Coast's liberal Massachusetts Institute of Technology with its globally top-ranked engineering and IT department. Four years in either environment is sure to affect your beliefs and values that, in turn, affect your decisions and choices.

Similarly, consider the vastly divergent cultural leanings of a General Electric corporation under the tough, unforgiving, and excellence-driven leadership style of a Jack Welch versus Google's college-campus-like atmosphere—complete with motor scooters, sand volleyball courts, and a "structured chaos" work environment. Under Welch, managers who didn't produce were quickly terminated. The company valued leaders who were prepared for a constantly changing business environment, embracing its varied challenges and freely pitching cutting-edge ideas. Welch's mantra of "We're either number one or number two in any business" fueled the decisions and choices GE's leadership made.

Google's own management culture has created a flexible work environment that gives its engineers the freedom to work on ideas they're most passionate about. They call it "20-percent time," and so far, it's given birth to new products like Google Suggest and AdSense for Content, among many others. Google's goal in managing its vast workforce "is to determine precisely the amount of management it needs—and then use a little bit less," according to a quote by Shona

Brown—a former McKinsey consultant–turned–Google senior vice president for business operations—in *Fortune* magazine.

The values and beliefs acquired and reinforced at two of the world's most admired companies undoubtedly influence their engineers and leaders' behavior and choices. This, in turn, affects the unique influence they exert on their surroundings.

The Powerful Influence of Context on People's Choices

When male CEOs in Denmark have daughters, the wages of their female employees rise (relative to male employees' wages). If the child is the first daughter, the effect is stronger, and if the first daughter is also the firstborn, the effect is stronger still.

Seeing someone yawn, hearing someone yawn, even reading about yawning can lead you—you guessed it—to yawn.

Customers primed with images of money before they shop tend to go with lower-priced options, while those primed on comfort images pick the more luxurious options.

Sensing a theme yet? Our environment and particular circumstances—the context of a situation—can have tremendous impact on our thinking, behavior, choices, and decisions.

Architects discussing government building structures in the context of the threat of potential terrorist acts are under a different influence than they would be if the discussion took place in the context of sustainability—a focus on a "green" environmental design.

Then there's the less-is-more approach to grocery shopping. Professor Barry Schwartz, author of *The Paradox of Choice: Why More Is Less*, observes that "people are worried they'll regret the choice they made. [They] don't want to feel they made a mistake." Among the reasons Trader Joe's has succeeded in a tough marketplace is that it limits customers' choices rather than giving them unlimited options. Thus, by limiting the number of, say, peanut butter options, Trader Joe's actually makes it easier for customers to pick an item. Stores that boast of "nearly unlimited" choices may lure potential customers in, but too many options can overwhelm, and people may leave without buying anything.

Malcolm Gladwell has made a career exploring how apparently small phenomena can lead to such large effects. He notes that contagiousness (as with yawning) is "an unexpected property of all kinds of things" and that, combined with the massive effects that may result in the accumulation of small changes, can lead to "epidemics" of behavior. A few well-placed individuals wearing a particular shoe or hairstyle may unleash a nationwide (or even global) trend.

Such observations might seem de rigueur to anyone with a background in marketing; the idea that people can be influenced by advertising, product placement, or celebrity endorsement is commonplace in the field. But as much as we'd like to think that such influence is limited solely to consumption, it's perhaps less obvious that these influences work on us in all kinds of situations.

For influencers, the consideration of environment and setting on decision making is critical to the outcome of the process. Choosing among brands of peanut butter is relatively low stakes, but move the setting to a boardroom meeting regarding a potential merger, and you have the potential for groupthink, which can lead to disastrous outcomes for a company.

Avoiding the Contextual Influence of Groupthink

Journalist William Whyte first coined the term *groupthink* in the 1950s, but the phenomenon is most often associated with research psychologist Irving Janis, who defined it as follows: "A mode of thinking that people engage in when they are deeply involved in a cohesive in-group, when the members' strivings for unanimity override their motivation to realistically appraise alternative courses of action." While some features have since been modified, the basic notion that group members might reach premature agreement still holds.

The scholar Robert Baron reviewed groupthink research and offers a revised model. In his version, social identification with the group, salient or shared norms, and low self-efficacy or lack of confidence in the group's ability to manage the issue at hand may interact to produce groupthink. Unlike Janis, Baron believes that groupthink operates not just in intense and highly complex situations (such as an international foreign affairs crisis), but in everyday situations as well.

That's the bad news. The good news is that groupthink can be avoided, especially if the influencer-in-charge explicitly directs her colleagues away from premature decision making. She might play the devil's advocate or introduce contrary evidence to disrupt the apparent consensus, and by making sure her group has the time, resources, and confidence to address the issue, she reduces the potential pressure to reach quick agreement. In other words, she changes the context and influences participants away from a possibly negative outcome for all.

Professors David Garvin and Michael Roberto suggest that influencers try to build "constructive cognitive conflict" into the decision-making process as a way both to try to head off affective or personal conflicts and to inoculate against groupthink. They suggest creating a "point-counterpoint" or "intellectual watchdog" process, whereby some members of the team are tasked with creating alternative proposals (point-counterpoint) or are designated critics of any proposals (watchdog). The process is repeated as proposals are revised to meet objections until all members reach a point of common agreement.

And while coming to agreement can be a good thing, undue contextual influence like groupthink may trip up the smartest group. Garvin and Roberto offer the example of General Motor's Alfred Sloan, who once famously told his assembled GM executives, "Gentlemen, I take it we are all in complete agreement on the decision here." Everyone nodded yes. Sloan shot back, "Then I propose we postpone further discussion of the matter until our next meeting to give ourselves time to develop disagreement and perhaps gain some understanding of what the decision is all about."

Whether it's the dreaded groupthink phenomenon that results from a particular context or any other choice that you see as a threat to your ideas or business, try to influence the setting or change the environment so you have a chance of influencing the outcome.

Structuring Complex Choices to Make Decisions Easier

Hollywood likes architects. From Henry Fonda in *12 Angry Men* to Tom Hanks in *Sleepless in Seattle*, Liam Neeson in *Love, Actually* to Steve Martin in *HouseSitter* to Adam Sandler in *Click*, when storylines need a character who is both artistic and logical, architects seem to be the go-to choice. Or perhaps the architect is the wizard behind the scenes—as in the last two *Matrix* films—the one who directs or otherwise controls events. Even in "Seinfeld," hapless George Costanza wanted to be an architect!

If you ever shared George's dream, when it comes to decision making and influence, you too can be an architect—a "choice architect." According to professors Richard Thaler, Cass Sunstein, and John Balz, "A choice architect has the responsibility for organizing the context in which people make decisions." The store owner who places impulse buys like candy bars to breath mints next to the checkout line; the bookseller who highlights an author by placing all of his books on an endcap, the table that meets your field of vision on entering the store; the museum docent who steers visitors to the gift shop—all of them are choice architects who attempt to shape the decisions of their customers. (Marketers, needless to say, are professional choice architects.)

But doesn't this mean that everyone is a choice architect, insofar as we all try to influence others? Yes and no. We do try to sway others, but choice architecture is not just about the attempt to influence; it's about the *specific shaping* of that attempt.

I mentioned in Chapter 3 that people often go with a default option, even when there are other, clearly better, options. Thaler and his colleagues, however, note that choice architects can use this tendency in their favor by making the default the superior option. When you install computer software, for example, you are usually urged to choose the default option; for those who are not programmers, this is often the optimal choice.

What counts as the default can be controversial. For example, there are far more people in the United States on hospital waiting lists for organs than there are organs available. When they get their driver's license, people may indicate that, upon their untimely demise, their organs may be donated, but the default position is against donation, or opt-out. Some organ donation advocates suggest switching the default position to "presumed consent" or opt-in, so that those who do not want to donate will have to take the extra effort to opt out.

But presumed consent presumes too much for some people. Thaler, Sunstein, and Balz point to Illinois's "mandated choice": before people can get or renew a driver's license, they are required to say if they're willing to be donors. Illinois's sign-up rate is 60 percent versus the 38 percent national average.

Other ways to influence behavior? Expect that people will make mistakes and build in corrections. The checklists recommended by the doctor and *New Yorker* writer Atul Gawande, for example, are designed to decrease medical error. Both the information superhighway and the old-school concrete highway system provide feedback—"Are you sure you want to delete this file?" and "Last gas station for 180 miles"—as ways to signal the consequences of your (in)actions.

What about more complex decisions? Thaler and his colleagues recommend mapping: "A good system of choice architecture helps people improve their ability to map and hence to select options that will make them better off." One way to do this is to make the information about various options more comprehensible, transforming numerical information into units that translate more readily into actual use.

Technical language can be useful, but most people are just looking for the "upshot." For example, choosing appropriate health insurance from the various options your company provides can send anyone into fits of rage thanks to the confusing presentation of the relative benefits of different plans. Bullet points and jargon-free language with graphics depicting factors such as the number of family members covered can narrow down options and speed up the process of elimination, guiding the decider to the right choice for him.

Mapping is conceptually similar to the construction of the consequences tables and swaps discussed in Chapter 5; the point is to lay out your options in a manner that allows you to see and compare relevant variables. Such simplifying strategies help to lessen the anxieties of Schwartz's paradox of choice by reducing the concern that you will make the wrong choice, thus enabling rather than disabling your decision-making process.

Choice architects should also pay attention to incentives: who uses, chooses, pays, and profits? Sometimes the person who uses, chooses, and pays is the same (as with buying consumer items), while those who profit are the store and manufacturer. In other areas—most notoriously, in medical care—the number of stakeholders may be so high as to turn the decision-making process into a muddle.

One way to cut through this type of muddle is to introduce a kind of salience meter: "Are choosers aware of the incentives they face?" Sometimes they are, but sometimes—as with the undervaluing of opportunity costs—they are not. Increasing awareness of these and other costs may make people more mindful of the trade-offs inherent in the choices they make. For example, cost-disclosing thermometers may do more to decrease household energy use than rate increases.

Choice architecture can be tremendously useful in any sort of system design, from software to road construction to public policy, but what about other kinds of nonsystemic activities? Garvin and Roberto don't use the term *choice architecture*, but in considering the dangers of groupthink, they do suggest ways to structure the decision-making process itself to produce better outcomes. They note that "advocacy" models of decision making, in which a leader clearly signals his preferred outcome, tend to short-circuit the process in ways that lead both to disgruntled colleagues (who may think they participated in a charade of decision making) and to worse outcomes.

Instead, the authors suggest an "inquiry" model, which "is a very open process designed to generate multiple alternatives, foster the exchange of ideas, and produce a well-tested solution." It's a collaborative approach in which discussions are meant to test and evaluate claims rather than simply validate them; team members are critical thinkers rather than cheerleaders; proposals are debated and revised; and alternative and critical views are cultivated. The point-counterpoint and intellectual watchdog structures, discussed in the preceding section, are ways to counter what Garvin and Roberto admit are the more usual advocacy structures. It's also what GM's legendary leader Alfred Sloan routinely practiced in the boardroom as demonstrated by his quotation earlier in the chapter.

Some thin rationalists despair of the apparent inability of most of the human race to make decisions according to elegant algorithms and see the problem as residing in the people making the decisions rather than in those elegant formulae. But by recognizing that human beings are human—that is, complex, conflicted, and sometimes confounded—you can guide people toward making decisions that work for them *and* for you.

Environmental Control: Seven Contexts You Can Influence

By now you know that when I say "environmental control," I'm speaking of the influence of context—the arrangement of context to more effectively influence people toward better choices and decision making. And for anyone who raises the idea of Machiavellian motives here, I'll save you the time. The challenges I'm offering in this section are situations and environments all professionals, managers, and executives face in the daily quest to meet their goals with and through other people. The solutions that follow are simple and ethical responses to the human tendencies that can make real progress difficult at times. I'll start with a familiar one touched on earlier.

1. Groupthink

The challenge: Decision making becomes easier when we know how others in the same situation would act. That's why groupthink doesn't even have to be observed in person—just a perception of consensus from our peers will naturally sway us in the direction of the majority. Even in person, all that's needed is a small group of three to five to initiate the pull of groupthink. This can pose a problem when you are introducing new ideas or a reason for change for which you as yet have no real peer support and everyone sticks to their equally strong tendency to favor the status quo. Watch in particular those team members who exhibit a strong need for structure—they are more likely to conform than those who are more comfortable with uncertainty, creative chaos, and ambiguity.

How to influence the context: Cultivate dissenters. Find the one person you can count on to play devil's advocate who's also part of the group. Better to have more than one, but even a single dissenter—that person's credibility is critical—can reduce group-think by 61 percent, according to research. Next time you find everyone agreeing to something that disagrees with your better judgment, call on the dissenters to bolster your case and punch holes in the group's resolve. Then you have a chance to make your case and sway team members to your side by getting the majority to see the merit of your idea.

2. Irrational Escalation

The challenge: In business and politics, we sometimes realize that we've gone down the wrong path, that we've invested money, time, and effort in a decision that's probably going to turn out badly. Sometimes we feel it in our gut, and sometimes the gut feeling is supported by clear evidence. Yet, against all that evidence to the contrary, the people around you rationalize that more money, time, and effort need to be invested to bring about the desired outcome (based on the fact that the sizeable investment already made would make abandoning the idea, project, or effort a complete loss). It's variously called irrational escalation and sunk cost effect, but the results are the same: to avoid the pain of accepting the loss, we keep a project on artificial life support until we run out of resources.

How to influence the context: Step up; pull the proverbial plug; and say with authority, "Enough!" It's tough and a bitter pill to swallow, but sometimes we're wrong and fund a poor decision. Once that becomes more likely than not, it's time to cut losses and save what can be saved. Develop a simple presentation with as much evidence as you have—such as all those wasted resources—to illustrate the depth of the current sinkhole. Show why your group initially went down the wrong path (likely for a good reason) and contrast that with new evidence that shows why these initial reasons are now invalid or have been proven false. Take it to the extreme by showing the damage that would be done by further escalating investment in that direction. And make acceptance of the sunk cost and loss easier to bear by (1) designating it a valuable learning experience; (2) removing blame and feelings of guilt; and (3) introducing ideas for a new direction—a better future—based on the new evidence. It helps to get others with authority and credibility on your side first. The more the better, since others will look to them for input on the decision (see groupthink).

3. Disengagement at Meetings

The challenge: Another workday, another meeting. There are plenty of unpleasant stats out there that remind us how much time, productivity, and money is wasted with unproductive meetings. And you know this intuitively, because you participate in or run many of them yourself. It's usually the same scenario. The introverts hang back, the ones who usually have something to say speak up, and the objective gets lost in a tangled web of tangents woven by the leader and the participants—they have everyone's ear so they think they can just bring up whatever crosses their mind, much to everyone's confusion and frustration. How often do two or three participants engage in a very vocal and public across-the-table minimeeting within the meeting that stops the flow and has nothing to do with the purpose of the original meeting? You know the answer.

How to influence the context: Set and follow a clear objective. It sounds deceptively simple, but I've witnessed numerous meetings of all stripes where informal chatter among participants alone accounted for a good amount of time wasted from everyone's day. So let everyone know that whatever isn't pertinent to the objective— say, a decision to be made, the brainstorming of ideas, knowledge to be shared—needs to be relegated to a different setting or taken up with a specific individual after the meeting. In addition to a clear objective with which you'll start and end the meeting, involve those who are typically more reserved. Get their opinions on the table. If they're part of the meeting, they are important team members.

Make them feel included and hear their ideas. Look for the minorities in the team, and make sure they have a voice. Whether it's gender, race, rank, or some other group affiliation, make sure you get the full benefit of a diverse perspective. Those in a minority can feel that their contributions are less relevant, so make them relevant for everyone's benefit. Your influence on the context of the meeting will directly affect the choices of whether and how others participate in that meeting.

4. Complex and Detailed Information

The challenge: A fair number of business presentations involve some complexity and detail that we need the client or team to understand. Too often, however, our audience drowns in detail, fails to grasp any kind of coherent structure, and suffers through a monotonous delivery. Complexity stays complex and never makes it into the audience's awareness. The presenter's credibility is directly affected by this inability to simplify complex information. And since audiences don't like to feel incompetent and confused, they reject both the information and the presenter and start tuning out, tuning in instead to their iPhones and BlackBerries to see what they're missing on e-mail.

How to influence the context: Take anything that's complex and turn it into a story. Stories resonate, particularly those in which we can see ourselves as the protagonist. They also capture our attention more than a column of numbers. Take what's complex and overly detailed and wrap it in a story that has enough emotional resonance for you—the more you feel it, the more they will—and the audience; at the very least, they'll pay attention. More likely, however, you will be helping them make sense of what they're hearing by adding context. The degree to which you'll reach their hearts and minds depends on your ability to make the story personal and relate it to their lives and travails. Keep asking yourself as you look at the data you're trying to get across, "What does it mean to audience members on a deeper level? How will it impact their lives, their work when they get back to their desks, their health, their incomes, their families?" Remember, the more personal the information is, the more relevant it is—and vice versa, if they understand it. People make choices and decisions based on things that move them emotionally. Show them—don't tell them—how the detail in your presentation matters as part of a story that resonates.

5. Subconscious Bias Against People Who Are Smarter than You

The challenge: This one is about influencing your own choices as well as those of others. Research has shown that many of us like to surround ourselves—particularly when making hiring decisions—with people who don't compete with our unique strengths. It's referred to as the social comparison bias, and it is the antithesis to the very intelligent proposition of hiring people smarter than us so we can achieve our professional goals. The motives can be anything from protecting our special turf to not wanting to feel inadequate in contrast to someone who's more qualified in our field of expertise. Fair enough. But we may be impeding our own progress by keeping talent at arm's length instead of increasing team strength with another strong player.

How to influence the context: Recognize this bias in yourself if you're the decision maker, and keep the focus on strengthening your team with needed skills, even if one of your hires matches your prowess in the field. If you see the bias in others—most likely subordinates—flag it. It doesn't help the organization or your team if talent is chosen with ego as a filtering or deciding factor. Pull the threatened one aside and let him know you value him for the sum of his abilities, skills, and attributes, not just for one special skill. This obviously only works if you are at a rank or position that makes this a feedback session rather than an embarrassing presumption.

6. The Seeming Entanglement of Outcome and Process

The challenge: Many of us are guilty of judging decisions not by their merit at the time they're made, but by the outcome they produce. This outcome bias affects everyone from presidents and prime ministers to middle managers and professionals across the spectrum. It's easy to lash out at someone whose decision produced an undesirable outcome. But it produces another problem altogether, and that is that people become afraid or unwilling to make bold decisions on anything of consequence for fear the outcome may disappoint or worse. That's certainly understandable given the prospect of punishment or social backlash.

How to influence the context: Stress that as long as the decision-making process is sound and makes good sense, taking all pertinent available information into consideration, everyone has the support of the team and management. Decision making is a critical leadership skill, and those in charge of making decisions should be as educated and trained in the art of it as possible. They should also feel empowered to pull the proverbial trigger when a decision must be made, without facing retribution when the outcome isn't the result everyone hoped for. Taking full stock of a decision-making process after the fact and when the results are in makes good sense as well—both to learn the details of the decision that led to the outcome and to plan for the future.

7. Delicate Matters That Need Careful Language

The challenge: Language is used to create understanding and meaning. From the media to politics to the workplace, our word choice, presentation of facts, and recounting of an experience can create the reality we want others to consider. Those who are unable to frame effectively are at a disadvantage compared to those who can. Executives will take offense instead of accepting coaching as part of their leadership development if the offer suggests incompetence on their part; employees may *reduce* efforts toward reaching goals if the language meant to motivate them is more inspiring to the board of directors and the CEO; and initiatives meant to move the organization to change certain behaviors can fall flat if the language used in its presentation doesn't connect to people's values. Identifying the right language for others to accept ideas and proposals is crucial for success. This is particularly true because others are working within their own frames—or cognitive structures, as they're also called. And they can easily work against you if those frames are left unchallenged.

How to influence the context: Understand what resonates with people and use language that gets people to accept one meaning over another. In the case of executives who need coaching, you can frame it as providing them with better awareness and communication tools to succeed in the executive suite as opposed to "fixing inadequacies" or even "minimizing weaknesses"; both of these terms denote that something is wrong. Framing also dictates what you leave out when you "recreate reality" for someone else and what you choose to include when you describe an event or course of action. Describing an argument between colleagues as "an ugly fight between a production supervisor and a team leader" creates a different meaning than saying it was "a spirited disagreement among professionals." The words we use to create context and reality have an impact on others' perceptions and, with that, their choices and decisions.

In the next chapter, you'll improve your understanding of what it takes to master organizational politics. You'll learn why this is a critical management skill and how you can quickly learn any organization's unique political culture. You'll also discover how to assess your actual power—formal and informal, social and professional—in the organization.

CHAPTER 7

Mastering Organizational Politics

W hy can't I just practice medicine?" Robert, a highly credentialed anesthesiologist, asked me this exasperated rhetorical question in an impromptu coaching session over the phone. At that point, I had been working with him for almost three months on rebranding himself after he'd been asked by his former hospital's chief of staff to resign. As the chief had put it, Robert didn't "fit into the culture."

For Robert, who had gained a reputation as a brilliant clinician, this had come as an ego-crushing shock. He'd always worked hard, graduated at the top of his class at medical school, and performed with excellence in the operating room. He didn't know what had hit him.

The chief had explained that not fitting into the culture meant that Robert kept alienating people with his abrupt personality, curt communication style, and aloof attitude. What Robert viewed as being "laser-focused" on the well-being of his patients involved sparing the social niceties and doing his job to the highest standards. But others seemed to view him as an antagonistic, unpleasant colleague who was not a team player, much less a leader.

Save for one friend, Robert didn't have any allies at work, which meant he had nowhere to turn to counter the sentiments levied against him. Unable (and perhaps a bit unwilling) to navigate the political landscape that spanned the floors of St. Elsewhere, he resigned.

We started working together shortly after, when he started a new job as one of three anesthesiologists in a small hospital in a Chicago suburb. Robert now understood that his current personal brand wasn't working for him and that he needed to rebrand himself while learning to embrace the challenges of organizational politics.

By the time he asked his rhetorical question, he'd become more skillful at forming relationships with the right people and avoiding making enemies. But even as we worked on his executive presence and a more socially intelligent communication style, he still found it frustrating to play the political game.

Organizational Politics

These days, the term *politics* has become a four-letter word for many, in part because it represents a fraternity that spends more time defending itself than abiding by its dictionary definition: "activities associated with government." The word has evolved to mean the relational dynamics associated with influencing and governing—be it a country or a company—that become the currency of executing and trading favors and fostering opinions.

Rex C. Mitchell, Ph.D., professor at the Department of Management at California State University, observes that organizational politics, while neutral until touched by human perception, are usually viewed by players and observers alike as a negative. The common perception is that organizations should work to minimize politicking. For those of us with a keen political awareness, however, the importance of communication via sympathetic belief systems and shared goals is a part of organizational life that is ignored—or dismissed as manipulation—at our professional peril.

What gives the game of organizational politics the occasional dark turn is how people perceive and respond to threats, territorial boundaries, clashing worldviews, personal tastes and biases, and the sense that rubbing the right elbows will only lead to better things. While the less politically inclined undoubtedly wish that they could be judged and progress on contribution and merit alone, the stark reality is that organizational politics is an inescapable, significant factor in job performance and career trajectory. Thus, managing those politics becomes a skill set you can and should seek to understand and cultivate.

It's easy to understand that when it comes to organizational survival and success, influence is everything. The more political the organization, the more important such influence is.

Why Organizational Politics Are a Critical Management Skill

Managing organizational politics is part and parcel of the ability to exert 360-degree influence in the workplace. The 360 context here refers to the benefits of exerting this influence upward into more senior management, laterally to peers, and downward (in terms of the organizational chart) to those you supervise or otherwise are exposed to in the course of navigating your responsibilities. So no matter what skills the job calls for, regardless of the breadth of your intra- and interpersonal awareness and sense of how you are perceived by your corporate comrades, the presence of organizational politics is always at the top of the list of variables you need to contend with to come out smelling like a bonus check.

The ability to navigate the political waters of your organization is as critical to your success as is a diver's ability to swim. Politics define the cultural and relational workplace waters in which you dog-paddle every day. From the simple act of walking into a room to the critical moment of making a presentation to a team to the way you defend strategic decisions to the executive board in highly charged conversations, you are being judged by how you are perceived, and there is always a political factor in play. At one end of the scale, you may be perceived as a threat or a risk, at the other, as an ally or a go-to player. That spectrum of perception is something you can manage and improve—*if* you understand the dynamics of these politics in the first place.

"Politics are an organizational fact of life," echoes executive coach and author Gill Corkindale, the former management editor of *Financial Times.* Managers who believe they can avoid or ignore them are, she says plainly, naive.

Intuitively, you might think that a preponderance of organizational politics is concentrated in the hallways, corner offices, and cubicle farms of the big firms, the multinationals and corporate juggernauts that employ thousands of the best and brightest on sky-reaching floors. Not so, according to Corkindale. In fact, she says, some of the most political organizations she's come across are charities, nongovernment entities, and even local bridge clubs. Add the operating room to that list, as my client Robert the anesthesiologist learned.

A cynic might say that when two or more people are gathered within a context of competition for promotion, money, and plum assignments, feelers come out seeking to identify fault, vulnerability, and something that can be exploited. And while that is certainly a very real part of the political game played in any organization, there is a flipside to this coin.

Organizational politics can be a constructive and positive aspect of a manager's career, if it's properly understood and practiced. Rather than engaging in behavior that undermines trust and seeks to gain personal advantage with oblique maneuvers, enlightened professionals influence organizational culture in a more principled way. They cultivate mutually productive relationships with key players; they recognize and negotiate existing power structures; and they purposefully seek buy-in for ideas with more than a peripheral understanding of people's individual agendas and personal values.

To refuse to acknowledge the value of constructive political behavior is to leave yourself unprotected and vulnerable to having your agenda blindsided and your best efforts derailed by prevailing forces. Cynicism and resulting behavior that leads to defensive and possibly underhanded politics in return is self-serving rather than in service of the organization, which leads to a culture-defining deterioration of trust, teamwork, and the greater good. Likewise, capable and upstanding executives and managers who persistently view all politics with suspicion may routinely watch their more politically savvy colleagues pass them by for otherwise deserved recognition, rewards, and increased responsibility.

The Double-Edged Sword of Organizational Politics

Even for those who know how to navigate the political terrain masterfully, organizational politics is a tough thing to define accurately without prejudice. Ben Dattner, Ph.D., and Allison Dunn at Dattner Consulting, LLC, take a good swing at it: organizational politics is "a process through which people represent different interests, agendas, and perspectives and then compete, come into conflict, and/or collaborate in order to interpret and evaluate information and make decisions; to allocate and claim scarce resources and rewards; and to structure or restructure the organization."

Dattner and Dunn warn that overly political organizations allow a bias on self-focus and territoriality rather than on the greater good of the organization. This leads to an inevitable lack of trust, rules that are enforced without consistency, and selectively shared information. What happens then is inevitable. The organization is left with spotty and compromised loyalty and is riddled with pockets of interest pitted against and thus threatening to one another. Defensive, guarded employees tend to make more mistakes, not to mention the added workplace stress and anxiety due to overcompetitiveness and strained relationships.

So what's an overly political organization to do? How do managers and executives mired in a dense web of political activity exert lasting influence to promote their ideas and get things done through others? A stern hand is usually polarizing, which contributes to even further politicization. Dattner and Dunn suggest working within the organizational culture and system while seeking to improve it. However we exert our influence within the corporate confines, the organization's interest should serve as a compass and always trump a self-interest that doesn't support it.

It's Never a Level Playing Field

Ask people working their way up in an organization with a complex flowchart what they dislike most about the political climate and they'll most likely put the inevitable gossip and backstabbing near the top of their list. But is gossip in the workplace more than just an unpleasant by-product of human beings working together? Can it impede or support influence? These are questions that challenge most organizations, because few dynamics influence intraorganizational perception like the proverbial grapevine does.

Evidence suggests that gossip has a potency far beyond watercooler entertainment for the bored and that it often takes place not just in casual office encounters, but in more formal settings as well. A recent study by Indiana University sociologists Tim Hallett and Brent Harger, published in the October 2009 edition of the *Journal of Contemporary Ethnography*, shows that people who are the targets of gossip in informal settings tend to be evaluated more negatively in formal meetings as well. Simply put, the perceptions created about someone during those "watercooler moments"—the off-the-record, informal banter during meetings—carry over to the way someone is represented in on-the-record, work-related discussions. The target of gossip is often compared unfavorably to a nontargeted colleague, and any criticism of the target tends to be accompanied by an undertone of sarcasm.

This study's authors recommend quickly derailing negative gossip by subtly changing the subject, focusing on a different target for criticism, or diffusing the negative gossip with a pre-emptive strike of something positive that can be said about the person. Astute managers recognize the appropriate moments and use these techniques, while the unwilling participant or bystander to such gossip can have similar influence by following the same strategy without giving away his or her agenda of political damage control.

Hallet and his colleagues also recognize the positive aspect of gossip; he notes that gossip "can also be a gift. If people are talking positively, it can be a way to enhance someone else's reputation." Still, gossip is generally used as an indirect means of criticism, especially of one's superiors. Paying attention to the discrepancy between how people behave both in front of and out of sight of the target may tell you a great deal about both the target and those engaging in the gossip—and who really wields the power.

Learn Your Organization's Unique Political Culture Fast

The key word in this heading is *fast*. When you come on board, you are most vulnerable to the forces of organizational politics, as people are assessing where you stand, where you might land, your threat quotient, and your potential as an ally. They may recruit you or wait for you to seek them out, but even while politically unaf-filiated, you are nonetheless subject to the cultural forces around you. The quicker you identify them, the better equipped you'll be to make choices that serve you and the organization—a one-two combo that always goes hand in hand for successful influencers.

If you accept that culture is synonymous with organizational politics, then you are buying into the notion that cultures, which are defined by their political stances and preferences, are the stuff that make any subgroup unique. If it is politically advantageous to go out with the boss after work and you don't, you are not adapting to the subculture of that unique group, and at least on that count, you risk becoming a political outsider. A newbie is best served by keen observation of the dynamics that define these subgroups, a process that involves active listening. This works in your favor in two ways: first, you learn about your colleagues and the general office culture; and second, people love to be listened to, and the favorable impression you make on them by listening intently will gain you points in the overall perception game. Once you're more tuned in, you'll begin to notice things such as intragroup hierarchy, intergroup dynamics like "us versus them," a sense of what's funny and what isn't, who is endorsed and who isn't, what the group considers empowering and embarrassing, and who's cool and who's a frequent target for gossip or ridicule.

This isn't the time to hide in your cubicle or office behind safely closed doors. Proactive engagement and social interaction with different groups of people—as opposed to relying on e-mail, memos, and other electronic means of communication—is necessary for integration into a politically sensitive environment. Through keen observation and casual but focused conversation, you can assess general job satisfaction levels, the response to new ideas, whether innovation is encouraged or stifled, how (and how quickly) and by whom decisions are made, and how contrary opinions are received.

Politics have always relied on key players—so-called movers and shakers—to forward an agenda. The observant new arrival quickly discovers who these key players are and decides whether to ingratiate or distance themselves accordingly. These cultural veterans may actually be recruited through soliciting their views and advocacy.

To get a crash course in cultural dynamics, you can tap these key players about their opinions and views of the organization's history and potential. Listen for bias and attempts at recruitment—you just might hear it.

Mind the Unwritten Rules

Of course, you may not hear everything there is to tell. Every organization has unspoken expectations and rules of culture that need to be discovered, learned, and navigated before the corporate ladder climb can commence in earnest. Do people leave work at 5 P.M. sharp, or is that a slow form of political suicide? Is it customary for executives to consume lunch at their desks while powering through proposal drafts or for small groups of three to five to bond over salads and sandwiches? Is it OK to fraternize with employees a couple of rungs lower on the organizational chart, or is that an unspoken taboo? Your ability to influence within your organization can grow or take a hit, depending on how well you heed the unwritten rules of workplace behavior.

Over time, this sort of thing becomes second nature to most, an adopted basic level of workplace *being*. Newly arrived hires need only look to their peers and immediate supervisors for clues and behavioral examples, and in most cases, those same folks are looking back at you to see if you're paying attention.

Laura Sabattini, writing for Catalyst, the organization that promotes the advancement of women in the workplace, conducted interviews with 65 men and women on the topic of unwritten organizational rules. The results showed that both formal and informal networks were accessed to get the lay of the land. Nearly two-thirds said they used informal networks to learn cultural expectations, while just over half included more formal networks in that process. Just under half used mentors for the skinny on what to do and what not to do, and more than a third wished that they had learned more and quicker when they had just arrived.

The information and modeling is out there. Once you know where to look, you have a better understanding of what your own path needs to be.

Assess Your Actual Power—Formal and Informal, Social and Professional

Once you've been with an organization for a while, you get a sense of the office culture: who to cultivate and who to ignore, what skills and behaviors are rewarded. At that point, you are in a position to figure out where you fit in the organizational structure. This isn't just about what box on the flowchart has your name in it; it's about what other kinds of leverage you bring to your workplace.

The position you hold *does* matter. Fifty years ago, the social psychologists John French and Bertram Raven outlined five different types of power, an outline that is still used and cited by organizational theorists today. Some of these power types are attached to a specific position in the office hierarchy, some to the role played in collegial networks, and others to particular skills.

○ *Legitimate power* is clearly attached to hierarchical position. French and Raven note that such legitimacy comes from having the authority to request that others behave in a particular manner. It is important to recognize that the authority adheres to the position, *not* the person. Any deference is given to the title; lose the title, lose the deference. While such power is undeniably useful, it is not enough on its own to make the person wielding it powerful in her own right.

○ *Reward power* may also be attached to hierarchical position, as the person with this power may both bestow high-value rewards (vacation time, promotions, and so on) and remove any negative sanctions. Like legitimate power, reward power is limited; for example, company policy may dictate the maximum

128

allowable salary increase or the maximum number of vacation days. Finally, there is a fair amount of evidence that, over time, workers may see rewards more in terms of their rights or something they've earned than as something given; as such, the person offering these rewards is not credited for having done so.

- *Coercive power* is the flipside to reward power and is even more limited. A boss may threaten to demote or fire someone, but while the threat may lead to short-term gains, over the long term, employees are likely to work defensively, putting their efforts into avoiding trouble rather than advancing ideas that could lead to gain. In addition, constant threats to punish subordinates are likely to be discounted, especially if the threats are rarely fulfilled. French and Raven note that you cannot expect to build your leadership based on punishment, whether it's warranted or not.

- *Expert power* is more under the control of the individual. Those who possess skills and abilities that are of use to their coworkers can quickly gain influence with and over their colleagues, either through teaching those skills or by contributing to a colleague's project. You may also use your initial expertise in a particular area to expand your knowledge either deeper into that topic or into similar areas in neighboring fields.

- *Referent power* is, like expert power, attached to the individual. Unlike expert power, however, referent power inheres in the individual as a form of charisma or personal magnetism. While we tend to think of charisma as something you either have or don't have, it is possible to cultivate referent power over time, as colleagues come to value your interpersonal skills and see you as a useful ally. It is important to recognize that this power can be abused, especially if your charm or likability is unmoored from an ethical sense; the best con artists, after all, are often the most charming.

129

Discovering your real power within an organization, then, means being aware of more than just your title or whether you have a cubicle or a corner office (although, to be honest, the corner office should be a pretty big clue). Pay attention to what kind of resources you command, how people react if you request something (big or small), and how often your boss or colleagues come to you for information or advice.

Jeffrey Pfeffer, who teaches business at Stanford University, concurs that one must pay attention to both organizational structure and relational power. Mere competence is not enough to catapult a person upward, nor is it necessary for someone to be unusually gifted. What is necessary is a willingness to take risks in order to accrue power. While you may not hold a formal position of authority, you can—by cultivating valuable work-specific and interpersonal skills—cultivate your own sphere of influence among your colleagues and superiors alike.

Pfeffer has observed over the years that many of his students are initially uncomfortable with the ideas he teaches. Rick Nobles of *Stanford Business* quotes Pfeffer as saying, "They [the students] believe the world is a just and fair place, and if they work hard and do a good job, they will be successful."

In my own experience with coaching clients, I have learned that many nominal leaders, from the supervisor to the C-level executive, actually reject the notion that they have power over people. Some of them find the notion downright distasteful. I believe that power, however, no matter what position people occupy in the organization, should be embraced and embodied by those who hold it. Otherwise, it serves no one—not the leader, the organization, or its stakeholders. Nor does it serve the objectives that good people have set for themselves and others. I agree with Pfeffer when he says, "Stop waiting for things to get better or for other people to acquire power and use it in a benevolent fashion to improve the situation." So understand the power you have, and use the influence it gives you to accomplish your goals, both personal and professional.

Know the Leaders Around You— Enforcers, Narcissists, and Bullies

Getting the lay of the land is an intuitive reaction for either a new arrival or someone seeking to change his or her status within an organization. With an informed view of this landscape, you can leverage your awareness of several archetypes of leaders based on their power and intentions. Knowing these types well can help you manage the landmines of leadership behavior and aim your influence upward.

Beware the Big Bad Wolf

Perhaps most easily spotted is the *enforcer*. Every powerful organizational bad guy in the movies has one, referring the dirty work to this person while he sits back and counts the money. This goes for good organizational types too. The enforcer's role is to punish wrongdoers and rid the halls of injustice, or at least anything that is contrary to his own agenda. There can be a martyrlike quality to this, which invests the sacrificing-for-the-greater-good enforcer with a certain power and status. Such folks are strong and assertive, with authoritarian nuances. They are the watchdogs of the culture—where most will bite their tongues, the enforcer speaks out.

Innate enforcers can be stress junkies, thriving on pressure and stimulation. They can also be suspicious and hard to please or convince; when not laying down the law, they are mostly extroverted and otherwise noticeable. They are also obediently submissive to superiors in the organizational hierarchy and controlling of those lower down.

If you work for an enforcer, it is important to recognize what is often the motivation behind enforcement, that is, the need to "hold the line" against real or perceived transgressions. Don't argue with the enforcer about the lines themselves (making the rules is not his concern), but don't be bullied either. Instead, make clear your agreement that standards matter and that you're willing to abide by those standards.

Meet the Narcissist

In the cubicle next to the enforcer, you might find the narcissist. These people can be successful because they are risk-tolerant. They can be charming and influential, and they aren't afraid to apply clever rhetoric to push boundaries and recruit supporters. They demonstrate deep feelings of superiority and entitlement, as well as a constant need for attention and positive reinforcement.

All this leads to some predicable hot buttons. Michael Maccoby, author of *The Productive Narcissist: The Promise and Peril of Visionary Leadership*, notes that narcissists are often defensive, better at talking than listening. They can lack empathy when the matter at hand has nothing to do with them and reject help and mentoring. Also, because they are competitive, they like nothing more than to come in first.

Gladeana McMahon and Adrienne Rosen, writing in a recent issue of *Training Journal*, note that narcissists can be extremely difficult for even professional coaches to manage, which means that you as a coworker are unlikely to be able to affect such a person's behavior. If you are unable to avoid or minimize your interaction with such colleagues, your best bet may simply be to recognize that they are narcissists and avoid behaviors that are likely to challenge their self-regard. In short, your ability to exert influence will depend on your knowing their cultural pathology even better than they do.

Steer Clear of the Bully

Nobody likes a bully. But only few are able to influence them. Bullying is an epidemic of even wider implications than harassment and incompetence, because it exerts precisely the wrong type of influence within an organizational culture. The opportunity to influence around, and in lieu of, the bully is a key skill that will not go unnoticed and might ultimately be rewarded.

The bully's position insulates him from feedback and consequences, as well as providing the false empowerment of inconsistent boundaries and inherent vulnerabilities. "Good organizations won't tolerate bullies," notes the author Robert Sutton, if for no other reason than that they are costly. They elicit subpar responses and work due to fear-based power wielding, and at an extreme, they are the causal factor behind turnover and litigation.

None of that organizational intolerance, however, helps the victim of managerial bullying until the negative consequences are noticed and quantified. Cheryl Dolan and Faith Oliver admit that there is little you can do to change a bully's behavior, but there are steps you can take to protect yourself from that behavior. First, bullying should be documented and defined. Care should be taken here, especially among genders, because there are many stigmas that include female bosses being perceived as "too bossy" when they are simply emulating the energy of their male peers—who are praised for their "strong leadership qualities."

Second, you need to consider and weigh the options. If the culture actually supports and even rewards a bullylike management style, perhaps a change of employer or scenery is in order. Dolan and Oliver cite the psychologists Ruth and Gary Namie, who state, "Much of the repeated mistreatment that characterizes bullying relies on a poisoned, sick workplace to permit and sustain the madness." When bullying is a symptom of the culture, the problem is bigger than the bully; it is cause to consider your tolerance of and fit within that culture.

Third, new employees have the opportunity to halt bullying the first time they encounter it. Your response to public bullying—staying calm, using the bully's name, not showing that it's getting to you—can go a long way toward diffusion. Bullying can be a habit, so don't let the bully get used to pushing you around.

Finally, Dolan and Oliver recommend that you seek out and cultivate a support system. Bullying is rarely targeted, and others with the same sensitivities as yours should be easy to find. Bounce feedback, feelings, and options off each other to make sure your response isn't as emotionally fragile as is the bullying you seek to counter.

Political Strategies and Tactics to Increase Your Influence

There are a number of ways to strategically leverage your cultural influence, some as old as humanity itself and others the product of modern research into human dynamics. Rex Mitchell has reviewed a number of texts on organizational politics and how to manage them, noting methods, ethical and otherwise, for making your way through them and leveraging your influence. Since there are already too many examples in the real world of how not to behave, I'll focus on the ethical approaches; after all, to be truly and authentically influential requires ethical behavior.

Working off the insights of Andrew Durbin, Mitchell notes that there are three main types of strategies: those aimed at gaining power, those aimed at building relationships, and those designed to avoid political errors. It is important to recognize what your goals are within your organization. Do you seek to move up or to expand your range of responsibility? Or are you more interested in networking across the organization and throughout the hierarchy? Those tactics necessary to move up—displaying dramatic results early and often, mastering key information, and controlling lines of communication—may not work as well if you seek a power base built on relationships. In the latter case, you want both to consult and to be consulted, as well as to develop a reputation as someone who's both knowledgeable and willing to help. There is overlap in these two types of strategy, particularly in the necessity of demonstrating your mastery over a knowledge base or skill set, but how you leverage that mastery may vary with your goal.

Executive presence and 360-degree influence is based on what you know about the needs, values, and perceptions of others, and information is the first line of both offense and defense in that department.

The Art of Selecting Allies and Building Coalitions

In a relationship-driven environment like the organizational culture, the people with whom you choose to surround yourself can define you. So take care that your choices reflect your intentions.

Leadership is an art of give and take. You must strive to have a balance of both on your personal relationship ledger. Once again, Durbin (via Mitchell) is useful. He observes that favors should never be granted simply to gain an upper hand or a future favor in return, but a favor given is also a favor banked, and everyone understands the unspoken nature of this game. If you play it under the rules of developing a positive 360-degree sphere of influence, your favors will reflect your essence rather than your agenda.

Loyalty and a positive attitude play huge on the cultural landscape. Loyalty is valued by managers and peers alike, while staying positive makes you the individual managers want others to look up to. Impression management is a way to enhance such an image, but be careful that your actions aren't perceived as self-serving or agenda-driven.

If you deal with customers, vendors, or outside entities, and you know you've served them well, there's nothing wrong with coming right out and asking for a note of approval for your manager. Likewise, sending thank-you notes is a solid basis for ongoing relationships and equity building.

When you are expanding your sphere of influence, it's sometimes easy to overdo it, to allow your enthusiasm to expose your intentions in a way that may be perceived negatively. Remember, the core of your personal campaign to expand your influence shouldn't be blatantly self-serving, or at least not *just* self-serving; it should be primarily organization-serving or at least in equal measure. When you do this continually, you will be in a position to build solid coalitions of like-minded players who will support and appreciate your contributions, just as you will theirs.

Leverage Your Influence to Achieve Organizational Goals

It could easily be argued that any strategic intentions where your personal perception is concerned are self-serving and contribute to your position and status rather than the organizational good. But the opposite is the case, as each of these strategies can create an organizational win in the process. It's an entirely positive phenomenon when people strive to build influence by doing things right, collaboratively, and with little tolerance for the darker side of office politics.

Influence gained can easily be lost if the process by which it was attained is not maintained going forward. Like a rookie who doesn't play up to her potential after that sparkling first year, executives must grow into their sphere of influence as much as they grow into the nature of their job description. The two always coexist, marching hand in hand down a career path that depends on the success of self as much as it does the success of the organization.

Gill Corkindale, whom I mentioned earlier, provides a number of useful tips on how to manage organizational politics. Remember to learn your company's system and work with it or around it as necessary. Cultivate relationships sincerely but with an eye toward the right partners. Seek to understand the agendas of others, as this will empower your ability to serve them and the organization. Always remain highly principled, and never be judgmental or elitist. Expand your network and information sources, and avoid making enemies at all costs. You may selectively avoid hooking up with people for reasons that align with these principles, but take care not to alienate them in the process.

The basis for workplace relationships is often ideas and roles as much as chemistry and aligned values. Build support for your ideas, and consider those of others with an open mind. Your reputation is your influence equity, so care for it as if it were on your performance review—which, for an executive, it is and in many ways that don't appear in a list of key competencies. Be fair, even if you need to be tough. Leverage influence rather than authority; it always fosters a deeper commitment and better results.

Become a master of meeting management and contribution. Learn to negotiate without alienating, and because it is inevitable, master the art of conflict resolution and managing the unmanageable.

If all this sounds hard, it is. Which is precisely why not everyone can pull it off. But not everyone approaches the management of their workplace perception with this level of strategic and tactical awareness. When a sincere desire to be of service is matched with being a good teammate and a contributor to a positive culture, the sky becomes the limit. You need to truly understand the dynamics and the upside of cultivating a 360-degree sphere of influence in an organizational environment that is always infused with political overtones and consequences.

In the next chapter, you'll learn ways of influencing up in the organization as well as proven strategies that will help you bring your bosses around to your way of thinking. You do this in no small measure by understanding what captures the attention of decision makers and what is truly important to senior management.

CHAPTER 8

Influencing Up: Bring Your Bosses Around to Your Way of Thinking

O ne of the first things we discover on departure from school—business or other—where we thought we'd heard and learned it all, is that life isn't always fair. Not even close. In the real world, those coveted "attaboys" or "attagirls," promotions, and good press don't always go to the hardest worker or even to the overachiever with the best idea or the consistently superior numbers (though that latter tangible always seems to help). Nor do they manifest according to any timetable or tenure; just as often, it's the pure blind luck of being in the right place at the right time.

And how fair is this? Every organization on the planet has someone who can outthink the major players in the C-Suite on a regular basis but who nonetheless never gets a seat on the upper deck. It's easy to let this state of affairs get you down, but there's a better way to get what you deserve. First, though, you have to give any residual cynicism the boot before that path becomes clear.

Life may not be fair, but for the most part, it runs by a certain set of relational dynamics, all of them based on the fact that the human beings inside those C-Suites are just that—human and therefore somewhat predictable. And while it may be tempting to conclude that the inherent inequities of career trajectory require us to "play the game" as cunningly as the next guy, the truth enshrouding success is altogether the opposite. The fast track to getting things done resides in the evolution of a cliché, also mentioned in the auditoria of business schools: "Work *smarter*, not necessarily harder."

That cliché is outdated, by the way. Because in today's highly competitive organizational cultures, it should more accurately read, "Work smarter *and* work harder."

It is the former—work smarter—that becomes an imprecise yet critical variable in the outcome of our career agenda. Because the smartest thing you can do in your career may not have anything to do with the tasks and responsibilities you are assigned, the products you sell or make, or the numbers you crunch. No, the smartest way of working in today's culture of fear of failure, and the most universally reliable when it comes to advancing an agenda and/or a career, involves how you are *perceived*—by peers and, most important, by superiors. And *that*, unlike external factors over which you have no control, is something that is completely within your power to manage, evolve, and optimize.

It's called *executive presence*, and I wrote an entire book about that topic. If you hope to seize your full potential and squeeze every ounce of upside from all that hard work you're putting in, it's the ultimate and critical skill set you need to understand, cultivate, and master.

Got Executive Presence?

At a glance, and particularly when described by those outside the microcosm of the workplace, your score on the executive presence scale is the collective interpretation by your peers and managers and anyone else with whom you interface on who you are, what you've got to offer, how viable your ideas are, how well you present them, and to what degree you are worthy of a closer look and further consideration. It's your "it factor," your degree of cool under pressure, a level of social grace, boldness with a parallel sense of appropriateness. Your *essence*. It is your timing, your likability, the power and viability of your ideas combined with the quantification of your contribution.

Executive presence is what happens when you walk into a room—or not, which is precisely the point. Some have it, others don't. Those who do tend to demonstrate both style and substance, and they do it with the full understanding that neither quality alone will get you there.

Executive presence is the complete and total absence of two career deal killers: a lack of confidence and an overabundance of misplaced and mishandled bluster. Executive presence is the thing that makes people listen to you, take you seriously, and want to hear more from you on a consistent basis. It is the sum of where you went to school, how you look (relax, in the truest essence of the word *presence*, this too becomes something you can manage), who and what you know, and how well you can communicate what you know. It is the opinion your bosses and peers hold of you. It is the combination of all the variables and nuances that lead to that judgment. Your virtual score on the executive presence scale is plainly measured by how you are *perceived* in any given moment or situation.

Building Your Executive Presence

It is accurate to view your executive presence as nothing less than your career equity. In some eyes, it will be seen as talent; in others, as potential and credibility. A few people with new age leanings will call it your *energy*, while others with lingering old-school sensibilities will call it your *schmooze factor*. However it is described, executive presence requires and will benefit from no less of a mounted effort than your grad school thesis or your ongoing program at the local gym. It is something you discover and then learn about, prepare for, practice, and evolve into.

Left to chance, you must rely on unmanaged perception and serendipity, the cousin of blind luck. But you need not bet your career on that strategy. Because even the slightest shift and intention toward the cultivation of a powerful presence can create a significantly optimized view of who you are and how influential you might be.

Executive presence is, in essence, more about your skill in crafting a moment than it is about selling, showcasing, or otherwise demonstrating capabilities. Some might argue that it is the triumph of form over function, but the real empowerment of this cultural nuance comes when the two combine. According to Glenn Llopis, author of *Earning Serendipity: 4 Skills for Creating and Sustaining Good Fortune in Your Work*, it is the stringing together of these moments that defines the organizational player. It is developed and mastered over time, propelled by self-confidence, sustained by self-trust, and managed through an understanding of the needs and priorities of others. At the heart of executive presence, says Llopis, is the ability to be a good listener and a master connector of conversational patterns to get inside what others value, need, and appreciate. Most of all, Llopis stresses that executive presence isn't about you, it's about the other guy. It's about being included, valued, and trusted because you have something that others want more of.

Llopis lists several cues that your executive presence is at work—or not. People notice you when you enter the room. They like you, they trust you, they seek your opinion and approval, and they value both when they get them. They want to know more about you, both within and outside the context of the workplace. They want to get closer to you, develop a relationship, even a friendship.

These are earned responses, growing from a seed of what will become your executive presence. You get there by asking provocative, illuminating questions. You spark dialogue and exchange without judgment. You are easy around others, highly social, with fresh and timely opinions; none of it is forced, all of it's perfectly natural and easy. People remember what you say, and they consider your take on things. This esteem knows no hierarchy or prejudice; you are well thought of at all levels and among a breadth of personality types.

And you are just as effective when things get serious, exhibiting a consistent yet less-than-chaffing candor always tempered with clarity. You are open with your thoughts and with your willingness to consider what others think. You are passionate about it all, yet with a sense of poise and cool; you're always sophisticated, without the slightest whiff of pretension or bluster. Your confidence is void of hubris, always tempered with sincerity and thoughtfulness. Your countenance is warm and welcoming, even when the air in the meeting room is chilly.

It's a tough bill to fill, certainly. But look around at the people you already recognize as seemingly on career steroids, and you'll see it all there. These folks wear their perceived confidence and charisma naturally, as if it were a birthright rather than a skill set. But don't be fooled. Sincere and comfortable as it truly is and needs to be, to sustain the pressure and flak of a workplace full of diverse needs and opinions, it's always the product of a personal code and a commitment that has evolved into a core identity. It's a choice that transcends strategy to become your default mode of navigating the waters of the workplace. It's also what will capture the attention of those who can catapult your ranking into the upper echelon of the organizational flowchart.

Become an Expert at What Is Important to Senior Management

The objective of pleasing your boss is nothing new to the science of career advancement. But with everyone aiming for that goal, a keen understanding of the issues that keep senior management up at night and sequestered in daylong meetings becomes the context for performance excellence and project success, rather than something you learn about in sterilized form in weekly departmental assemblies in conference room C. Showing genuine interest in what senior executives are dealing with as they chart the course and navigate the treacherous waters of business competition in the battle for market share lets upper managers notice the performer as well as the performance.

Getting there isn't solely about giving management what they want. While it may seem a subtle difference at first, success comes from actually *wanting* what they want and making sure your aligned desire is visible so that it contributes to your career equity as much as any tangible results you deliver. In a 2009 survey of 444 global CEOs, 10 criteria for excellence among their highest-ranking managers emerged, the top two being excellence in execution and consistency of top management strategy. Notice these two front-runners are qualitative rather than exclusively quantitative metrics, trumping priority issues such as top- and bottom-line growth, customer loyalty and retention, productivity improvements, regulatory compliance, and the ability to adapt to changing markets. While the sum of these abilities defines executives' performance, it is the two highest priorities that define their executive presence. Their place in this pecking order of must-haves is no idle coincidence.

When you genuinely want what your leaders want, you have successfully adopted *their* agenda, not merely promoted yours. That's half the ball game when it comes to influencing the perceptions of upper management.

Build Confidence When It Counts the Most

Because perception management is such an outward-facing strategy that depends on your accurate read of what others need and value, it connects to the issue of confidence in risk taking. It affects your offering of ideas, mounting challenges, or merely creating an opportunity to grab some face time. Before going there, you'll want to take both the contextual dynamics of the situation and the personality and immediate priorities of the targeted party or audience into account.

Successful managers are not archetypical. They come in all sizes and shapes and, more important, from all points on the personality scale. Some are effluent and aggressive extroverts; others are more thoughtful and introspective by nature. Your perceived confidence, then, is not merely one of cultivated extroversion, but rather the adjustment of your natural style to those you work with and under. In the case of a specific influencing approach with a near-term goal, this assessment becomes a critical variable—you need to know what values, beliefs, and predispositions you're walking into in a personal sense as much as you need to have your act together for the pitch itself.

Wharton management professor Adam Grant led a study showing that introverts are just as likely to succeed as extroverts. The variable isn't as much their personality on this issue as it is that of subordinates, not all of whom are sensitive to the difference. Extroverted managers often collide with equally extroverted and proactive staff, whereas the same extroverts' management of an introverted staff has a high likelihood of smooth sailing and increased profits, according to the Wharton study.

This matching of -verts, if you will, becomes a variable in the success equation. In a study of a large national pizza chain, the evidence showed that proactive workers responded better to more introverted leadership, presumably because they felt they had the latitude to create and innovate. When the situation was reversed—more passive workers reporting to an assertive boss—this too yielded higher results than when the social factors and personalities were level across the team. Putting opposite personality types on the same team can, however, also lead to conflicts and resentment when managed poorly, igniting power struggles and polarization.

Clearly, a keen understanding of others' personality and communication style is the key to making relationships work, including the optimal pairing of introverts and extroverts in teams and leadership. The power of influence is available and attainable for both personality types.

Another study illuminates the true source of response and behavior when these dynamics start to dance. As told in an article by Joseph Grenny, coauthor of *Influencer: The Power to Change Anything*, the Harvard economist Felix Oberholzer-Gee conducted an experiment in which he offered folks waiting in line at the airport a cash incentive in return for their consent to cut in front of them. Predictably, more people who were offered $10 accepted the proposition than did those offered only $1. But less predictable, and the catalyst for closer examination, was the fact that the $10 offerees were also less likely to take any money at all, they just stepped aside with a smile and allowed the cut-in to happen. Grenny suggests that the reason behind this resides in the fact that the transaction was actually more social than economic. The more money offered, he postulated, the greater the perception of need, and thus, the higher the personal obligation to help without charge. Grenny advises, "We grossly underestimate the power of making simple public requests," and, "a polite and public invitation transforms already-formidable social influence into a tsunami-like propulsion to commit."

Of course, most socially intelligent human beings presumably understand that how we present and sell our underlying need can make all the difference in successfully influencing our contemporaries. But Grenny's observation certainly helps drive that point home.

Sell Your Ideas the Way Senior Executives Buy Them

The holy grail of any influencing attempt is achieving *buy-in*. Your evolved influencing power leverages building consensus, credibility, and a power bank on which you can draw when it counts. Buy-in takes many forms, from nodding heads in genuine agreement to signatures on the dotted line, but getting there is always more than simply a juxtaposition between risks and rewards, upsides and downsides, and the impact on the political barometer. Rather, it is often a merging of two drivers: facts and feelings. The latter is, unsurprisingly, contingent upon relationships and driven by bias and emotions.

This, too, has been the subject of much research. Another Wharton professor, G. Richard Shell, teamed with management consultant Mario Moussa on a study of the phenomenon of buy-in, coming up with five barriers to acceptance of ideas that—not coincidentally—are all antithetical to achieving influence. They are (1) unreceptive beliefs among the target audience; (2) conflicting interests at the time of potential buy-in; (3) negative bias based on the state of the relationship; (4) a lack of credibility; and (5) a disconnect between sender and receiver based on communication style and preferences.

Getting buy-in from an individual is one thing, but it rarely launches anything organizationally significant. To make your mark and successfully pitch your ideas, you need wide managerial and executive buy-in leading to commitment. Shell's research more specifically shows that, at an organizational level, you'll need at least eight people of influence to line up behind you before the proverbial mountain can be moved, or even before the anthill warrants a feasibility study.

Executive coach Marshall Goldsmith, in an article for Linkage, a global organizational development company, paraphrases the late management guru Peter Drucker. He writes that knowledge workers—who generally know more about their assigned tasks than do their managers—are often less than effective at influencing upper management. As a poignant example, he cites Columbia University's Warner Burke, who tells of the outcome of a managerial effectiveness survey from NASA—employees evaluating their managers—that occurred just before the Columbia Space Shuttle exploded. The survey highlighted a dismal last-place showing among all ratings for the criterion "Knows how to influence up in a constructive way." Given that "up" is what NASA is all about, this is perhaps as disconcerting as it is illuminating.

Ten Ways to Influence Upper Management

Goldsmith offers the following considerations to anyone looking to sell ideas to upper management. All of them, by the way, work even better when delivered within a context of stellar executive presence on the part of the influencer.

1. Look at your presentation this way: it is incumbent on you to *sell*; it is not the responsibility of anyone, including upper management, to buy. Don't assume alignment; strive to earn it.
2. Consider the larger good in all things, pushing your own considerations far to the side unless they align completely with and—most important—are a viable element of the proposal. The organization not only comes first, it comes first exclusive of anything else that may trickle down into your win column.
3. Pick your battles and focus on the big ones. Upper management has a nose for the trivial and irrelevant, so don't allow them to sniff it out in your presentation. Also, don't leverage any "psychological capital" that might become fallout or even an implication of what you're selling. Time is money in

these situations, so spend it on the main dish instead of the trimmings.

4. Benefits are good, but how they juxtapose to costs is even better. Benefits without a corresponding cost analysis can actually be detrimental to your purpose, as are costs offered without substantiation. Tie the two together and then help your audience do the math. Remember, what you are proposing might come at the expense of something else, which is another layer of cost that should be considered and quantified.

5. A moral compass knows no hierarchy. Don't be afraid to "challenge up" when something tweaks your sense of ethics. If you can, tie that logic to the organization and attach costs to it rather than personalizing it. Also, don't assume disagreement to be an issue of ethics. Welcome and facilitate debate and discussion with the confidence that it will land on ethics if that's the squeaky wheel. Courage is always admired, especially when tactfully and productively demonstrated.

6. Regardless of titles, upper managers are people too. Never use the phrase, "someone at this level" to frame an issue as being out of sync with the organization's goals. Strive to help, not judge.

7. Find a comfortable middle ground between respect and sucking up, one that never comes near the vicinity of disrespect. Less is more, but too little will get you just that—too little.

8. If you don't get your way, don't take the bad news back to your team and then throw the rejecting managers under the bus. This is always a bad, self-defeating move. You are a leader, not a messenger or an advocate for divisiveness.

9. The objective isn't to win, it is to contribute. To take the organization forward. To make a difference in a positive way. Even if it means allowing some of the love to spill over onto someone else's performance review. Individual ideas that

don't ultimately contribute are more counterproductive than shared ones that do.

10. Keep it forward-focused. The past is gone, or as Shakespeare said, it's just prologue. Letting go of the past is synonymous with embracing the future, which always uses the past as context. As should you.

Mastering the Critical Art of Small Talk with Your Boss

Make no mistake, you are always being evaluated and judged. From your cool in front of the executive team as you justify quarterly results to your banter on the tenth tee. Your ability to influence is partially dependant on how socially intelligent you are perceived to be in the presence of another executive, regardless of the pressure or agenda.

Just as with any presentation opportunity, you need to be prepared for either a planned or a chance encounter with a manager or an executive who is on the short list of people who can impact your career for better or worse. It bears repeating that executive presence isn't a mask or a pretense; rather, it's a cultivated essence that you proactively bring to the workplace and commit to as your default source of energy, which means you don't pick and choose when and where you turn it on. It's not an act—it's *you*, which means it's for everyone, every day.

If you know you're about to rub elbows with someone who has an office on a higher floor, your homework has two realms. In the first, you should be aware of that person's sphere of influence and interest, then come with some thoughts, observations, and (above all) baseline awareness. The other realm is an awareness of who that person is: his life, values, belief systems, story, and worldview. Anticipate what he might ask you about—your projects, opinions, past, life—and offer a relaxed, thoughtful response that defies any appearance of rehearsal. Isolate a key message in each area, then consider all the ways you can frame it within any situational context.

Above all, though, be yourself. Remember, these are—with obvious exceptions—sharp, sophisticated folks you're dealing with, and they can smell a poseur from the next building. The oldest Dale Carnegie technique in the popularity manual applies here: show interest, ask questions, listen, engage, add value, be empathetic, . . . and by all means, be yourself. I'd adjust that to being your *amplified* self. Your read of the situation drives everything that happens in these moments, and your nuanced ability to influence up is rarely more visible than in the fleeting, one-on-one social encounters that determine your likeability in the eyes of someone in charge.

Neutralize Your Critics

To come out ahead when it counts, sometimes you have to think like a trial lawyer. Put yourself in the skin of the listener or, better yet, the opposition, and apply their context and priorities to what they're about to hear from you.

In their book *Buy-In: Saving Your Good Idea from Getting Shot Down*, authors John Kotter and Lorne Whitehead encourage you to invite criticism and debate. With your ducks in a tight row, this allows you to deepen the logic and appeal of your pitch and can attract even more attention and energy if you can pull it off without a stare-down. Nothing engages an audience more than disagreement, with everyone on the edge of his or her seat to see who will jump the shark first. This perhaps counterintuitive strategy not only opens the door to your upside, but it speaks assertively to your understanding of the power of influence in high-stakes situations that can go either way.

When the counterpoint arrives, the best defense isn't always a good offense weighed down with data and case studies. Short, clear answers are usually best; bottom-line what the data illustrate, transforming your response from a spreadsheet to common sense. Executive presence keeps you respectful and mindful of your audience in these moments, and you will win the day through both the merits of your argument and how good a winner you appear to be. Nobody appreciates—and few tolerate—chest thumping and end-zone dancing bluster in the boardroom, and bullying is always the great killer of buy-in, especially when it trickles down.

They key here? Anticipation and preparation. A confident countenance alone won't save you if you aren't ready for an assault. Anticipate the angle of a critic's onslaught and prepare for every other possible angle on top of it. Improv is for the stage and has limited application when you're facing a prepared opponent whose single-minded goal might be to discredit your idea in support or absence of her own. And if there are cracks in your confidence and cool, it is precisely in these situations where they will show. Deep preparation will keep the strain of anxiety out of your voice and face, and it will allow the strength of your argument and passion to survive any incoming flak and neutralize the grenade throwers.

Manage the Perceptions of Your Peers

You may have used them yourself, or you may have heard them used. Labels like *suck-up, brownnoser, sycophant*—these are the most obvious and resented of all species of coworkers, and they'll kill your social standing faster than a chronic itch and garlic breath.

Here's one of the golden rules of organization life: loyalty counts. Allowing your loyalty to shine through, even in your most constructively critical mode, is vital to maintaining executive presence and the ability to influence in all directions. The career coach Randall S. Hansen, Ph.D., says that workers with a shaky track record of loyalty are the first to go when times get tough, even when they may have stronger numbers beside their name.

One of the most obvious tools in the influencer's tool chest is the sincere use of compliments. The line between being complimentary and manipulative is a thin one, however, so tread carefully in this realm.

Flattery can work to your advantage if handled right. A study by Ithai Stern of Northwestern University's Kellogg School of Management and James Westphal of the University of Michigan's Ross School of Business supports this notion and gives it credence. Seeking advice, they say, is a safe way to communicate admiration and endorsement, as is showing doubt or confusion just prior to suddenly understanding, thus allowing the mentor to feel as if she's been heard. Also effective is a kind word about someone to a friend who is likely to pass your compliment along, especially if the message is glowing to the point of risking embarrassment to both you and the receiver.

Another way to get your complimentary point across to achieve social influence, according to Stern and Westphal's findings, is to acknowledge mutual values or some common ground, perhaps common social affiliations and interests. These remind the listener that you are on the same page, the same team, which sets the stage for your expression of admiration, gratitude, or appreciation as lateral rather than aspiring. It's always better to be complimented by someone from your own camp than by someone who doesn't "get" you.

Manipulative? Not if you mean what you say. Practice *that* and you're on the path to cultivating a decidedly more robust perception of your influence and social power than if you carelessly sprayed the flattery in all directions for purely selfish reasons. Intending to compliment and complimenting well (in a way that enhances rather than unfavorably skews perception) are two different things; the latter isn't as much calculating as it is just plain smart.

Success is all about seeking out opportunities and optimizing them. This is as true for interpersonal moments as it is for the nuts and bolts of conducting business. Social influence is to organizational success what fitness, strength, and speed are to athletic success; what knowledge, experience, and intuition are to medical triumphs. It's all about being the best you can be in any given moment, and in a competitive organizational world, embracing the tools and techniques of doing so is the best win-win strategy of all.

In the next chapter, we'll look at how we can influence the other gender for mutual success. We'll uncover what neuroscience tells us about the brain differences between men and women; take a closer look at the different leadership styles of both sexes; and discuss which strategies work best in influencing the opposite sex in meetings, during presentations, and in conflict situations.

CHAPTER 9

Influencing the Opposite Gender for Mutual Success

S trap on your bulletproof vest, pull on your flak jacket, and prepare for the battle of the sexes! Or so you might think. Much has been made of the allegedly vast chasm between men and women (you may have heard we're from different planets), so much so that you may wonder how we manage to live or work together at all. It's almost as if we're different species. Almost.

There *are* differences between men and women, both biological and social, and these differences may affect how someone's perceived by his colleagues and how well they receive her message. If you want to influence people, male and female, it makes sense to recognize those differences and *adapt* to them.

That part is key: adaptation. We humans are a highly adaptable species and capable of modifying our own behaviors and outlooks to succeed in any particular environment. Those of us who are able to call on an entire repertoire of skills and behavior, including those associated with the opposite sex, will find ourselves far more at ease and thus more likely to connect with more people.

So shrug off the flak jacket, and unbuckle the bulletproof vest. Whatever our differences—and they do exist—we're also a lot alike; even better, both men and women are capable of adapting the skills of "the other side" as a way of making themselves more effective leaders of everyone. Gender doesn't have to be a battlefield.

The Brain Differences Between Men and Women

"All sex differences result from the imbalance of X and Y genes." So notes a recent Institute of Medicine (IOM) report on sex differences in research, tracing the biological differences between men and women to the genes on our sex chromosomes. Under most circumstances, women carry two X chromosomes, while men carry one X and one Y; genes on these chromosomes trigger a series of events that influence not only our reproductive organs and body shape, but also our brain organization, neurotransmitters, and the kinds of hormones that course through our bodies.

Plausible, you say. "Except the story is about more than X and Y chromosomes. Sometimes genetic and hormonal differences manifest themselves in our bodies, but sometimes, as the IOM reports, "Sex-specific mechanisms cancel each other out and make the sexes more similar" than different. To add yet another level of complexity, biological differences, be they structural or functional, do not always lead to different social or behavioral outcomes. Biology matters, but if you want to influence the men and women around you, you have to understand *how* it matters and when it might not.

So let's consider some of those differences, particularly as they relate to the brain. The one undisputed difference between men and women, researchers agree, is that men's brains are, on average, larger than women's. Christiana Leonard of McKnight Brain Institute, University of Florida, and her colleagues noted that the cerebral volume of men is 13 percent larger, and that "men had 17% more cerebral white matter, 10% more gray matter and a 10% larger corpus callosum." Women tend to have a higher ratio of gray-to-white matter, and the proportions of the different areas of the brain vary according to sex as well.

The kicker, however, is that these variations may have more to do with the *physical size* of the subjects than with sex. How's that? Leonard and her colleagues suggest that a larger brain, with its bigger surface area, requires a scaled-up structure in order to transmit information as efficiently as a brain with a smaller surface area. In other words, if you want to fling a pebble across a longer distance, you need a bigger slingshot.

Women's and men's brains also differ in terms of the relative size of various parts of the brain and the architecture of those parts. Hannah Hoag, writing in *New Scientist*, says researchers have found that the decision-making, problem-solving parts of the brain are proportionally larger in women, as are the sections that manage emotion, short-term memory, and spatial navigation, "perhaps surprisingly given women's reputation as bad map-readers." Those areas that process information from sensory organs, are involved in spatial perception, and control emotions, as well as social and sexual behavior, are proportionally larger in men.

These variations have real physical consequences. Larry Cahill, Ph.D., University of California, Irvine, observing that "sex differences exist in every brain lobe, including in many 'cognitive' regions such as the hippocampus, amygdala and neocortex," goes on to detail how these differences may affect the health and well-being of men and women. Addiction, sensitivity to pain, and the risk of anxiety and other mental disorders may all vary by sex, a conclusion backed up by the IOM report.

Yet these structural differences may not lead to markedly different outcomes. Consider the issue of directions. Hoag notes that whereas a man might simply trace a route on a basic street map, a woman will "get you there, too, but using a different technique. Drawing on her hippocampus, she'll offer you physical cues like the bakery, the post office and the Chinese restaurant."

Cahill concurs, referring to brain organization as a complex "mosaic" of two distinct types, male and female. But even with these clear distinctions, "the way that information is processed though the two mosaics, and the behaviors that each produce, could be identical or strikingly different, depending on a host of parameters." Think of it this way: men's and women's brains are both vehicles; sometimes they head off in different directions, and sometimes they traverse alternate routes to the same destination.

So the sexes do have different brains. The takeaway from this emergent area of research, however, is not that we are neurologically incompatible but that we are neurologically *adaptive*. If, as the IOM report states, "the brain can get the same outcome in more than one way," there's no reason to think we can't be as adaptable as our noggins.

He Leads/She Leads: The Difference in Leadership Styles

Our brief trek through the field of neuroscience has confirmed that, underneath their skulls, men and women differ. But it's also shown that there is not necessarily a straight line between behavior and biology. An article in the *Economist* noted, for example, that "these differences in structure and wiring do not appear to have any influence on intelligence as measured by IQ tests. It does, however, seem that the sexes carry out these tests in different ways."

So let's look at those different means not in our brains but in our behavior. Social scientists distinguish between *agentic* and *communal* styles of leadership. Agentic styles are marked by assertiveness, even aggression, and tend to be forceful and confident, whereas a communal style is more focused on other people, with those who deploy it described as caring, nurturing, and sensitive. As one study put it, "In employment settings, agentic behaviors might include speaking assertively, competing for attention, influencing others, initiating activity directed to assigned tasks, and making problem-focused suggestions. . . . [C]ommunal behaviors might include speaking tentatively, not drawing attention to oneself, accepting others' direction, supporting and soothing others, and contributing to the solution of relational and interpersonal problems." Guess which style is associated with each sex.

This is not a trick question, nor is it a trap. There is, after all, evidence to support that men pursue more agentic styles, whereas women deploy a communal approach, and that each style has its own strengths. Yael Hellman, professor of organizational leadership at Woodbury University, observes that the strengths of female leaders center on teamwork, in particular, their encouragement of innovation through collaboration; because they tend to share information, they also increase opportunities for improvement. Male leaders, on the other hand, are more likely to make clear the roles and responsibilities of subordinates and to weed out those who don't measure up. Anne Cummings, a professor of business administration at the University of Minnesota at Duluth, concurs; she highlights the task orientation of men and the interpersonal style of women, noting that men are more likely to take intellectual risks, whereas women may focus more on problem solving.

Relying too heavily on these generalities, however, *can* be a trap, in terms of both how we treat others and what we expect from ourselves. Given that the default model of leadership is still that of the assertive male, when we internalize such gender norms to the point where we expect men to "take charge" and women to "take care," we may end up overlooking both the strengths of the communal style and punishing assertive women as "pushy"—truly a damned-if-you-do, damned-if-you-don't situation for female leaders. Hellman says this can have the devastating effect of keeping them out of leadership positions and allowing their talents to go to waste.

Instead of getting caught in this trap, recognize that taking charge and taking care are *both* positive attributes, and *both* are required for effective leadership. Consider military officers. Few organizations are as traditionally masculine or as ruthlessly up-or-out as the officer corps of the armed forces; if you want to rise in the military, you had better learn how to take charge. But just as important is your ability to take care of your soldiers, to keep your troops calm and focused while performing often-dangerous work. Leading soldiers under fire might be the epitome of the hard charge, but the success of the mission also requires that the officer take care of his men.

This might seem an extreme example (corporate officers tend to drop metaphorical rather than actual bombs), but it actually serves perfectly to illustrate two points: (1) good leaders both pay attention to and work with their subordinates; and (2) organizational culture matters. Female drill sergeants tend to be just as loud and demanding as their male counterparts, traits that have less to do with gender than the requirements of the position. Similarly, men and women who don't wear combat boots to work have to accommodate themselves to their particular corporate cultures, an accommodation that may lead to more similarities than differences among leaders.

Given different organizational cultures, then, it makes sense to think of the agentic and communal styles less as masculine-only or feminine-only, and more as distinct toolkits, each with its own set of behaviors. That the default model of leadership is still male—a model that may change as more women move into leadership positions—does mean that women have to pay more attention than do their male colleagues to how they act and how those actions are perceived by those around them. Mixing expected feminine styles, especially in terms of consultation with coworkers, with a more assertive or decisive approach may provide women the leeway they need to rise through the ranks.

Communication and Conflict: Influencing the Opposite Sex When It Counts

So men and women have different brains and different behaviors (except, of course, when we don't). Does the same hold true when it comes to how we communicate and when we conflict?

Simma Lieberman, coauthor of *Putting Diversity to Work*, cautions that communication styles exist on a continuum. Nonetheless, she does provide a broad outline of what are often considered typical differences in male and female styles of communication. Her findings coincide with those of other observers, not only in women's more interpersonal style, but also in their greater willingness to share questions, problems, and information. Men, on the other hand, are more likely to work through problems on their own and are less likely to ask for more information.

Men and women both build relationships at work, but they approach them from opposite ends. According to Lieberman, "Women get things done at work by building relationships. Men build relationships while they are working on tasks with each other." In both cases, work and relationships go together, but for women, the relationship may precede the work, whereas for men, the work precedes the relationship.

This approach to work relationships may help to explain why women and men may differ in their reactions to disagreement. Conflict in one area may affect the whole of a relationship between women, whereas men, in a form of compartmentalization, may simply drop the disagreeable topic and move on to another—perhaps over a beer at the corner pub.

Lieberman notes that the sexes are also unique in how they signal agreement: "At meetings women nod their head to show they are listening. Men think the woman is agreeing with them. He then assumes the women will go along with his idea. He is surprised when she later disagrees, since she nodded her head. She has no idea why he thought she agreed with him since he never asked her." Men, on the other hand, "only nod their heads when they agree. If a woman is speaking and she doesn't see his head nod as he listens, she assumes he either disagrees or is not listening."

Is one way better than the other? No. The problem centers less on the method than on the misunderstanding of that method.

Recognizing that the meaning of, say, a nod may vary gives you the chance to adjust your own behavior accordingly. If you're a woman speaking before a group of men, don't get thrown by their stillness, and if you're a man speaking to a group of women, don't assume the head bobs mean yes.

Too often, however, women are simply told to adapt their behavior to the expectation of what's correct: don't bother with chitchat; suppress your emotions; and, perhaps, don't even acknowledge that there is such a thing at work as (deep breath) "feeling." True, it's best not to burst into tears (or punch a wall) when you encounter an obstacle at work, but treating the so-called feminine style as less often translates into treating those who employ that style as less—not a good approach if you're trying to get the best out of yourself and those around you.

Overcoming Specific Influence Challenges for Women

All of this talk about adaptation and continuums might lead you to believe that, hey, there really aren't any gender issues in the workplace anymore. We're all getting along. It's all good. If only.

Unfortunately, gender stereotypes continue to work against women who lead and aspire to lead, and it's not just men who hold those views; women may also view either themselves or other women as incompetent to fill leadership roles. And while the old notion of having to work twice as hard to be considered half as good isn't necessarily true in its calculations, it does highlight the problem that women can't count on even superior performance to help them move up, not least because their contributions are often minimized. Finally, the strategies often suggested to women—comport yourself to male expectations—won't garner them respect from men or help them lead women either. Nicholas Kristof, writing in the *New York Times*, says of women, "If they're self-effacing, people find them unimpressive, but if they talk up their accomplishments, they come across as pushy braggarts." These are serious challenges.

More than 30 years ago, Robert Altemeyer and Keith Jones, University of Manitoba, Canada, conducted a study on the ability of someone in a group to persuade the entire group to accept his solution; I say "his" solution because in that study, women were far less likely than men to have their answers accepted. Fast-forward to the 21st century, and . . . women still have difficulty gaining acceptance of their problem-solving abilities. As New York University professors Madeline Heilman and Michelle Haynes put it, "Stereotype-based negative expectations about women's performance in traditionally male domains are tenacious." Those women who do manage to rise in male-dominated fields often work with men who are reluctant to credit their female colleagues for their contributions, especially when they work in mixed-gender groups.

One strategy women may employ to boost their reputation for competence—mastering the details of any particular operation—may work against them in evaluations for leadership. The complaint? She's too detail-oriented and lacks vision. A *Harvard Business Review* study found that even when women leaders are more highly ranked than their male counterparts on such attributes as "outside orientation," "rewarding and feedback," and "team building," their male colleagues nonetheless still think women lack the ability to be visionary leaders.

What accounts for this gap? Study authors Herminia Ibarra and Otilia Obodaru concluded that women may have an alternative version of vision, they may be unwilling to take the leap from the detail to the big picture, or they may simply be skeptical of the necessity of vision. Regardless, this lack may hold them back, as they are deemed not up to the critical task of inspiring others to follow them.

A Catalyst study on women and leadership showed that a supposed lack of problem-solving ability fed into perceptions of a woman's inability to lead, largely because problem solving, motivation, and team building are considered related leadership behaviors. Thus, the central stereotype that women are better at interpersonal relationships does not hold if they are seen as less competent with the building

163

blocks of those relationships. As this study observed, "Men's lack of faith in women's problem-solving competence (whether justified or not) may actually cause them to be less open, if not resistant, to the inspirational appeals and team-building attempts of women leaders."

Another challenge is the "niceness" problem, as Kristof points out. Men have to be competent; women have to be competent and nice, even if perceptions of niceness and competence don't always go together. Laurie Rudman, professor of psychology at Rutgers, the State University of New Jersey, New Brunswick, and Peter Glick, professor of psychology at Lawrence University in Appleton, Wisconsin, note that this phenomenon is widespread: "When faced with direct evidence that a female target has violated the niceness prescription, however, women—who consistently endorse sexist ideologies less than men—tend to react as negatively as men, or even more so." Men may engage an autocratic style without repercussion, but as the psychology professor Hilary Lips of Radford University points out, women who do so "are disliked and disparaged."

There's more. Lips also notes that people are more likely to take direction from men than from women; that women who express ambition or attempt to promote themselves are considered less likeable; that women may need external validation or a credential beyond their performance as a way to vouch for their competence; and that even young women, when asked to imagine themselves as leaders, tend to use adjectives such as *aggressive, power hungry, mean,* and *bossy,* among others. This sense of the imagined attributes necessary for female leadership carries over to the real world. An informal *Forbes* survey of female bosses elicited evaluations that women are more likely to let their emotions get in the way, have "female catfight instincts," or be "threatened" by female subordinates. All of these responses, by the way, are from women.

Finally, there is the granddaddy (grandmother?) of stereotypes: that some professions are for women, and some for men. This can actually work in women's favor if they seek leadership in traditionally female-dominated fields or those corporations that sell primarily to women. Nobody is surprised that Mary Kay Cosmetics is dominated by female executives. If, however, a woman wants to break through in a "man's" field, she not only has to work with colleagues who are unfamiliar with female leaders, she may have to fight the perception that she doesn't belong in that job. Furthermore, women working in positions traditionally dominated by women (such as human resources) may find their leadership abilities denigrated by their subordinates. It is, as Catalyst points out, a true "double-jeopardy" situation.

Given the obstacles, how can ambitious women even get out of bed in the morning? That they're ambitious might be one clue, and as we'll discuss in the next section, there are ways for women to clamber over these obstacles and move into influential positions. Discrimination exists, but it can be addressed by both individuals and organizations.

Overcoming Specific Influence Challenges for Men

Challenges—what challenges? Men have it made, don't we? Yes and no. If you look at executive suites or political offices or the members of the Joint Chiefs of Staff, the occupants tend toward the male side. But that some men have made it to the top doesn't mean that all men have done so; maleness may thus far have been favorable to success, but it is no guarantor of it. That men today are also dealing with far more diverse workplaces than in the past also means that methods that may have been just fine a couple of decades ago no longer propel them to the top.

And while diversity can lead to an influx of new ideas and differing perspectives, it can also pose challenges, particularly as we try to learn how our own behavior may affect the behaviors of our diverse groups of colleagues. Provided we have the emotional intelligence to even understand our own behavior.

Shaunti Feldhahn, author of *The Male Factor*, states, "When men see a worker taking criticism personally, seeming to push too hard for his or her ideas, or having a personality conflict, they automatically view that worker as less business-savvy and less experienced, or as someone who operates on emotion, not logic." In so doing, they let their own perception of that worker as emotional interfere with an assessment of true ability. As a result, they may overlook someone who could be a valued colleague.

The admittedly generalized perception that men should shut down their emotions at work also suggests that they're not always able to identify when they respond emotionally. As one male business leader told Feldhahn, "I don't think women realize that men have self-doubt running through their veins." Thus, when women ask a direct question to elicit more information, men may react angrily, as if their own worth and authority were being questioned. And because men do compartmentalize, they are less able to deal with the consequences of such compartmental "leaks": if they're not supposed to be emotional at work, they may deny that any emotion may adversely affect their judgment.

Stereotypes about men's inability to express themselves can also work against them. There is zero evidence that men are less verbal than women, but this notion of men as verbal kindergartners might lead them to downgrade their own abilities, which in turn leads to worse performance. It might also lead women to judge men as less able than they are. These are effects of *priming*—if people are told that their "type" (sex or race, for example) is bad at a particular skill, they tend not to perform well; furthermore, if those assessing a skill are told that a person of this "type" is less able, they will judge that person more harshly.

This may also mean that men are shut out of important conversations with their colleagues, especially if they are in the minority or if the topic is considered a "woman's issue." In some cases, these conversations may not be directly related to the work itself, but if you're one of a few or the only man in the office or division, this may mean that you are effectively kept out of the group itself.

This is one of the dangers of *tokenism*, that is, being the sole or one of a few representatives of your group; you are, in fact, perceived as representative of your group (be it of race, sex, religion, or some other identifiable characteristic) and thus "like every other man." Or a "typical woman." Women used to and in some cases still do worry that if they err or fail, no other woman will be given a chance, that their sex will be seen as the *cause* of the problem. Men, too, may find themselves in the situation where they are treated not as individuals but simply as an embodied mass of stereotypes. As Deborah Cameron, writing on *The Myth of Mars and Venus*, notes, men may lose out on jobs in which interpersonal skills—skills they allegedly lack—are considered key: "In today's increasingly service-based economy, this may not be good news for men."

Men can also be tripped up if they don't exhibit that take-charge, agentic, masculine style, especially if they are in a workplace in which masculine behavior is expected of all leaders, male and female. If they act outside their expected gender role—say, by asking a lot of questions or working more collaboratively than authoritatively—men may be "downgraded to feminine status" and overlooked by both men and women who expect leaders to be decisive go-getters.

Thus, men who seek to influence their colleagues have to recognize their own hidden biases, in terms of both sex and style. This is, of course, a challenge generic to everyone: we tend to favor those people who make us most comfortable and those methods with which we're most familiar. Because men have been so successful with the traditional methods, they haven't had to pay as much attention to alternative styles and may find it difficult to adapt to them when needed. This is understandable. If we're successful with the hard charge, we may have difficulty seeing the benefits of a more participatory approach, thereby overlooking the skills and competence of those who are more communal.

Complementing Styles: The Influencing Power of Mixed-Gender Teams

So much for not engaging in a battle of the sexes. We humans seem to want to hang on to our stereotypes, tucking men and women into their respective blue and pink cubicles and shrugging that this is how it has always been and will always be, period.

Such a conclusion, however, would overlook the not-insignificant fact that women didn't used to be represented much in the workplace at all, certainly not in white-collar professions. Women were secretaries and typists and assistants—pink-collar workers—and were thought unsuited to run even an office, much less an entire company. Yet now women run offices, businesses, even countries; so, yes, it is possible to break out of color-coded cubicles and on to a larger stage.

It is tricky, however, for both men and women. We may believe or want to believe that we see only individuals and are able to work with whoever can work, but our unexamined biases keep getting in our way. For example, on the topic of mixed teams, one study found that mixed-gender mutual fund teams performed worse than either all-male or all-female teams; one commenter suggested that this was due to communication problems across the genders.

The first step to working together, then, is to recognize that we *all* have biases. As I mentioned previously, we may each like to see ourselves as clear-thinking individuals guided only by evidence and reason, but alas, our biology and psychology conspire against such clarity. Clarity *is* possible, but you have to work for it.

The second step is to recognize that leadership skills are just that—skills. Assertiveness, verbal dexterity, and problem solving are not, in fact, exclusively encoded in our genes; they are behaviors that can be learned. How we make use of our attributes may vary, but there's no reason to believe that men are born leaders and women are . . . not.

The willingness to develop and make use of our entire repertoire of skills is the third step. There are advantages to both the
agentic and communal styles; cultivating our ability to make use
of every tool in the kit allows us to adapt to each particular situation, taking charge when that's needed and inviting participation
when that will lead to the best result.

That all sounds good, of course, but what of the fact—
demonstrated over and over—that men and masculine styles are
preferred to women and feminine styles for leadership positions? It's
important to realize that expectations are changing and that corporate
cultures are becoming more welcoming to a diversity of leadership
styles. Professors Nilanjana Dasgupta of University of Massachusetts,
Amherst, and Shaki Asgari of Fordham University, state that when
women are exposed to famous women who have made contributions
to their respective fields, they tend to interpret "the success of the
famous individuals as attainable for other women and themselves."
Happily, men who work with successful women may also alter their
sense of female capabilities, helping to normalize female leadership.

In the meantime, however, what specifically can you do to
influence your teammates who are of the opposite gender? Joanna
Krotz, a contributing columnist at MSN, offers a number of practical tips for good working relations:

○ Given that women are more likely than men to ask questions,
  women bosses should be sure to "verify that men have enough
  knowledge to complete a task." It also makes sense to consult
  often and early in a project. Male bosses, on the other hand,
  should pay attention to the questions female team members may
  ask, recognizing that the answers could provide good information
  about the overall task for everyone involved.
○ While both men and women like to illustrate a point with stories, each needs to make sure that these anecdotes are gender
  neutral.

169

○ When there's a conflict, don't assume that a more communal style makes someone weak or that the agentic style is bullying. Rather, identify them as styles and be willing to borrow from each.

○ When a problem turns up, women tend to want to go over an issue in detail, whereas men want to get to the point. In this case, "men ought to explain their thinking and not simply jump to conclusions. Women need to get to the bottom line more quickly."

○ Men and women may both treat workers of the opposite sex the way they treat their spouses or partners; needless to say, this does not always go over well. Know when to give yourself a time-out and make sure you're not importing your personal life into the workplace.

○ Facts and feelings are each part of most conversations; acknowledgment of this fact can serve as a bridge across communication misfires.

In other words, don't be afraid to mix it up in relating to your colleagues.

I offer one additional recommendation. Remember the earlier discussion of priming? I mentioned that studies suggest that expectations of failure for members of a specific group can lead both to worse performance and to harsher judgment. But priming can also work in the other direction: if expectations are raised, or if members of a group are told there is no difference in ability between their group and others, then performance levels can increase and assessments may be more equitable.

So raise your expectations. *Confront* the attitudes that men-in-general or women-in-general are worse at skill X or in field Y, and *actively counter* them by highlighting the contributions of individual members as evidence of competence and by pointing out success stories.

These general guidelines can work in both one-on-one and group situations, but it's important to know that certain dynamics particular to mixed-sex groups may impede the functioning of such a group and work to the detriment of its members. It is also important to stress that *discrimination still exists*. The individuals within a company may consider themselves, if not free from bias, at least willing to address their biases, but inequitable practices within the organization itself affect hiring, promotion, and assessments of performance. Highly competent women in discriminatory institutions cannot necessarily count on the idea that their individual abilities will be enough for them to overcome the existing prejudice. The good news is that there are ways for organizations to reform their own practices in ways that benefit all members.

Research suggests that mixed-gender groups can lead to worse *or* better outcomes than single-gender groups. How's that? If women (or men) are in a significant minority (tokenism) within a group, in-group communication may be hampered; in single-sex groups, the communication may flow more smoothly.

Note that part of the problem may be due to the *extent* of the minority status. A study out of the London School of Business suggests that teams that are more balanced between men and women—meaning there are equal numbers of both genders in a given group—may create better conditions for all group members. Professor Lynda Gratton, the lead author of this study, observed, "Too often, senior teams have just one or two women as members. This report highlights the detrimental effect this 'tokenism' has on women and indeed on the performance and innovation of the team." The evidence in favor of balanced teams is dramatic. In terms of both experimentation and efficiency, balanced teams performed better; in fact, with experimentation, having slightly more women (a 60:40 ratio) is beneficial.

Gratton and her team also studied the effects of context on team performance, in particular, the "spillover" from home life. While more women than men take the lead in household labor, in the businesses studied, more men than women had children at home. There were positive effects on work performance for both sexes if home life was going well; if home life was problematic, the negative effects were more pronounced for men than for women, perhaps because they were more likely to have small children at home.

To create better conditions for individuals and better performance for teams, then, the study recommended that companies take the following steps:

○ Encourage shared domestic labor in terms of family-friendly policies; this may also help with spillover.
○ Actively manage spillover in terms of reducing the conflict between work and home.
○ Manage and minimize the "minority experience" for both men and women, and encourage gender-balanced teams.
○ Optimize the team's innovative potential in terms of both gender and experiential diversity.

As this research emphasized, mixed-gender teams were particularly valuable for innovation. Men may generally deploy and respond to one set of behaviors while women may generally deploy and respond to another, but as Gratton observed, "It appears that in work men and women are remarkably similar in their attitudes and aspirations."

As you expand your ability to influence in all directions, firmly keep in mind that you're working with people who want to be respected for their particular skills and abilities, not viewed as stereotypes.

In the next chapter, we'll discuss the importance of managing the impressions of your organization on those whose opinions count, such as customers, clients, and the constituents who keep you in business.

CHAPTER 10

Influencing the Public's Impressions of Your Organization

live on the Upper East Side in Manhattan. It's where I buy my groceries and where I take my dry cleaning. It's also where I take my suits if they need tailoring and where I drop off my mail whenever I can't send something electronically. I frequently eat here too—either at Gracie Mews, the 24-hour diner around the corner, or at one of the hundreds of other restaurants within walking distance from my residence.

As a consumer, my impressions of any one of the places I frequent fall on opposing ends of the spectrum. On one end, there's a grocery store that appears to celebrate "disgruntled employee of the month," with a staff who couldn't be less delighted if they worked in the cafeteria of a maximum security prison, not to mention a disheveled manager who wears his shirts over his pants, watching bemused from a perch while his cashiers berate each other in various regional dialects.

A few blocks farther down, it's a different story. At Agate & Valentina, professionals man the counters, the atmosphere is friendly, lines move efficiently, and fully stocked shelves are a powerful contrast to the disheveled mess at the former place.

My tailor, Ban, a North Korean transplant, does business in a small store behind a simple shopping front on 1st Avenue. And while he hardly speaks any English, his warm and welcoming demeanor; kind, broad smile; and superb craftsmanship make his little shop seem like the Four Seasons of tailors.

The diner I mentioned seems perpetually overstaffed, and that's a good thing, because every person behind the counter and working around the many booths adds a smile and a little bit of comfort when you want to have a meal away from home. You feel welcomed 24 hours a day.

The impressions I take away from these and many other business interactions at home, while traveling, or on the phone determine my choices and behavior. Whether most people realize it or not, their decisions are shaped by such impressions as well.

Too many organizations have members who don't feel like they have a stake in their company's reputation. For reasons that range from being mistreated, underpaid, mismanaged, or mistakenly hired in the first place to simply not wanting to be there, these dissatisfied employees slowly but steadily proceed to taint the public image the organization wants to protect and uphold.

And because we're all consumers, and we all witness and experience examples like those I gave earlier, we need to understand that—from the cashier to the CEO—how we present ourselves and our wares to customers translates to how well or how badly we are regarded by a public that has infinite choices for taking its business and partnerships elsewhere. It isn't marketing or public relations or human resources or sales or senior management that is the custodian of the organization's impressions on the public. It is every human being on the payroll who contributes a piece to the narrative I tell myself about a company and to the choice of whether or not I want to be part of that story.

From Top to Bottom—Everyone's in Charge of Organizational Reputation

Organizations have two intertwined reputations: that of the overall firm, and that of the individuals who work there. In some cases, the most important people, reputation-wise, are those in charge of the company; in other situations, the front-line workers—sales- and servicepeople—are the ones most likely to leave an impression. Regardless, the behavior of whoever is the public face of the organization often blurs into a sense of the organization itself.

Some businesses have chosen to highlight their CEO or founder. Putting a specific face on the company—think Jack Welch and GE, Mark Zuckerberg and Facebook, or Steve Jobs and Apple—can work to humanize an enormous corporation (GE), give a new organization an identity (Facebook), or simply differentiate the company from the rest of the pack (Apple). In each case, there are costs and benefits to such identification.

Humanization can be critical, as when the legendary former CEO Lee Iacocca, attempting to pull Chrysler out of a financial ditch, shot a series of ads touting his integrity and, by extension, the integrity of Chrysler. The attorney Joel Hyatt appeared in ads touting his law firm promising, "I'm Joel Hyatt, and you have my word on it." And the Rooney family in Pittsburgh has cultivated a reputation as good stewards of the Steelers football team and the city in which they play. Interestingly enough, the field of sports also provides a few examples of the downside of such identification. Both Jerry Jones of the Dallas Cowboys and Dan Snyder of the Washington Redskins are often ridiculed and even reviled by their fans; their perceived interference in the management of the team can serve to loosen the bonds between the paying fans and the team.

Increasing and differentiating the profile of a company can also be helped along by a dynamic individual. Mary Kay Ash built her eponymously named cosmetics company, in part, by putting herself front and center. Facebook rose on the strength of its offering and its aggressive pursuit of new users, but the story that this enterprise was started by a college student in his dorm room helped feed the perception that this version of social media was by the young and for the young. Bill Gates and Steve Jobs at Microsoft and Apple, respectively, also benefited from the upstart-in-the-garage mythos; Jobs, in his second go-around as company head, had emerged as a guru of technological innovation at the company.

Again, however, there are downsides to this strategy. Jobs has recently resigned as CEO of Apple, leaving observers (friendly and not) wondering if the company can survive his absence. Other organizations tightly tied to a founder, such as the Moral Majority and Jerry Falwell, founder themselves when the leader moves on or dies. Of course, any institution that is linked to leadership involved in a scandal, such as the PTL Club with Jim and Tammy Faye Bakker, may not survive.

Clearly, then, for an organization to succeed, it cannot rely too heavily on one person. How well Apple performs in the future will depend in large part on the talent of the people in the company, as well as the company's ability to make use of that talent. Or to use yet another sports metaphor: you need a deep bench.

Some organizations are all about the bench. Companies that rely heavily on their sales force, such as Mary Kay Cosmetics or Amway, recognize that their workers must buy into the corporate ethos for both those workers and the company to succeed.

The same is true for service-oriented companies. In his *Harvard Business Review* article, writer Paul Hemp reported on his guest stint as a room-service waiter at a new Ritz-Carlton in Boston. The Ritz, of course, is synonymous with luxury, but Hemp noted that the luxury has less to do with the furniture or artwork than with the service its employees provide. Given its reputation, it is unsurprising that the Ritz-Carlton has an extensive employee-training program, a program so well regarded that the corporation offers its training services to other companies.

Hemp took part in a sped-up version of the program, a combination of classroom orientation and on-the-job training supervised by an experienced server that combine to turn employees into dedicated disciples to a corporate ethos: "We are ladies and gentlemen serving ladies and gentlemen." Though some of the precepts seemed a bit "hokey" to Hemp, he nonetheless recognized that "it is employees' emotional commitment—which is achieved in part through symbols and ritual that enhance employees' sense of identity with the company—that contributes most to superior performance."

Not all corporate cultures are as successful as the Ritz-Carlton in preparing their employees for the demands of the job, a lack that may result in lower-quality service. Groupon, for example, is a highly successful social media company that seeks to drive customers to businesses that take part in its discount programs. As Utpal Dholakia, professor of management at Rice University in Houston, observes, however, not all of the participating businesses adequately informed their employees of the program or prepared them for the higher volume or the expectations of discount-seeking customers: "Overworked or skeptical employees are less able (or inclined) to create a positive customer experience. Their behavior can make the Groupon offer backfire, since two keys to reaping profits from the coupons are getting the Grouponers to buy items in addition to the discounted one and to become repeat customers who will pay full price in the future."

And for those who dismiss the relevance of employee satisfaction, look to the aptly named *Sabotage in the American Workplace*, a compilation edited by Martin Sprouse. Here you can read nightmarish tales of employee theft, assembly-line slowdowns, product wreckage, and electronic disruption. One unhappy programmer explains how he planted a "logic bomb" in Bank of America's payroll program, with the result that "on payday, nobody got paid in Northern California's PayNet system. Granted, I [messed] with the workers, but I really ruined Bank of America's credibility." A worker at a large Christmas ornament company, distressed at the low pay and poor working conditions, "started destroying all the Christmas ornaments I could get my hands on," throwing boxes against a wall and then shipping them out "to the hundreds of soon-to-be-irate customers."

Some of the workers interviewed may simply have been criminal or incompetent, but one autoworker, who sabotaged carburetors along with other workers, mourned that auto companies "don't treat you like a human being"; wrecking the parts was "our way of equalizing the situation." That the "auto industry got a bad rap because of it" may have been counterproductive, but a workforce so alienated from its employer is unlikely to concern itself with the company's long-term financial health.

Examples like these—from the intensive company dedication program at the Ritz to sabotage in the workplace—exist at the extreme ends of the spectrum; most companies are likely somewhere in between. Regardless, each pole and intermediate point offers the same lesson: how you manage your workplace will affect your company's reputation—for good or for ill.

Understanding Organizational Impression Management

Bank of America holds more than a million bad mortgages; it has also, according to a fair number of its customers, done a bad job of working with those mortgage holders. Banks that received tens of billions of dollars from the federal government as a means of staving off widespread economic collapse should not be surprised that their customers might also want a bit of consideration in preventing personal economic collapse. What customers got instead, many of them allege, was a fraud designed to push them out of their homes. Bank of America has responded to criticism by buying up domain names that are critical of the company.

As a sarcastic piece in the *Huffington Post* put it, "The company seems to be buying up scores of domain names that portray the financial behemoth and CEO Brian Moynihan in a negative light. Want to start a website slamming Moynihan? Too bad! URL addresses like BrianMoynihanSucks.com and BrianMoynihanBlows.com are already gone." Of course, Bank of America must know that angry customers can be very creative in thinking up epithets or that trying to make criticism go away is *not* the same thing as fixing the behavior that led to the criticism in the first place. But with a preemptive strike, it's trying to take some of the wind out of its detractors' sails.

Perhaps Bank of America is entirely innocent of all wrongdoing, and if so, perhaps it should follow the advice of Eric Dezenhall, head of a crisis management firm: "If you are innocent, go on the offense and don't apologize if you didn't do anything wrong." On the other hand, if you have not had particularly good customer relations prior to any specific wrongdoing, don't expect customers to give you a break. Maybe former Medtronic CEO Bill George hits closer to the mark when he says, "If your company deserves some of the blame, your CEO needs to face reality. CEOs often go into denial, and that's the worst thing they can do. It's a huge mistake to hire a PR firm and ask it to restore your image. The CEO's job is to take the lead in restoring it."

I bet its shareholders wished that BP had heeded this advice. The year 2010 was not a good one for the energy company formerly known as British Petroleum, later trying to push the more "green" moniker of Beyond Petroleum. It was hit with a crisis when the Deepwater Horizon oil rig it had contracted blew up in the Gulf of Mexico, killing 11 people, injuring many more, and soiling coastlines from Louisiana to Florida. The mid-April explosion and spill were terrible news—a true crisis not just for the people of the Gulf region, but for the company as well.

How did BP handle it? Less than two weeks after the explosion, then-CEO Tony Hayward wondered to his board, "What the hell did we do to deserve this?" At the end of May, he apologized to Louisiana residents, supposedly empathizing with them by saying, "There's no one who wants this over more than I do. I'd like my life back." In July, as oil continued to pour into the Gulf, Hayward attended a yacht race.

None of these actions would be recommended by image consultants (or anyone with a firm grasp on reality), although to be fair, Hayward did try to use the tactic of shifting blame to Transocean, the corporation that owned the rig. While technically correct that most people don't know Transocean and do know BP, such finger-pointing not only didn't succeed, it seemed to magnify the impression that BP was shirking responsibility. Hayward did recognize that "reputationally, and in every other way, we will be judged by the quality, intensity, speed and efficacy of our response." Too bad that recognition didn't translate into effective action.

The fact that BP deals with a necessary product will likely limit the long-term damage to the firm's bottom line. Hayward, on the other hand, was determined to be a liability and was replaced.

Are strollers necessary? Anyone in charge of a small child might respond in the affirmative, but when strollers go bad, parents and nannies do have options, including the use of another brand. Thus, when the news leaked out that Maclaren strollers were being recalled for having caused serious finger injuries to children, management had to respond immediately.

Maclaran CEO Farzad Rastegar initially planned to release a statement on November 10, 2009. But on November 9, the *New York Daily News* headlined a story on the recall. While the company had prepared to meet demand for the necessary repairs—in this case, by producing more than twice the number of covers needed for the offending hinges, hiring extra customer service reps, and purchasing extra computer capacity—within the first 30 days after the official statement, "none of this was ready to go."

"It was a colossal oversight," Rastegar admitted, noting that the company should have been prepared for a leak. That oversight was costly: "Our communications system first jammed and then crashed. Callers got a busy signal. E-mails went into the ether. Our website froze." The headquarters' showroom happened to be closed the day the story hit, so that when reporters showed up, it looked like no one was around. "I had to run down from my second-floor office to catch the reporters," Rastegar says. He was in constant communication with colleagues, and the company hired far more people and produced far more hinge covers than it had originally planned. "We were in triage, dealing with one issue after another, and the frustration was deep." The frantic pace lasted two weeks.

Looking back, Rastegar bemoaned the long lag between the company's identification of the problem and the announcement of the recall, a lag due at least in part to negotiations with the Consumer Product Safety Commission (CPSC). As Maclaran used this time to prepare not only for the recall but also for a larger conversation about stroller safety, Rastegar admitted, "We did not invest in crisis management or communications advice. Given our reputation for safety and our work with the CPSC, we thought the PR would handle itself and that our money would be better spent supporting the recall. We were wrong." The result was that "when the news broke, our advice was completely ad hoc." Maclaran was behind the news curve, scrambling, and pilloried for the scramble as the criticism went global.

Despite the errors, the company *was* able to recover. It took a financial hit, but Rastegar noted in January 2011 that worldwide sales remained strong. He expressed admiration for Maclaran workers and customers and observed that "the recall demonstrated to Maclaren's senior management team that the company must become more cohesive." It hopes to consolidate almost all distribution by the end of the year. Finally, he stated, "we have realized that Maclaran must play a bigger leadership role in the industry. . . . Thanks to the recall, we have realized that Maclaran is a tiny company with a giant name."

Sometimes the problem truly is a problem of perception. Toyota initiated a recall in response to complaints of unintended acceleration. The first fix involved floor mats, which were thought to interfere with the gas pedal; when the complaints continued, there was a second recall to fix what was thought to be a sticky accelerator. Reports of problems persisted, leading some to conclude that there was a problem with the cars' electronics; a number of people blamed near misses and crashes on wayward acceleration. Given Toyota's reputation for safety and reliability, the accusations were devastating, leading to criticism of the company at many levels of the U.S. government, as well as falling revenues and a lower share price.

Andy Beal, an online reputation management consultant and coauthor of *Radically Transparent*, criticized Toyota for "denying" there was a problem, but a little over a year later, the National Highway Transportation Agency cleared the company. "The jury is back," said Ray LaHood, the transportation secretary. "The verdict is in. There is no electronic-based cause for unintended high-speed acceleration in Toyotas. Period." Share prices rose in response.

Toyota was tarred with a scandal that, in the end, turned out to be untrue. But even though the company may have been blameless for the accused acts, it did err in its phlegmatic response to the charges. Still, it's not hard to feel that Toyota may have suffered unfairly.

Fairness, however, is beside the point. Any organization that makes anything or provides any service or deals in any way with anybody—which is to say, every organization—will be criticized for its products, services, and customer or client relations; every organization is at risk of something going horribly, terribly wrong.

Even if such criticism is unfounded (as with Toyota) or in bad faith, the company and its leaders must be prepared to deal with both the day-to-day complaints and the possibility of crisis or else suffer the consequences.

Organizational Impression Management Gone Wrong

I could offer you a list of ways to manage your company's reputation, but why not a list of how to trash that reputation?

For Day-to-Day Operations

○ Consider yourself indispensable and pay yourself accordingly.
○ Consider everyone else dispensable and pay them accordingly.
○ Let everyone know that you have all the answers.
○ Don't bother learning about the general operations of your organization.
○ Eliminate quality controls.
○ Eliminate employee training.
○ Micromanage your employees so they know how little you trust them.
○ Subject employees to random disciplinary action.
○ Encourage discord among staff members.
○ Eliminate customer service, and make sure it's difficult for customers or clients to reach you with complaints.
○ Set up a phone system that keeps customers on hold and repeats the message, "Please hold. Your call is important to us."
○ Ignore complaints that do reach you.
○ Promise customers and clients you'll "get right on it" and then do nothing.
○ Tell dissatisfied customers to "take a hike" or "sue me."
○ Blame others for undelivered or defective goods.
○ Demand payment for undelivered or defective goods.
○ Never use your own company's products or services.

These strategies should help convince all employees, customers, clients, and other stakeholders of your utter contempt for them and create plenty of incentive for all of them to bash the organization.

While engaging in these activities will certainly tarnish your company's reputation over time, nothing can destroy it quicker than responding badly to a crisis; this applies to small-business owners just as much as to world leaders, with outcomes of varying magnitudes. What qualifies as a poor response? The following list of "reputation busters" will hopefully set you up to protect your most valuable asset—your good name:

○ Assume nothing will ever go wrong.
○ Deny there's a problem.
○ Wait for the problem to blow over.
○ Freeze out the people or division responsible for the problem.
○ Don't bring in extra people or extra resources to fix the problem.
○ Fire people at random.
○ Withhold information from employees, key stakeholders, and the public.
○ Make sure there's no way for customers or clients (or more rational minds) to reach you.
○ Stonewall the press.
○ When you do finally communicate, speak or write in the passive voice, as in "Mistakes were made."
○ Assure customers and clients or constituents that the problem is being "blown out of proportion."
○ Blame the customer, client, or your own people for the problem.
○ Blame contractors or allied organizations for the problem.
○ Let everyone know the personal toll this is taking on you.
○ Never explain, never apologize.

In short, close your eyes, plug your ears, make a wish, and point fingers. Mix and match as you see fit, and you too can destroy your company's brand and reputation. Oh, and *your* reputation as well.

Proven Strategies and Tactics for Influencing Perceptions

Now that we've got the faulty examples out of the way, let's take a look at how to make sure your company and its reputation are in the best possible shape. Andy Beal, coauthor of *Radically Transparent: Monitoring and Managing Reputations Online*, emphasizes the importance of reputation, reputation, reputation. He declares that everyone has a reputation, online and off; every reputation has its weak spots, and every reputation will come under attack (discussed later in this chapter). Although Beal focuses on cyberspace and the role of social media, it should now be common sense for a company to be actively involved in reputation building, maintenance, extension, and repair.

Two of the more important aspects of reputation management are strategy and tactics. *Strategy* is the overall plan, usually encompassing a goal or purpose; *tactics*, on the other hand, are the specific actions you take or tools you use to implement that plan. The distinction is important, as the strategy must guide the tactics, not the other way around. It also helps to think of strategies as long term and often behind the scenes, something developed over time and in sync with the products and ethos of the company, whereas tactics are more flexible and utilitarian, tools that can quickly be adapted to a changing environment.

President and CEO Carlos Ghosn highlighted the importance of strategy in an essay describing his turnaround of Nissan Motor Co. He sought both to make the changes needed to get Nissan out of its financial hole and to protect the identity of the company and the respect of the people who worked there: "Those two goals—making changes and safeguarding identity—can easily come into conflict; pursuing them both entails a difficult and sometimes precarious balancing act." He later observed that "turning around a company in Nissan's state is a bit like Formula One racing. To take the highest-speed trajectory, you have to brake and accelerate, brake and accelerate all the time. The revival plan, therefore, was as much about future growth (accelerating) as it was about cutting costs (braking)." The strategy was *what* he wanted to accomplish, the two goals; the specifics of *how* he did it involved tactics.

Advertising is considered a tactic. Some ads are designed simply to let potential consumers know that a product exists. Aflac, the supplemental insurance company, rolled out a series of ads using a duck to squawk "Aflac!" when people wondered how to protect themselves against income loss due to injury or illness. Stories of how the CEO persisted in using the duck against everyone's advice filled business magazines for a while. He comes out the hero, as you may surmise. Similarly on the ad front, more pharmaceutical companies are rolling out ads to alert consumers that there may be a "little blue pill" for what ails them.

Then there are ads that are meant to raise or maintain a company's profile. What does a gecko with an English accent have to do with car insurance? Not much, beyond a similar-sounding name, but when you see that little green lizard, you know you've stumbled across a commercial for Geico. Taco Bell was also quite successful with its Spanish-speaking Chihuahua, who ended every commercial with the tagline, "Yo quiero Taco Bell."

It also helps to distinguish *reputation* from *brand*, although there is a great deal of overlap. A company can have a sterling reputation for quality products but also be considered an unexciting or even an overlooked brand; another company may be a "hot property" with high brand-name recognition but flame out or get tangled up in bad business practices. And, as Andy Beal points out, "Companies rarely rebrand when they have a great reputation." Perhaps it helps to consider the brand at the leading edge of the reputation, the profile on the body—intimately connected but distinct, depending on the angle from which it is viewed.

In the book *Differentiate or Die: Survival in Our Era of Killer Competition*, by Jack Trout and Steve Rivkin, branding is how you avoid the latter option. The authors note that in a crowded market that offers consumers an overwhelming number of choices, your company has to set itself apart from the rest. This may involve a variety of tactics, most of which are focused around advertising, but it may also require an emphasis on your company's reputation.

Impression management can encompass both brand and reputation. Depending on its purpose, it may involve straightforward or indirect tactics, and it may be used as either a sword or a shield. A. A. Mohammed, professor of management at Indiana University of Pennsylvania, offered one such taxonomy of tactics, shown in Table 10.1.

TABLE 10.1

	DIRECT TACTICS	INDIRECT TACTICS
Assertive tactics	Ingratiation	Boasting
	Intimidation	Blaring
	Organizational promotion	Burnishing
	Exemplification	Blasting
	Supplication	
Defensive tactics	Accounts	Burying
	Disclaimers	Blurring
	Organizational handicapping	Boosting
	Apologies	Belittling
	Belittling	
	Restitution	
	Prosocial behavior	

Some of these terms are self-explanatory (*ingratiation, intimidation, boasting,* and so on), but others are less clear. *Exemplification* means you hold up your company as a paragon of social responsibility and integrity, while in *supplication,* you portray your organization as vulnerable in an attempt to elicit aid from others. When engaging in *accounts,* you attempt to minimize the severity of an existing problem, whereas you generally employ a *disclaimer* preemptively *Organizational handicapping* is a way of lowering expectations so as to avoid the blame for failure, and *prosocial behavior* is a way to claim credit for positive behaviors.

Indirect Tactics

Indirect tactics follow the same assertive and defensive split. *Blaring* is when you state what your product does *not* contain (such as artificial additives), while in *blasting,* you exaggerate the bad qualities of your competitors or of the industry image in order to highlight your strengths. In *burnishing,* you seek to link your institution to a favored cause or organization. The indirect defensive tactics are all focused on links to other organizations: you *bury* a link to, say, an unpopular parent company, you *blur* a link when you downplay a conflict with a favored organization; you *boost* when you downplay the negatives of a linked organization; and you *belittle* when you, well, belittle the positive traits of a competitor.

It is important to note that this list is, in fact, a menu of options from which an organization can choose. The key to the deployment of any of these tactics is to identify the nature of your problem and the status of your company vis-à-vis any of the other players.

Massey Energy (now part of Alpha Natural resources), which has been subject to environmental protests and mine safety lawsuits, has taken a very aggressive line against detractors, engaging almost all of these tactics in an effort both to stave off regulation and to promote itself as good for West Virginia. Recently retired CEO Don Blankenship has promoted health clinics in the poor counties in which Massey operates, while also promising in 2006 to do "whatever it takes" to elect friendly Republicans to the West Virginia state legislature and funding a candidate to victory in the state's Supreme Court. Yet even with the 2010 Upper Big Branch Mine disaster in which 29 miners were killed and consecutive quarters of operating losses, the fact that the company sits on billions of tons of high-quality coal means that Massey's reputation may matter less than the demand for its product. In fact, one could argue that Blankenship has successfully used this demand as leverage behind his hard-nosed approach.

Most companies, however, can't rest on the certainty of the need for their products and thus have to rely on less pugnacious strategies and tactics. Southwest Airlines, for example, has to compete with other modes of transportation, other air carriers, and the generally dismal reputation of the airline industry. Yet despite Southwest Airlines CEO Gary Kelly's blunt observation that the customer is *not* always right, the company routinely tops customer satisfaction surveys, in large part because it *has* been so responsive to customer requests. Now if it can only get those pesky cracks and holes in its planes fixed.

Inder Sidhu, a senior vice president at Cisco, writes in an article for Forbes.com, "The relationships that Southwest maintains with its partners help it deliver more love to customers. They respond, in turn, by giving Southwest more business, which leads to more opportunities for the company's partners." In short, the airline asserts itself through customer satisfaction, promoting as well as burnishing its brand as a highly competent organization and exemplifying the worthiness of its service.

Strategies of Strong Brands

So what should you do? Kevin Lane Keller, professor of marketing at the Tuck School of Business at Dartmouth College, notes that strong brands share ten attributes:

- They deliver what the customer wants. Do you know what your customers want?
- The brand is relevant. Does your brand fit your customers?
- The price strategy dovetails with customer expectations. Are customers looking primarily for a low price or a particular quality in your brand?
- The brand is well positioned. How does your brand stack up against the competition?
- The brand is consistent. Are all messages about your brand pointed in the same direction?
- The brand's position within the company makes sense. How does it fit with other brands in your company's portfolio?
- The brand takes advantage of the full range of marketing tactics. Have you compiled a complete package—brand name, slogan, logo, and so on—in support of your brand?
- Company officials know what the brand means to customers. How do customers use the brand, both concretely and symbolically?
- The company supports the brand. Have you devoted sufficient research, production, and marketing resources to the brand?
- The company engages in regular "brand inventory." Has the brand been eroded in any way? Should it be adjusted?

This checklist is just the beginning, as Keller himself says. Use it to generate even more questions and possibilities for your brand.

Key Lessons on Influencing Perception from the World's Top Brands

According to a survey by Reputation Institute, the ten most trusted large U.S. companies in 2010 were Johnson & Johnson,

Kraft Foods, Kellogg, the Walt Disney Company, PepsiCo, Sara Lee, Google, Microsoft, UPS, and Dean Foods; other notables near the top included Apple, Caterpillar, H.J. Heinz, and 3M. (Unsurprisingly, financial institutions dominated the bottom of the list, with AIG coming in last at 150.)

What accounts for the success of the top firms? *Forbes* reporter Laurie Burkitt says, "The secret to Johnson & Johnson's success rings true for all of this year's reputable companies: Each has direct connections to their consumers and their families." Food producers did well as more Americans ate at home, thereby increasing brand recognition in the process. Philanthropy also boosted reputations: the Bill and Melinda Gates Foundation, for example, helped lift the reputation of Microsoft. Such attentiveness to status matters: Anthony Johndrow, Reputation Institute's managing director, states that reputation translates into customer recommendations, "and you can bet you'll improve your bottom line."

Another survey, focusing on U.S. "thought leaders," put Apple at the top, followed by Google, Southwest Airlines, Amazon, Facebook, Microsoft, Intel, RIM, Coca-Cola, and Whole Foods. Trust, authority, innovation, admiration, and the competitive advantage of their products all helped to define these companies as the best.

What should you pay attention to? Different advisers recommend different metrics, but they generally agree on a few main themes:

○ **Reputation matters.** Yes, this should be obvious by now, but companies at the top neither take this for granted nor rest on their laurels. They integrate the concern for their reputation into the structure of their business rather than treat it as a public relations adjunct.

○ **Reputation management is an activity, not a slogan.** This follows from the first point. You must actively monitor media coverage about your company and be in a position to adjust your message as needed.

○ **Tell the story.** I almost wrote "control the narrative," but that isn't always possible; instead, recognize that if you don't tell the story of your company, someone else will. This doesn't mean all ad campaigns have to include your company's history or that spokespeople have to tell the same anecdote about the founder or CEO over and over, but you should have a sense of the general narrative and purpose of your organization and be able to call on that story to guide your actions.

Sometimes actions themselves can tell the story, as with Amazon. The online retailer invests little in offline marketing, concentrating its investments in technology, distribution, and good deals. One marketing specialist notes, "It's not about splaying their logo everywhere. They are all about ease of use." Similarly, Zappos built its business on inventory, delivery, and service; customers know that if the shoe doesn't fit, they can ship it back to the company free of charge. Unsurprisingly, perhaps, Amazon bought Zappos in July 2009.

○ **Know your base.** The companies that succeed are those that know what business they're in. Ritz-Carlton knows it's in the service industry, and Maclaran is in the baby-products biz, so each must concentrate on what sets their brands apart in those industries. Bill Taylor, writing about the "amazing" customer service of Zappos in the *Harvard Business Review,* observes that "it's the emotional connection that seals the deal." If you sell widgets, then those widgets have to be reliable and appropriate to your target market; so, too, with the services you provide. Fit matters.

○ **Earn the trust of all stakeholders.** Aloof no longer cuts it in the wide-open, social media age. Employees have always kibitzed with one another about the job, but now they can go online and let the world know their thoughts. Consumers, too, can click around for information on a product or corporation; Randall Beard, former global chief marketing officer of UBS, notes that "it's really easy for consumers to check and verify a company's behavior to find out if a company's actions match its words."

Trust is particularly important to companies that operate exclusively or largely online. Would you shell out a hundred dollars for a pair of shoes or a sweater that you didn't know would fit you if you didn't know you could easily return it? And wouldn't you want someone knowledgeable to guide you through the fitting process? Lands' End, L.L. Bean, and Zappos each have generous return policies and a surfeit of customer representatives. The L.L. Bean customer service web page leads with a quote from Leon Leonwood Bean: "A customer is not an interruption of our work . . . he is the purpose of it. We are not doing a favor by serving him . . . he is doing us a favor by giving us the opportunity to do so."

○ **Acknowledge error.** Most errors are small—a cold meal, the wrong size shirt, a broken shelf—and don't require the intervention of the CEO. Those employees who are in a position to fix the problem should be adequately trained and empowered to do so. The Ritz-Carlton allots every employee $2,000 to spend satisfying each customer with a complaint. Human resource director John Collins states, "You'll never get in trouble for taking the extra step." (If the error is big, try to do the opposite of what is suggested in the earlier "Organizational Impression Management Gone Wrong" section.)

○ **Fix the error.** Another no-brainer—or so you'd think. But does your organization have a way to identify problems over time, to track whether an error is isolated or part of a larger and more persistent problem? Do employees have a way to bring this information to management's attention, and are they rewarded for doing so?

○ **Recognize emergent concerns and respond to them.** Are your customers concerned about the environment? Do they pay attention to working conditions at your overseas facilities? Have any of your business partners or stakeholders been targeted for protests or boycotts?

○ **Never complain, do explain.** Stakeholders don't want to hear about your hard day or that you want your life back; they have their own lives to worry about. Workers want to know about production expectations and a rewarding work environment; shareholders want to know that their investment is managed by smart, forward-thinking executives; and consumers care about value in the end product—period. It's never good to get a reputation as a whiner. No excuses.

There's a common theme running through all of this: *pay attention.* Really, it starts and ends with the attention you give every aspect of your business, from the people on the front lines to the person in the corner office and everyone and everywhere in between. You have the opportunity every day to get it right or get it wrong. Pay attention to getting it right.

In the next chapter, you'll discover how you can influence with words, whether in speaking or writing, and how you can frame language to move closer to your goals.

CHAPTER 11

Using Your Words to Influence and Change Minds

My philosophy in helping my clients successfully craft and convey a powerful message can be summed up in a frequently circulated quote, once used to great effect by a not-so-gifted orator, the former prime minister of the United Kingdom, Gordon Brown. Paraphrased it is, "When Cicero spoke to the crowds of ancient Rome, people said, 'Great speech.' But when Demosthenes spoke to the crowds of his day in ancient Greece, they said, 'Let's march.'" I don't care how eloquent or lovely a speaker is, but I do care that a speaker's words and message spark something—make people "march."

As you look for ways to broaden, develop, or start building your sphere of influence in all directions, the power of speech is part of the foundation you have to master. It's more than public speaking and giving presentations, which most people have learned to see as necessary evils and unpleasant spectacles best performed on autopilot with a navigator named PowerPoint in charge.

Speaking to influence and change minds takes more than a routine approach. While useful for any man, woman, or child, it's most critical to those up-and-coming leaders and professionals who passionately care about making a difference and who won't stop before they've succeeded in stirring the emotions and engaging the minds of those who can help make it all happen.

Framing: Master the Language of Influence

It's not enough, however, simply to stir the emotions of your audience if you want to influence them; instead you have to *shape* their emotions to direct them to your preferred outcome.

That's where framing comes into play. The skill of framing is critical in the tool chest of anyone looking to influence others because people automatically look to assign meaning to the communication signals they perceive around them. And to frame strategically is to manage the meaning people take away.

When we attempt to frame an issue, we carefully choose our words in a way that focuses attention on a particular meaning—the one we want to convey—among several possible meanings. The facts are spiffed up, dressed up in partisan clothes, and lined up as part of the consideration.

We also frame when we want someone to see only one particular aspect of an issue—for example, when we want to influence or persuade an audience to buy a particular product, vote for a particular candidate, or solicit cooperation from colleagues. We don't change the facts, because that would be lying, but we choose what we present to shape the meaning others take away. This applies to performance reviews, the discussion of someone's qualities as a leader, and an employee's suitability for a new position or a spot on the team.

Considering the impact language can have in creating meaning in people's minds, and considering the ways language affects the way they perceive reality, we have to be aware of how this influence is exerted. Even in a free speech society, it becomes incumbent on the sender of words to understand and weigh how those words may be interpreted and acted on. Otherwise there is no difference between words and a potential deadly weapon in influencing someone's life.

Why do frames affect us in such a powerful way? Contrary to the rational choice theory in classical economics, which says people make choices that are realistic and rational, framing theory suggests people are carried away by the frames used in communication and that how something is presented (the "frame") influences the choices people make. Scientists have found conceptual structures in the brain. These structures are like our personal dictionary to which the brain refers whenever it has to understand an issue or make a decision. It can be a decision to buy a home theater or to vote for a specific political candidate. These structures are present in the form of metaphors; value systems; traditions; beliefs; personal experience; and theorizing picked up from textbooks, bedtime stories, or any other source. Think of the building of these mental structures this way: when you exercise, you build the muscles in your body, depending on the area you work out. Similarly if you think again and again with a particular angle and conceptualize an issue, then a brain tissue (formation of several synaptic connections of nerves) may develop and remain as a structure in your brain.

As simple proof for the existence of frames and his theory of cognitive structures, professor George Lakoff, a cognitive scientist and linguist at The University of California—Berkeley, routinely gives the following experiment to his audience to show how cognitive structure can be observed in action. You can test it on yourself right now. Take a deep breath; clear your mind; and after a couple of seconds, follow the instruction given. OK, here's the instruction: Don't think of an elephant.

In the classroom, after a couple of minutes, the instructor addresses the audience: "Those of you who did not think of an elephant, please raise your hands." Very few hands typically go up. It's now easy for the instructor to explain how all of us have a cognitive structure, a mental image, regarding the concept and

197

specific characteristics of *elephant*. Once we hear the instruction "Don't think of an elephant," the frame or mental structure of *elephant* automatically gets activated, making most of us think of it whether we want to or not. It's virtually impossible *not* to think of an elephant as long as the elephant-related cognitive structure is active in our brain.

Another quick test: Don't think of a Mattwollzinope. You get nothing, right? It's a made-up word, and you therefore wouldn't have any cognitive structures I can activate. So you'll draw a virtual blank on that one.

You can start to see how framing something affects reality itself. Since people can experience only a very small portion of the reality that affects them personally (meaning the information they take in through the five senses), they rely on others to convey most of the "reality" outside their own realm of experience—such as events, facts, news, conversations, and stories—to them. And how it's conveyed or framed is how they "experience" reality.

Framing, in other words, is not just about shaping the *perception* of the situation; it's about shaping the *reality* of the situation. You don't have to be a cognitive scientist to see the power of that.

Why Frames Matter

So how do you frame an issue to your advantage? If you want to be effective, you have to keep in mind *who* is your audience, *what* is the product or idea you're bringing to their attention, and *how* you want them to respond. A brilliant frame meant to rally supporters is unlikely to work in winning over skeptics, and someone concerned about budgetary matters won't be moved by appeals to organizational image. Of course, you have to give direction (Buy! Vote! Register! Volunteer!) at the end of your pitch. Once you've figured out the who-what-how triad, you can consider the best words or images to use in constructing that frame.

The frame will fail if you lack a sense of *who* your audience is. Are you trying to convince your colleagues? Your boss? Your subordinates? Are you reaching out to a natural constituency or trying to reel in those who remain outside your orbit? Or perhaps you want to garner attention from the media as a way of expanding the audience for your message. Regardless, you want to know what preconceptions they carry (which you can either reinforce or attempt to evade or erode), as well as whether they will respond to moral language, gentle humor, sarcasm, sentimentality, and so forth.

What is the focus of your framing exercise? This might seem to be the most obvious question, but don't take the answer for granted. Are you selling a particular product? Are you competing directly or indirectly with another product? Or maybe you're selling a state of mind, such that you want your audience to associate, say, "comfort" or "luxury" or "efficiency" with your brand. Or maybe it's an innovative practice or idea, a reorganization, or the pursuit of a new research agenda; regardless, you have to know what exactly it is you're pitching.

How you want people to respond to a proposal is also less straightforward than it appears. Do you want people to respond positively, negatively, or neutrally? Do you want them to act in your favor, act against someone or something else, or desist from acting altogether? Electoral campaigns usually contain both positive and negative messages: vote for me and not for that jerk. But campaigns around more general political issues may simply seek to keep constituents on the sideline, to encourage a wait-and-see attitude, or even to suppress voter turnout.

And don't forget that you may need to identify multiple triads in any one campaign. In electoral campaigns, for example, you seek to motivate supporters, persuade the undecided, and demoralize or deactivate opponents. You need to coordinate your frames over time and as appropriate to each audience.

199

Complicated campaigns—a new venture, renovations of a damaged image, or a multifaceted policy—will require both a strong central frame and a number of ancillary frames. Take, for example, the controversy surrounding human embryonic stem-cell research. In the United States, public funding is prohibited for any research on human embryos, although privately funded research is legal. Given that the derivation of stem cells necessarily destroys the embryo, it's clear that no public funds may be used for such derivation; what has been less clear is whether public funds may be used for research on the stem cells themselves.

That's just one piece of the controversy: how to interpret the Dickey-Wicker Amendment (the provision that outlaws embryo research) is a complicated issue in its own right. But there are other pieces as well, involving such matters as the biology of the stem cells, their potency, and how to control their development (so that, for example, they don't cause cancer); the relative merits of embryonic versus adult stem cells; how soon and how likely are medical breakthroughs; what is the purpose of federal funding for biomedical research; and, of course, the whole set of moral issues regarding the status of the embryo and the obligation to relieve suffering.

It is, in other words, complicated.

So how did proponents of embryonic stem cell research manage to convince a pro-life president, George W. Bush, to allow for limited public funding for the work? One scholar argued that those in favor of public funding managed to frame the debate in terms of a biomedical imperative, offering a central narrative of scientific research as wedded to medical progress, such that even those opposed to the research were required to fight the battle on the merits of the science rather than on their preferred ground of the personhood of the embryo.

Due to the ability (called *pluripotency*) of embryonic stem cells to become almost every other cell in the body, proponents were able to parry the opponent's argument that adult stem cells (which are multipotent, or only able to become some cell types) could serve as a worthy substitute to embryonic stem cells. It also helped that proponents also favored research on adult stem cells: they were able to portray themselves as seeking to expand *all* promising areas of research; opponents were portrayed as restricting such promise.

Furthermore, proponents were able to establish a moral basis for scientific research by tying that research into the medical obligation to relieve suffering, and in so doing, refused to cede the ground of morality to the pro-life opponents. This was a key part of their framing: proponents didn't just argue for the good of scientific research, but for *scientific research as a necessary part of medical progress*. Such medical progress, in turn, could lead to therapies for injuries and for diseases such as diabetes or Parkinson's, that is, could lead to making peoples' lives better—a clear moral good.

Opponents argued that any research that requires the destruction of embryos, which they consider human beings, is inherently immoral: you cannot kill some people in order to benefit others. Yet they were disadvantaged in this argument in a number of ways. First, while it is true that all humans begin as embryos, not everyone agrees that the embryo is itself a person. Second, and related to the first point, the embryo is microscopic, and images of embryos don't much look like people. Third, while people disagree regarding the moral status of embryos, they generally agree that those who could benefit from stem cell research *are* people. In short, the late *Superman* actor Christopher Reeve and Michael J. Fox connecting on an emotional level with audiences are going to beat static images of embryos every time.

Finally, proponents also brought in general notions of liberty and choice—potent ideas in American political life. They argued in favor of the freedom to pursue scientific research and, more important, for the expansion of choices of treatments for all Americans. Some patients who opposed embryonic stem cell research testified before Congress and various bioethics panels, but because the opponents were seen as seeking to restrict freedom, those arguments did not resonate as well as those that sought to expand freedom.

By framing the issue as one of scientific and medical progress, augmenting this frame with the moral imperative to relieve suffering (and prominently featuring people who could benefit from the work in their testimonies), and tapping into larger American themes of liberty, proponents were able to shape a complicated discussion in ways that opponents could never fully overcome. While opponents were able to influence the outcome—President Bush limited funding to research on stem cell lines already established—they were unable to sufficiently shift the terms of the debate to overcome the advantage of the frame established by those in favor of the research.

Paint Clear and Powerful Images by Telling a Story

The most important thing to know in creating meaning is that *narrative works.* You have to tell a story. Whether it's an uplifting story of redemption or a cautionary tale regarding inaction, whether you want to push your organization in a new direction or convince your colleagues of the importance of a new technology, whether you want to encourage or discourage an activity, you *have* to tell a story. It can be biographical or historical, speculative or forward-looking, negative or positive, or factual or clearly fictional—as long as it is relevant to your audience and objective. Telling the right story for the situation at hand is what matters. And a story beats straight argument or statistical presentation every time, because it infuses your data with a soul.

We're not talking about "once upon a time." Think of this more in terms of narrative arc: where you've been, where you are now, where you're going. At its most basic level, a story has a protagonist the audience can identify with, any number of obstacles that must be overcome or are in the way of the protagonist meeting his objectives, and a moral or a lesson to be learned.

Why do stories work? Simple. People remember them. People relate to them. People see themselves in them.

Say you want to sell a particular brand of car, one that gets good gas mileage. Do you show a still of the car, have the spokesperson mention that it's reliable and comes in many colors, and then announce the miles per gallon? Or do you show a carful of friends zooming past gas station after gas station to the sounds of a jaunty soundtrack, cruising though small towns and big cities, farmland and desert, up and over mountains? Do you maybe have a shot of an envelope labeled "gas money" that still has a fair amount of cash in it at the end of the trip? You can flash the miles per gallon and gazillion-mile warranty on the screen as the friends grab the cash and head out for a day or night of fun.

OK, so that's a bit of a no-brainer, but the reason it's a no-brainer is because we've become so accustomed to narration that we take it for granted. Some company slogans offer a précis of a story: "Like a good neighbor, State Farm is there"; "It's Miller time"; "Imported from Detroit"; and a throwback to yesteryear, "It's morning in America." These slogans flip a narrative switch in the audience: this insurance company will look after me; work's over, time to kick back with a beer; Americans make cars as good as the imports; Americans have a bright future ahead with Ronald Reagan. These are snippets, not novels, but what the slogan offers in preview and the story delivers is what evokes meaning for your audience.

Fellow consultant and organizational storytelling expert Stephen Denning advises using specific story structures to accomplish important objectives via narrative:

203

- If it's swirling rumors and conjecture you need to deal with because they're distracting people in the organization, frightening them into paralysis, and making productivity nosedive, try this. If the rumors have a basis in reality (reorganization seems to be what people are worried about), put it in its proper perspective, define the issue, and let people know how they will be affected in both positive and negative ways. Don't wait and make everyone worry about their jobs. If the rumors are completely false and the product of watercooler fiction, make fun of it and put everyone's mind at ease. Point out the ridiculousness of it all.

- When it's action you need, getting people to move in a new and perhaps an uncomfortable direction, tell a little success story. The key here is to make it short and short on detail (let your audience's imagination complete the picture); show that this situation has happened in the past and that it had a successful outcome. Remember, the story doesn't have to be your own; it can be any story you've heard or read that fits the bill and does the job. Personal experience is less important than the inspirational tone and outcome.

- If you simply have to share knowledge, the influencing challenge is to see that it's retained and understood so it can be useful when needed. This is where you add a generous helping of "what went wrong" to the tale you're dishing up. Negative stories are particularly useful in training situations and where learning is a critical outcome. Narrative that talks about mistakes that led to bad outcomes is effective because humans love drama and language that includes things like ". . . and in a moment of distraction, he loosened the wrong valve, causing pressurized hot vapor to burn his entire . . ."—you get the picture. We're riveted, and at the same time, we get to replay the scenario in our head, doing it the "right way" in contrast to the hapless protagonist in the narrative.

○ If you need to meet important leadership objectives and influence your team, it is critical to have the visionary story structure in your arsenal. This is a leadership staple, and leaders who aren't visionaries will have a difficult time painting a picture of a future into which their subordinates are to follow. So how do you paint that vision? Keep it simple and believable. When you describe a better future, make sure it looks enticing and bright enough that your listeners can see themselves there, but don't get into so much detail that much of it may turn out to be wrong. After all, no one can actually predict the future.

Whatever the form of communication, if you want to influence your audience toward a particular way of thinking or goal, you have to give listeners an incentive to follow you. Telling them a strategic story can give you a major edge in getting there.

The Core Message

Stories and framing won't do you any good, of course, if you don't have a solid point to make. While you will have to tell different stories and deploy different frames depending on the situation, it is your desired end result that dictates the way you get there.

Start by identifying your core message. That's the thing that determines everything else you say. It's your unique point of view, your angle of attack. It's also referred to as the thesis, theme, or governing thought you are trying to explain, promote, and drive home.

Speaking with influence requires that you do some homework. Who will listen—literally and figuratively—if you haven't any experience, expertise, conviction, or credibility in your topic and haven't narrowed that topic sufficiently to arrive at the core of what you want others to understand? What impact will your presentation make? When it's all said and done, the last person is shuffling toward the door, and you're collecting your things from the podium, what will they remember? What will have stuck to their intellectual walls that will cause them to support a proposal or resist your opposition's efforts at influence? Ideally, it's the key points you pinned to that wall in unimpeachable support of your core message.

If your message is fuzzy, they'll take that away and won't know what to do with it. Maybe they thought you spoke well—great even like a Cicero—but can't recall about what. Maybe they caught one point but not the others and definitely not where you were going with the whole thing, so they are confused and unable to think in the direction you want them to. So dig deep for what it is you *desperately* (italicized for drama) want your listeners to consider, put it in the plainest terms (always better than the most complex), and support it with plenty of rock-solid reason and evidence.

Jack Welch, former CEO of General Electric, had a core message—I mentioned it in Chapter 6—for his conglomerate of business units within GE. It was, again, "We're either number one or number two in any business we're in or we get out." His prescription for business units that underperformed was "Fix, sell, or close." It was a simple message in powerful words that every one of GE's thousands of managers understood.

The key in getting to your core message is that you fully believe it yourself and conclude that it is the one statement that says pithily what you want to get across.

Say It in Powerful Words

So let's get down to the nitty-gritty: How do we shape our narratives and frame our presentations around our core messages? It all begins with the words: The words we use with our clients and families, bosses and peers, colleagues and business associates largely determine how much influence we gain or lose at any moment. Most of us aren't yet on the public stage where words are carefully weighed and analyzed for meaning, honesty, and attitude—not to mention impact with any particular constituency.

Financial markets can rise and fall when a single phrase is misinterpreted or interpreted correctly. Organizational rumor mills can switch into overdrive with a careless remark about "reorganization" dropped in the wrong place; boardrooms and cabinets call emergency sessions in light of an announcement, presidential or otherwise, that threatens the status quo. That's why each U.S. president employs boiler rooms of speechwriters and media trainers—as do most Fortune 500 CEOs, albeit in smaller measure—to make sure that the intended message is put into words that get it across. The bigger the stage, the more influence words have.

That doesn't let us more common business and professional folk off the hook, however. It's my experience that most business executives and middle managers pay little attention to the language they use, just as long as it's part of the business jargon they're comfortable with. So they sound like pabulum-generating clones, each repeating what they glean from business reports, corporate brochures, memos, and e-mails from and to each other. We should be allowed to fine offenders anytime they use verbs like *architect* (yes, it's being used as a verb!), *disintermediate, e-enable, envisioneer, incentivize, reintermediate, facilitate, interface,* and *repurpose.* Adjectives, too, should get stuck in a speaker's larynx if they sound remotely like *clicks-and-mortar, holistic,* or *user-centric.* And if we add some nouns like *action items, bandwidth, convergence, supply chains,* and *e-services,* we may just suck the life out of any living organism within earshot.

What many who've trained in business, economics, politics, and the professions need to relearn is the simple language of the storyteller who captures and conveys meaning culled from the 650,000-word gift that is the English language. Famed writer Rudyard Kipling once said, "Words are the most powerful drug used by mankind. Not only do words infect, egotize, narcotize, and paralyze, but they enter into and color the minutest cells of the brain." So we want to choose wisely when deciding on words for influence.

Let's look at some concrete examples. *Concrete* is the key word here, as words that have concrete meanings typically have more visceral influence than words that are abstract. That's because the more concrete the words are, the clearer the meaning your listeners take away. Concrete words can often be translated immediately into a sensory perception, because they are based on the five senses. *Touch, hear, smell, taste, see,* and *think* are all concrete words. *Perceive* is an abstract word that registers with our logic versus our emotions.

Did you ever step on a beetle and hear it crunch? Just the word *crunch* almost makes you recoil in disgust. That's sensory perception via a simple, concrete word. *Killing* a beetle is more abstract; no sensory perception there.

Similarly, we use concrete and abstract terms when speaking of our competition. Football coaches may speak of "crushing the enemy's defense" or "decapitating" their leadership. It is language meant to influence players to perform at a higher level via the feelings that are aroused by concrete language. "Neutralizing the other team's defensive strategy," which is more abstract language, just doesn't pack quite the same punch.

Business is filled with sports, war, family, and relationship metaphors that convey a particularly strong meaning to audiences. Abstract words like *autonomy, elimination, contribution,* and *reward* are more high-level words and leave lots of room for interpretation. They don't immediately inspire images that translate into emotion—a key component for influencing with words. To influence people, you'll have to guide their thoughts directly where you want them, and that is best done with concrete language.

The good news is that we use this kind of language all the time, most of it in private conversation with friends, family, associates, and other confederates. Well, those words need to put on some business clothes and go to work with you, because they're desperately needed at the office. Incidentally, they're the tools of influence you'll find more often in the C-level suites of business where patience for jargon and doublespeak is in short supply. Executives want straight language in the boardroom (ironic, isn't it?), and if you try to snow them with "utilize impactful methodologies" or "synthesize out-of-the-box functionalities," they'll come after you like famished wolves after a bunny. Notice something else about these concrete words beyond their punch? It seems counterintuitive, but one of the reasons these words are so powerful is precisely because they evoke an established frame in our minds. When we combine them to create *metaphors*, we transform that image from a flat screen into 3D. Metaphors are powerful as they immediately connect to what we already know. We immediately get the message without wasting energy and time on processing words for comprehension. Just compare phrases like "slamming the brakes on spending" versus "halt spending." While *halt* is a concrete word, the message's meaning is intensified by using "slamming the brakes," a metaphor that conjures up images that engage on an emotional level. You can visualize being thrown forward by the force of a vehicle coming to an abrupt stop in that phrase. Likewise, "exploding at someone" is more visceral than "reacting with anger."

To be sure, check your language for appropriateness in any particular situation, but choose the most visceral, image-laden, and sensory-rich words you can get away with to better influence your audiences.

Frank Luntz, the pollster and message strategist to the Republican Party, came out with his own list of the 11 most powerful words (and phrases) for 2011. In an article he wrote for the

Huffington Post, he has a message "for those who care about words." Count us in, Frank! He says, "I'm going to make it easy for you. No need to dig through my trash or shuffle through my papers. I will voluntarily open up my computer files." Nobody ever accused him of being reticent. According to Luntz, the following are "the words that matter most in business, politics, the media, and culture":

- *Imagine* makes the list "because it's inspiring, motivating, and has a unique definition for each person."
- He likes *no excuses* because it "conveys accountability, responsibility, and transparency."
- *I get it* is on the Luntz list because it shows "a complete understanding of the situation" as well as "a willingness to solve or resolve the situation."
- He thinks *If you remember only one thing* is what politicos should say when they want to make certain that "voters will remember the one point that matters most to you."
- Luntz cites *uncompromising integrity* as a double whammy, because it captures two powerful words for those who look for integrity but are cynical and want integrity to be absolute.
- He borrowed *the simple truth* from Las Vegas billionaire developer Steve Wynn. Luntz thinks it's one of the most powerful phrases for the year, as it "sets the context for a straightforward discussion that might otherwise be confusing or contentious."
- The remaining words and phrases he feels trump all others for power are *Believe in better, real-time, you decide, you deserve,* and *Let's get to work.*

See if you agree and these words resonate with you. What I can absolutely agree with is their simplicity and straightforwardness of meaning.

As you look for your own power words, I suggest looking for the following characteristics:

○ Words that are specific and carry the meaning you want

○ Words that are universally understood and don't require a dictionary

○ Words that resonate with the feelings and values of your audience

Speaking for Impact

Who are you trying to have an impact on?

Knowing your audience matters for writing, but it is absolutely crucial for speaking. Audiences are fickle, busy, and very often distracted individuals with any number of preconceived notions about anything and everything. Making your material relevant to their situation and understanding their particular belief systems and the things they value most can be an express lane to their hearts and minds, or at least their precious attention.

There are times when you will try to influence an audience whose members don't feel they have a stake in the ideas or proposals you're offering. They're not opposed, but they're not particularly interested either. They're more on the neutral side. When you're selling, you're often in this position.

Any time you speak to influence, it's imperative that you establish and project credibility and likeability. Both are crucial to your success in getting people's attention and, in the best case, their vote for you or your idea.

Generally speaking, to get someone's attention or pull someone out of a state of inertia, the WIIFM (what's in it for me) has to be plausible; strong; and the more immediate, the better. People hate to wait for payoffs. Your language has to be aspirational, positive, and not too detailed in its description, so your listeners can paint themselves into the picture of this future scenario you're advocating. Once they have a sense of how much they could benefit from your solution or offer, the status quo is a slightly less alluring place.

And it's the status quo—the existing situation they were comfortable in—that you're trying to make undesirable.

This means, in addition to speaking in aspirational terms about a desirable future scenario that aligns with their beliefs and values, you need to find equally sensory-laden words that show them what they could be losing out on due to inaction or by sticking with the status quo. No one wants to be left behind, and the more people you can get interested in your ideas, the more interest you'll attract from others. We talked earlier about people wanting to conform and seeking input on important decisions by watching others. The situation is slightly more complicated when it involves people who are outspoken against, or perhaps even hostile to, your ideas. There will be resistance. The good news is, the resisters are talking. They are not mute about their opposition, and they want to let you know why they're resisting your plans and ideas. That, along with your research into their prevailing values and guiding beliefs, gives you plenty to work with.

There are many reasons why people may resist or show hostility to your offers; the key is that you get right to their values and beliefs. Lay them bare. Point them out. Say, "From what I understand, such-and-such is very important to you. And so is this-and-that." If you're right, they'll tell you with gusto.

It's at that point that you'll connect with them—by repeating their own words from their unique cultural or professional lexicon back to them—and find overlapping agreement or common ground. Find the areas where your values merge and focus on those when you speak to influence. Getting your foot in the door by initially focusing on what you have in common is an important step in inching your way to broader understanding—and hopefully acceptance—of your ideas.

Of course, there are other factors than just the attitude of the audience. Size, for example, matters. How big is the audience? Are you speaking for a crowd in an auditorium? A group of 30 or 40 in a conference room? Your team at a weekly meeting? Here are ways to get your audience to lean in rather than lean back in each of these situations:

○ **For the larger crowd:** Like a theater actor, you'll have to amplify your presence. Your gestures should be appropriately bigger, and your voice should carry to the last row for your message to get heard with all the nuances of vocal tonality and nonverbal signals. The style of your talk—conversational, passionately aspirational, or lecturing—depends on your objective and the reaction you want from the audience.

○ **For the medium-sized group:** As with larger groups, you need to assess how easily you can connect with the audience with your voice and body language, given their size and individual members' distance from your dais. The key to success is the appropriate adjustment of your "instruments." This is made easier by the employ of lapel microphones and projecting screens, but nothing fires the emotions like human-to-human eye contact when you're making a pitch.

○ **For the team meeting:** Consider the dynamics of the team members and take your cues from them. What is the mood and how do they feel about what's being discussed? As an audience they're often vocal and your agenda determines the direction of the discussion, if you're in control.

And while you don't always want active and vocal audience participation—even in team meetings—you certainly can integrate discussion into even larger crowds. Think of the "town hall meetings" so popular with U.S. politicians over the last couple of decades. The easiest way to connect with an audience here is to adopt a question-and-answer format, with either you or the members of the audience being the ones asking the questions. You have to be at the top of your game—be able to recall facts and

213

arguments off the top of your head, to improvise and riff—to take questions from your audience, but it's an incredibly powerful way to pull your listeners toward you. If you're not sure you're ready to take on all comers, you can still involve your audience by directing your questions to them, and asking for their input. Either way, by inviting your audience to participate, you're a little closer to creating an important emotional bond with them.

The following are 10 common speaking traps you can avoid:

1. Disconnecting by turning your back to the audience as you stare at PowerPoint slides on a screen or write excessive amounts of text on flip charts and whiteboards.
2. Offending individual members of your audience by making inappropriate jokes
3. Losing the attention of your audience by using irrelevant or obscure examples and data
4. Using language and jargon that is not in the general lexicon of your audience and therefore wasted on those not clued in
5. Letting more vocal members of an audience hijack the meeting with sidebar questions and discussion items
6. Appearing flustered in question-and-answer sessions because you're unprepared or intimidated by certain members of your audience
7. Missing a clear objective in your talk, leaving the audience wondering about its purpose
8. Failing to structure your talk logically in a way the audience can easily follow
9. Neglecting to put data into context via storytelling that makes your talk relevant to audience members
10. Ending without a strategic conclusion that lets the audience know exactly what you expect from them and what they should be thinking or doing next

Heed these tips to speak for better results, and you amplify your own power to influence.

How Writing Can Influence People and Change Minds

While writing hasn't been around quite as long as speaking (a fact that cannot, ironically, be proven because it's not written down anywhere), both writing and speaking predate recorded history. Words, spoken and written, have a unique power to penetrate the awareness and subconscious processes of an audience, and they thus become both weapons and tools in the eternal battle between human will, special interests, and often inertia and ignorance.

As with the spoken word, the essence of effective written communication is *voice*, the unique personal brand of the writer's use of language and presentation of the underlying thought and agenda. In fiction and nonfiction alike, this voice becomes the unique product an author is selling, drawing in readers as much for the sharing of style and emotional resonance as for the story itself. The writer may use first- or third-person narrative, adjective-free street vernacular spiced with euphemisms and racy imagery, or eloquent elaborations of the sublime. In persuasive writing in particular—be they essays, position papers, advocacy journalism, or editorials—the goal is clear: to reach into both the conscious and subconscious mind and install or alter a belief system that leads to a desired outcome.

One of the most powerful techniques of influential writing is to leverage the phenomenon of *rhetoric* in the narrative. Rhetoric is, in essence, language that is tricked out and honed to a specific edge. It is the marriage of the familiar with what is relevant, like associating good food with home cooking. Rhetorical writing takes the much-maligned cliché to a new level of credibility and effectiveness by legitimizing it within the flow of a written message, much like a coach who compels his team with the heat of a

215

locker room half-time speech. In the moment it works, it gets the desired result over and above some less familiar choice of words.

Like speaking, effective writing depends on understanding—and most of all, *empathizing* with—the target reader. The more you know about how the audience thinks and responds to your issues going in, the more strategically you can craft a plan to persuade different or evolved thinking going forward. Persuasive writing always sounds as if it comes from inside the audience's allegiance, rendering new information as coaching and upside instead of threat and disapproval.

One instance is the influence exerted by the work and writings of the late Saul Alinsky, a lifelong American community organizer, activist, and writer, whose teachings influenced a young Hillary Clinton, as well as Barack Obama in his efforts at community organization for social change in Chicago. Alinsky's work over several decades was aimed at improving social conditions among America's poorest communities and helping them organize in ways that gave them influence and power. His groundbreaking and controversial book *Rules for Radicals* provided a framework for activists in the volatile 1960s on how to organize the masses for social change. He was called a "Prophet of Power" by *Time* magazine and is often quoted or referenced by modern media pundits from Chris Matthews to Glenn Beck.

Alinsky was controversial to say the least but still highly influential, and the opening lines in *Rules for Radicals* hint at why: "What follows is for those who want to change the world from what it is to what they believe it should be. *The Prince* was written by Machiavelli for the Haves on how to hold power. *Rules for Radicals* is written for the Have-Nots on how to take it away."

And long before Facebook, Twitter, and Google executives became key players in revolutions and mass movements for change, Thomas Paine, a British resident living in the American colonies, published a series of influential writings in 1774 that instigated and inspired public debates about American independence from England. Paine's fiery pamphlet, *Common Sense,* was published shortly after the beginning of the American Revolution; it fueled the colonists' passion for independence and against tyranny with its simple and passionate style that was intelligible for the less-well-read majority of citizens at the time. At a historically perfect moment, Paine employed the kind of rhetoric and strong argument in his writing that simplified complex ideas for his readers and helped influence events in the most dramatic way for America's future— and perhaps the world's. As he said, "The cause of America is in a great measure the cause of all mankind."

Far from the days of Paine's ink and quill and small-run printing presses, technology has changed the way we write and read, and it seems to continue to do so at a moment's notice. We've moved from e-mail to blogging to texting to Tweeting so quickly that a phone call or letter seems oddly old-fashioned!

Writing Yourself from Obscurity to Influence

So what is it that renders writing influential? Thomas Paine had a historic moment that elevated his writing from merely relevant and on point to highly influential and change making. So with time to shape and trim and juice the words themselves, how does your writing take flight from the page, something that changes minds, moves people to action, inspires hope, and sparks paradigm shifts?

The answer is something that writing has in common with verbal communications, even when they are spontaneous and reactive in nature. The magic pill is *relational strategy*—the seizing of common ground followed by the drawing out of options and opportunity within it. Influential writing is rarely an unfounded attack or a hollow criticism; rather, it is more a game plan, a commiseration, and the illumination of a better path. It is written from an intimate understanding of the reader's initial point of view, acknowledging its reality or at least empathizing with it before shining a light on a different perspective.

The great secret weapon of influential writing is the delivery of awareness and options to the reader. Options can be positioned and skewed in a specific manner that serves the author's agenda. Or not. Some works explore issues with clarity and objectivity (such as John Irving's *The Cider House Rules*), using consequence and emotion to help readers weigh the variables and place them within their own real-world context. While genre fiction in particular pushes issues to a moral background in favor of plot exposition, rest assured those authors were in complete command of their powers of influence on a thematic level—just as much as essayists and bloggers use imagery and analogy as a tool to forward their agenda. In both cases, it is that common ground context—from politics to historical cultural issues, such as slavery and women's suffrage, to right to life and capital punishment to the equity of our criminal court system—that becomes the fodder of influence.

Op-Ed Articles: How to Write and Place Them

Whether you're blogging, writing white papers, or drafting inspirational guidelines for revolutionaries à la Paine and Alinsky, the goal is pretty much the same: to demonstrate *thought leadership*, to brand yourself as a source of inspiration and expertise the moment your name appears.

In general, bloggers are known for taking a stand and telling it like it is. Their presence becomes an ongoing issue of branding, which means the potential powers of influence grow with consistency and quality. The power of such bloggers, as well as the whole of what is known as the blogosphere, is not to be trivialized or ignored—it has brought down politicians, exposed crime and fraud, pressured social change, and prompted networks to reinstate programs with low ratings. As influence goes, blogging is a Titan missile in a war waged with darts and thrown eggs.

Influence is fueled by thought leadership, since the differential between the status quo and a vast delta of fresh and compelling thinking is, in fact, the sum of the power to change minds, alter opinions, and move readers to action. And nowhere is influence via writing more obviously on display than in the realm of the op-ed, formerly the province of the astute but now—thanks once again to technology—an open door for all.

Op-ed stands for "opposite the editorial page," and publicists everywhere are keen on getting their roster of experts into the op-ed columns of the top-tier papers and online markets. And while I stand by the idea that crafting an op-ed is open to everyone now thanks to the Web, there is some highly preferred and hard-to-obtain op-ed real estate that can spell riches in readership and prestige, not to mention attention from the news media and others you might deem important and influential to your career—should you get in, that is. The *New York Times* op-ed page is one of them; the *Wall Street Journal* is another. So is the *Washington Post, USA Today*, and the *Christian Science Monitor*.

The circulation for the *Wall Street Journal* is around 1.8 million, similar in number to *USA Today*. The *New York Times* prints close to a million papers per day, while the *Washington Post* isn't far behind with about 600,000. That doesn't include global online views, which range in the millions for each of these publications. And while the *Christian Science Monitor's* print circulation doesn't quite break 70,000 per the most recent data, its online views are respectable, a term that understates the reputation of the magazine and the prestige bestowed upon those lucky enough to have their op-eds published in it.

Even if you won't get the opportunity to grace the pages of these prestigious publications—or if you're looking to build up to a national audience—there are plenty of opportunities for you to deliver your opinions. Check with your favorite bloggers, local newspapers, or with the most prominent papers in your state. If you're a member of an alumni, business, or civic association, submit pieces to them. And don't forget about the plethora of daily and weekly online magazines, all of which are looking for sharp and fresh material.

Like a blog, an op-ed has a tight window of opportunity; readers are prone to judge the headline and then, if it grabs their attention, give the copy only a few seconds of consideration. The lead should never be buried; it should be the essence of the opening line and crafted like a killer literary hook. Also like a blog, the writing should be succinct and punchy, with short paragraphs and stripped-down rhetoric.

An op-ed need not mince words or tiptoe around its agenda. It should, in effect, ask for what it wants with a direct plea for mind-share and belief, doing so with unassailable logic backed by credible research, evidence, and most important, a strong opinion.

Unlike much of the oeuvre of business writing, an op-ed need not and should not shy away from the personal touch. Passion and humor can contribute here in ways that would imbue a white paper with an unprofessional bias; thus, it becomes immediately and closely associated with the writer's outward-facing brand to whatever constituency it is addressed. If you sound like the guy sitting at the back of the House shouting anonymous insults at the Speaker, that's how you'll be perceived—as a nobody with nothing to say. Instead, a great op-ed takes a proud seat in the front row of reflective thought and, through a process of impassioned case building, morphs into a powerful source of influence by the time the last line hammers the message home.

Writing an effective op-ed has become, via the traditional press, a bit of an art form, though one sustained through a combination of craft and strategy. The challenge is embodied by certain question-based criteria that's calling on op-ed writers to have their topical ducks in a row, preferably in some sort of private syllabus that names the objectives with specificity.

As an op-ed writer, you need to completely understand the nature of your target reader, not only in general but particularly on the issue under consideration. The first step in earning trust is to demonstrate empathy and understanding, and influence is rarely within reach until trust has been attained.

White Papers

Another way to get your message across is with a white paper. White papers are unique in that they represent an organization's position, often in the context of competing messages. Part of the strategy that wields influence here is the length you go to in researching your topic to master all the facts, to understand your target readers' industry better than they do, and to offer creative solutions to specific problems that readers can't find by spending hours upon mind-numbing hours brainstorming in a conference room fueled by pizza and Pepsi. An abstract or brief summary that delivers the goods for short attention spans or seriously time-challenged readers is de rigueur these days and should be right up front. Keep in mind that this type of writing is influential because it teaches and whets readers' appetites for more. You're most influential if you make it all about them.

How to Establish Yourself as a Thought Leader

Regardless of the media venue, thought leadership resulting in effective influence is a product of craft colliding with opportunity. An unskilled writer can turn a smooth ride into a rocky road with jumbled logic and cluttered narrative, while the skilled op-ed writer can bring the sharpness of a gleaming razor to issues otherwise considered complex and laced with blurred lines. The key to this is zeroing in on the sweet spot of the reader's need with a prepared salvo of optimized credibility and polished sentences.

The path toward thought leadership and influence has two lanes, both of which require an apprenticeship. One is immersion in the arena of battle, the earning of credibility through seasoning, properly reined-in passion, and clarity of purpose. The other is the mastering of the strategic craft of writing persuasively, which includes a basic list of proficiencies and nimble literary skills that allow the writer to navigate the tricky waters of complex issues.

Concurrent with this twin-mission apprenticeship is the seizing of opportunity and a sense of timing. Practice is more than essential; it's the minor league, where performance is noticed and rewarded, paving the way to the majors. To the brave goes the crown of boldness, but to the unprepared goes the dunce cap—a sartorial addition that doesn't quite go with the expertly tailored cloth of the thought leader.

It's lucky that, in this era of electronic media that brings opportunities faster and with clearer access than ever before, finding your practice games isn't the challenge. It's stepping up to the plate and hitting it out of the park once you're in the game.

Shared Human Experience

No matter what business you're in or what profession you practice every day, you can influence people with the power of the shared human experience. The easiest and most effective way to get most people interested in and paying attention to what you have to say is by using an interesting personal story or an anecdote about one person's experience that may initially appear to have nothing to do with the issue you're about to discuss. But you'll connect the dots for the audience quickly and bring the experience you lead with back to your main issue. What this anecdotal attention-getter does—and does powerfully—is draw your audience into your topic with images you conjure up with image-rich words, images the audience is almost forced to envision due to the power of the shared human experience and our inescapable social fabric that is spun from frames and narrative.

In the next chapter, you'll learn about managing your personal brand to influence others and how to avoid damaging your personal brand and reputation with simple yet harmful mistakes.

CHAPTER 12

Managing the Influencing Power of Your Personal Brand

At first glance, John Millard, M.D., seems like the prototypical successful plastic surgeon. His impeccably clean and stylish practice in Centennial—a small suburb of Denver, Colorado—teems with beauty. From the three receptionists to administrative staff and medical personnel, everyone looks as though they were live advertisements to the would-be-patients anxiously waiting for their consultation. Millard himself matches the image. Tan, fit, and muscular, he looks nearly a decade younger than his actual age. His small office is cramped and cluttered with medical journals, hi-tech gadgets, various frames with pictures of a stunning wife and three beautiful kids. Like many successful professionals, he works way too many hours and wishes he could spend more time with his family. It's when you get into a deeper conversation with him that you realize he's not your average plastic surgeon at all.

The discovery of medicine turned his life around. "I was a complete failure in high school, graduating in the bottom 20 percent of my class," Millard says. Then, at age 19, he found his purpose. "It took me figuring out what I wanted to do in life—being a physician—to really awaken my motivation to work toward something. Once I figured out what I wanted to do, the hard work was easy." Along the way, he became a voracious student and immersed himself in the study of beauty, the human form and sexual attraction, and the role these play in everything from natural selection to history to science and art. "The more I dug into the study of medicine and more recently the study of body sculpting and antiaging and preventive medicine, the more curious and driven I became to keep learning more and more and to think of new ideas to contribute to these fields."

Dr. Millard's primary specialty is in the field of liposuction. Lipo, as it's often called, is, according to various studies, either the number-one or number-two most requested and performed surgical procedure in cosmetic surgery. Millard's drive and relentless curiosity eventually led him to discover and learn a far less invasive and aesthetically more powerful method—liposculpture. This new procedure enabled him to truly start transforming patients' lives by providing the most anatomically realistic and desirable results of anyone performing liposuction in the United States. With his newfound knowledge and the latest technology, the artist in Millard was now able to sculpt people's bodies in high definition—he trademarked the term "VASER® HI DEF"—respecting, not removing, people's natural beauty and individual curves.

It is in this field that he's influenced peers and clients, changing the conversation permanently; not only revolutionizing the way modern liposuction is performed in the United States, but also influencing what patients increasingly ask for and what his colleagues feel compelled to provide if they want to keep current in their field. In other words, he's created a powerful personal brand and along the way changed the game of his specialty and profession. Physicians from all over the world want in on the conversation—the new game—and come to Millard's practice to learn the procedure and thinking he has pioneered.

And he's just getting started. In true game-changing fashion, he has recently created a virtual think tank of global experts brimming with cutting-edge ideas and people, including the country's foremost experts in preventive medicine, antiaging, and immune-related specialties. He's keeping specifics confidential for now, but his overall plan is no less ambitious than to motivate people to more personal responsibility regarding their health care and to provide powerful tools—culled from the brightest minds—to help in this regard.

This book is for the John Millards of the world—people who have big dreams and little dreams, short-term and long-term goals for which the ability to influence others' choices is critical to achieving those goals. Legendary U.S. journalist and newscaster Tom Brokaw put it succinctly when he said, "It's easy to make a buck. It's a lot tougher to make a difference."

Many of us are happy just to make a buck. Especially if we have mortgages to pay and families to support. Security first. We can always dream later, we think. But what if a nagging little voice in our head keeps reminding us of all the great goals we once had or that mark we wanted to make when we were fresh out of school, ready to set the world on fire with our ideas?

John Millard faced many obstacles on his way to the top. Among them were a poor academic record in high school and a lack of direction and motivation. Even once he found his purpose and established a successful career, colleagues and peers attacked and dismissed his innovative ideas and proposals. But Millard successfully managed his personal brand and influenced his way to the top of his profession using many of the techniques provided in this book.

Not Everyone Can Be Oprah

You're shocked, I know, saying to yourself, "You mean I *can't* run my own media empire, complete with talk show, production company, magazine, and cable network? Really?" Don't forget, however, that Oprah wasn't always "Oprah." She overcame a rough childhood and started working in radio while she was still in high school. From there, she snagged a talk show, which she transformed into the incredibly popular mix of confessional, celebrity hangout, and self-uplift that it eventually became.

There was no magic involved. Perhaps some luck (like right place, right time for that first radio job), persistence, and certainly talent. But even more than that, she was able to combine these elements into a formidable brand. "Oprah" didn't just happen; the woman worked to make it happen.

Again, whatever our innate talents, it is unlikely that any of us will replicate Oprah's success. However, she did set an example for the rest of us: identify your talents; hone your skills; and work, work, work toward creating a name for yourself.

That's really what personal branding is in a nutshell—making a name for yourself. Just as an organization must shape the impressions others have of it, so too can you be in control of creating the image others will have of you, along with their associated emotions, perceptions, and knowledge about you.

Your compatriots who rely on just "letting the work speak for itself" are at a distinct disadvantage, because if you want to move up in the world today, your personal brand has to sell you just as hard as your accomplishments do. Without an effort toward personal branding, those accomplishments will often be left unnoticed and uncelebrated by those who can catapult you to the next level.

"Accidental" Branding

There are times when your deeds do come through loud and clear—and it's not always in your favor. Consider a restroom. We use them every day and, for the most part, don't notice them. What we do notice, however, are sinks that haven't been cleaned, mirrors that are splotchy, dirty floors, a lack of soap or hand towels, and most disastrous, no toilet paper. Clean restrooms don't make an impression; dirty ones do. Similarly, being a good worker may not get you noticed, but showing up late, constantly missing deadlines, having nothing to contribute to group efforts, and backstabbing colleagues will, and not in a good way.

You will have been *accidentally branded*. This term involves the creation and reinforcement of perceptions that you do not intend to create and that, for the most part, would hurt your chances of success in personal and professional situations of consequence. Careless behaviors and the associated emotions and perceptions they create in others result IN accidental branding that can follow you throughout your career.

Remember Robert the anesthesiologist, the former client I mentioned in Chapter 7? He created an accidental brand by making nurses cry on a regular basis, barking out orders, being impatient, and otherwise clashing with peers and direct reports. He was asked to resign because he didn't fit into the culture. The brand he inadvertently created for himself hurt him professionally and personally. I worked with him to create a new personal brand, thus helping him get a fresh start with a new audience.

A colleague of mine related a somewhat more humble, but no less humbling, tale of impression mismanagement: She had worked on her high school yearbook staff since her freshman year, and she both wanted and expected to be named yearbook editor her senior year. She was stunned when she didn't get the position. When she asked why, the faculty adviser basically said, "You never told me you wanted it, and you messed around. Nothing in your behavior indicated that you took the job seriously. Why would I give it to you?" At least she learned the lesson young: if you want responsibility, you have to act responsibly.

There are any number of other examples of branding, both intentional (Richard Branson, entrepreneur and adventurer) and accidental (Eliot Spitzer and the exposure of his dalliances with prostitutes). Politicians, in fact, cannot afford to focus only on establishing a brand; they have to fight off efforts at sometimes-defamatory counterbranding.

First-term senator Barack Obama had to win over partisans in a hard-fought race with Senator Hillary Clinton for the Democratic presidential nomination. He appealed to young voters and gestured toward a vision of a more promising future. Once he had won the nomination, he then pivoted to convince independent voters of his gravitas, deploying his "cool" personality as a means of demonstrating that, despite his relative youth, he was levelheaded enough to handle whatever was thrown his way. His Republican opponent, Senator John McCain, relied on a narrative of the wise old warrior and sought to portray Obama as simply too inexperienced to handle the pressures of the presidency.

Books are written about why individuals win or lose the presidency; allow me to note only that Obama was able to control his persona, maintaining a kind of cool detachment throughout his debates and after the financial crisis hit, whereas McCain at times seemed less wise than frantic. McCain did help to raise doubts about Obama's qualifications; unfortunately, he also helped to raise doubts about his own.

McCain's running mate, then-governor of Alaska Sarah Palin, is another lesson in both intentional and unintentional branding. She has assiduously tended to her brand as a "Mama Grizzly," starring in a reality TV show, taking a job as a regular commentator on Fox News, delivering speeches to conservative audiences, and commenting regularly on politics in general and Obama in particular. She has cultivated a vociferously loyal following in the United States. Yet the fact that she resigned her governorship a little more than halfway through her term and has not curbed her tendency toward verbal gaffes has given the impression of accidental branding. For the astute observer, personal brands among public figures are fascinating case studies of what to do and what not to do, no matter where you are on the career path or socioeconomic scale.

Most of us don't have to worry about things that concern politicians and other polarizing figures: the issue for many of us is less adversity than apathy. No one is trying to impugn our characters, largely because we're not in the public eye. But in our own corners of the world, the people around us do have a sense of our character. If and when we seek to move up and whenever we exert our influence over others, we should expect scrutiny to increase. Prospective employers and clients may not care to impugn us, but they may discover that we have accidentally impugned ourselves.

Accidental branding can happen to the most image-conscious among us. You're at an industry conference, and you've just been introduced to a senior executive from a major corporation you'd like to land as a client. You launch into your oft-rehearsed elevator speech touting benefits over features and emphasizing your experience in this would-be client's market. But as you hear yourself speak loudly against a wall of deafening noise, you suddenly realize you sound oddly nervous and giddy—like a sales rookie pushing a little too hard, talking a little too fast, and making technical references an engineer would have trouble following. Before it's over, you sense you've just offended and annoyed someone who can open the door to your dream client but most certainly is thinking about changing the locks instead.

Accidental Branding Online

Another example of accidental branding is the story of the would-be Cisco employee who tweeted, "Cisco just offered me a job! Now I have to weigh the utility of a fatty paycheck against the daily commute to San Jose and hating the work." A Cisco employee responded, "Who is the hiring manager? I'm sure they would love to know that you will hate the work. We here at Cisco are versed in the Web."

You would never be so careless, would you? Well, what about your online persona generally? Yes, that Facebook account you set up in college contains all kinds of good memories, and who wouldn't want to immortalize that night you did seven tequila shots in a row and ended up shimmying on the bar? Who could fail to be impressed by your moves? Someone considering you for a job, perhaps?

Many of us are fortunate that social media wasn't around when we, let's just say, learned what our limits were (mainly by blowing way past them); there's no proof of what happened at that party or on spring break. But for just as many of us, Facebook and MySpace accounts were the bulletin boards to which we pasted our party photos and snarky insults, an online spot where we could kick back and relax with friends.

Yet for better and for worse, they're not just that: unlike actual cork bulletin boards, they're also readily available glimpses into your life, open to potential bosses and clients alike. As more of the social-media generation moves into managerial positions, it's possible that there will be some kind of understanding or pass given for high school and college-age behavior. In the meantime, however, you should clean up your online persona, either by deleting your social media profiles, editing the personal information out of those profiles, or perhaps simply increasing the privacy settings on your social media accounts and removing your profile from search engines.

Oh, and that fun e-mail address sexyhotmess@isp.com? Yeah, you want to change that.

Knowing How You Want to Be Perceived Is Critical to Influencing Others

"When an individual enters the presence of others, they commonly seek to acquire information about him or to bring into play information about him already possessed." So begins Erving

Goffman's 1959 classic, *The Presentation of Self in Everyday Life*. Goffman spends the next seven chapters discussing how we perform our roles, how context affects these performances, and what happens when the roles or communication about the roles don't match expectations. He also elaborates on "The Arts of Impression Management."

Other social scientists have extended his work in considerations of both organizational and personal impression management. While some note that Machiavellian approaches (in which individuals intentionally misrepresent themselves) can be effective, such pretense can be risky; the discovery of misrepresentation may lead to being discredited or socially sanctioned. In any case, if you're trying to sell yourself, it's much less complicated if *yourself* and the *presentation* of yourself are in alignment.

Such concordance is especially important if you must always be "on": it's far easier to assume the persona of someone who loves teaching yoga or owning a restaurant if you actually do love yoga or the restaurant business. Billie King, Jr., founder of the Bow Tie Cigar Company, noted that he "injected my personality into as many aspects of my business as possible. . . . Bow Tie Cigars is me, and I am Bow Tie Cigars." Jill Donenfeld, founder of The Dish's Dish, agrees: "I am invested in the idea of respecting our bodies and treating them well. And those leanings naturally come through in everything I do, especially within the brand. It's easy if you believe in it!"

King and Donenfeld were among 10 business owners who were asked by *Entrepreneur* to share their lessons in branding. Most of them echoed the importance of aligning your sensibilities with your business to create that strong personal brand. As the wine expert Gary Vaynerchuk, another of the chosen entrepreneurs, argues, "Everybody today is in the branding and customer service business. Whether you know it or not, you already are."

A lot of us do already know this. A quick online search of "personal branding" will quickly overwhelm you with more than

233

3.9 million related sites, many with advice on how to build your brand. Less apparent, however, is how to leverage that brand into real influence. This is key: recognize that your brand is not simply a kind of label but also a *process*, one that you continually manage to expand your opportunities; a brand is not the end but the *means* to the end.

Creating an Influential Brand

So how do you create an influential brand for yourself? First, cover the basics. Many of us have been in situations where one guy talks about how hard he works, and one guy simply works hard—and we all know who we'd rather work with. Yes, when you want that promotion you do have to highlight your effort and results, but it will only resonate *if you have actually produced those results.* Shouting "I'm impressive!" is unlikely to impress your colleagues, at least not in the way you intend.

Which brings me to the first step, and that is figuring out what you do intend. What do you want to accomplish? Where do you want to go? How do you want others to perceive you? As I discussed in previous chapters, it helps to think in terms of narrative: what is your story, and what character do you play in your story? Create a vision or big picture that has you as the protagonist, and use that as a guide for your behavior.

The second step is to get a sense of your environment. Find out what makes your associates tick—and what ticks them off—and adjust your behavior accordingly. Some firms frown on exuberant self-promotion, whereas others expect it; some have tight hierarchical structures, while others are more open; some assign new hires a mentor with whom they are expected to work closely, whereas others take a sink-or-swim approach. Figure out what's rewarded and what's punished, then do your best to cultivate the former and avoid the latter.

As a general exercise, it helps to think in terms of "If you want to be perceived as . . . you need to . . . ; in order to influence others, you need to . . ." Here are some examples:

○ If you want to be perceived as an expert, you need to demonstrate credibility; in order to influence others to accept your claim, you need to tailor your message with the audience's beliefs, values, and predispositions in mind.

○ If you want to be perceived as reliable, you need to show up to meetings prepared, meet deadlines, and consistently produce good work; in order to influence others, you need to work with those others and be willing to share what you have learned.

○ If you want to be perceived as innovative, you must keep yourself informed of new strategies in your business and find ways to adapt them to your particular work environment; in order to influence others, you must be willing to take the risk of proposing something new while providing additional information and evidence to support your proposition.

○ If you want to be perceived as a leader, you need to demonstrate a willingness to take charge, make difficult decisions, and accept the additional obligations of leadership; in order to influence others, you need to take advantage of leadership opportunities that are presented to you, asking to head a team or volunteering to take the lead on solving a long-standing or emergent problem.

You can continue to elaborate on these scenarios: if you want to be seen as good in a crisis; if you want to be seen as indomitable, unflappable, honest, compassionate. Whatever value you want others to associate with you, you must first demonstrate it in your behavior.

Recognize, too, that as your position changes, so should your behavior. Deferring to long-standing employees when you first start a job is both courteous and smart; you demonstrate respect for their experience while learning about both the work and the workplace. After a while, however, you'll need to assert yourself, to demonstrate that you have actually got hold of the reins of the position. Similarly, as you move up, you must recognize that what might have been considered overreach in a lower position is expected in a higher one.

Positioning Your Personal Brand Against Your Competition

Many of the principles that apply to tangible products and services as far as organizational brand positioning is concerned can be applied to personal brands—being first, specializing in your market, emphasizing the demand for your skills, taking advantage of word of mouth, and so on. The name of the game here is to stand out and to do so in a way that influences consumers, clients, constituents, and colleagues to choose you and your ideas and wares over someone else's. Period! So what can we learn from successful personal and professional brands that leave their competition playing catch-up?

Be Unique

Successful personal brands identify a unique dimension where they can claim a sustainable advantage over their competitors. Fashion designer Ralph Lauren has been at the top of his particular niche in the fashion industry for decades because he understands that his customers yearn for a *lifestyle* as opposed to merely wanting to own a safari jacket or equestrian boots. To claim your own mindshare in a unique dimension of your calling, you have to learn what people want deep down, what they aspire to, and what values they hold as most important. Makes sense for a fashion designer, you might think. But how do I position my personal brand in the decidedly less exotic category of, say, accountancy? Maybe by making a name for yourself in the area of forensic accounting, the number-crunching sleuths who uncover and untangle the complexities of high-finance fraud and other white-collar crimes. Or maybe you can become the go-to professional—the ethical one—for business owners with tax problems, helping them stay clear of the Internal Revenue Service's bad side. Whichever way you take to carve out an edge over the competition, strive for a unique dimension that makes it easier to lead and excel.

Be Consistent

The chance to host the Academy Awards is one that any entertainer would covet. For the organizers, the choice of who to have head-line a show that is seen globally by billions is a weighty one, and much rides on its success. Billy Crystal is widely considered one of greatest Academy Awards show hosts ever, delivering consistently smart humor, expertly timed punch lines, and charismatic gravitas that made him a sure bet for eight shows. Even today, Crystal's personal brand stands for the Academy Awards, so indelible was the impression he created as host. And just like this beloved comedian, a human resources manager can build her personal brand on a reputation of consistently delivered quality. If it is within your responsibility to manage the talent in your organization, to make it easy for workers to choose among a variety of health-care plans, to develop training programs that increase productivity and bring out the leaders in the organization's ranks, and you are consistent in your ability to do so, you are creating and reinforcing a powerful personal brand. If you're that manager, remember what I mentioned earlier about just letting the work speak for itself. You have to fight for mindshare and find ways to elegantly communicate your contributions to the right people; otherwise your more charismatic colleagues may over-shadow you right onto the sidelines.

Offer Value

People make choices in favor of their preferred brands because they derive a certain value from these brands. Whether those values include safety, prestige, respect, joy, freedom, love, power, peace of mind, or any other subjective and uniquely personal value, if you can offer values that resonate on a deeper level with people, you are in an excellent position to build a solid personal brand. To observe this on a personal level, think of the people in your life who offer such values to you. Does the family doctor you've been seeing for years offer only medical care, or is it more than that? Are all the teachers in your past the same, or does someone stand out as having added more value to your life than the rest combined? Did you choose certain colleagues as mentors or wish you had others to guide you through the politics of organizational life?

Regardless of which area you focus on, chances are someone stands out for contributing a tremendous value to your life that resonates with and matches the values you hold important. And the personal brand that person represents in your mind, the feelings and associations you conjure in thinking of him or her, is something you can cultivate in yourself for the benefit of others. You just have to listen and learn what others hold dear and tailor what you have to offer to be precisely that. The result will be your personal brand built around value that burnishes itself into their consciousness.

Be Visible

Part of any thriving brand's success is that it is ubiquitous. From the daily barrage of product brands we consume (such as Starbucks coffee, Apple's mobile devices, and the labels we choose to slip into before we leave the house) to the public figures—both famous and infamous—we encounter in the media, the fact that we engage them by clicking on the latest scandal story about them, purchasing their latest book, or tuning in to their reality show is part of their success. But positioning your own personal brand against the competition doesn't necessarily require Donald Trump's public relations savvy. It does require, however, that you come out from the shadows and get seen by people of consequence—often. The social sciences refer to it as the mere exposure effect, the predictable human response to repeated exposure to people or things in order to induce a positive feeling. It's important to note the science's caveat: without the presence of a negative prejudice. In other words, someone must be at least neutrally disposed toward you, if not favorably inclined, or the mere exposure effect can backfire. This is proved when you think of your attitude toward someone you can't stand the sight of and who somehow seems to be everywhere. You'll start liking that person even less. So to distinguish your personal brand and position yourself through visibility, get out front whenever there's a chance to contribute something of value, verbally or otherwise. By contributing value, even those whose feathers you've ruffled may see the light sooner or later.

Ten Ways You Can Sabotage Your Personal Brand and How to Avoid Them

You've done the work, you've paid attention, and you've assiduously built up and capitalized on your personal brand. Now how do you protect it?

Consider a case of a good brand gone bad. Hollywood is pretty forgiving of off-set bad behavior, at least on the part of its stars. Getting arrested for driving under the influence or being tossed out of a club for brawling might land you in the tabloids, but unless your personal behavior affects your ability to work, chances are you'll continue to get jobs, especially if the audience continues to tune in.

Still, even Hollywood has its limits. Exhibit A: Mel Gibson, who was a wildly successful Academy Award–winning action star and also received good reviews for his straight dramatic roles. Today, however, he's toxic. While he still has supporters in Hollywood (few of whom are outspoken), among the general public, he's better known for his drunken insults to a female police officer, repeated anti-Semitic rants, and threats to (caught on tape) and alleged assault on a former girlfriend. What director will want to hang a 50-million-dollar movie on a star who's more likely to turn off moviegoers than get them to turn out? Aside from longtime Gibson friend and *The Beaver* director Jodie Foster, that is.

Perhaps Gibson will redeem himself and work his way back into the good graces of both the film industry and the public. Perhaps. Regardless, he serves as a cautionary tale (admittedly in the extreme) to the rest of us: good work can be swamped by the deluge of a messy personal life.

Again, just as we are unlikely to ascend to Oprah-esque heights, we are—hopefully—unlikely to descend to Gibson-esque depths. Still, each of us is human, which means each of us is likely to err. As long as you recognize that possibility, you have the opportunity to avoid or at least minimize those errors. Here are some of the obvious mistakes:

1. **Being inconsistent:** You just pulled off the impossible and brought that important project in on time and under budget. Don't follow up this success by blowing off what you think is a relatively trivial project. If you want to give the impression that you can deliver, then deliver on everything, great and small.

2. **Overpromising and underdelivering:** On the other hand, don't tell colleagues or clients you can bring in that important project early and at half the cost if you're not absolutely sure that you can. Even then, you're better off ensuring that the

project is done right and on time. Make sure your promise matches your delivery.

3. **Setting false expectations:** Along the same lines, don't set the bar so high that there's no way you can reach it, much less vault over it. Don't wave off help if it's offered or refuse to take a break if you need it. Don't pretend you can do everything perfectly. You can't.

4. **Engaging in careless social media practices:** I noted the example of the almost–Cisco employee earlier, but there are, unfortunately, far more examples. Here's one: the designer Kenneth Cole thought he'd be clever and tie his new collection into the liberation movement in Egypt. He tweeted, "Millions are in uproar in #Cairo. Rumor is they heard our new spring collection is now available online at http://bit.ly /KCairo." Unsurprisingly, people responded just as fast as he could tweet, and they did. Furiously. Cole quickly issued an apology.

   Twitter can be a powerful communication tool, a great way to relay information fast and efficiently. However, since it is so enticingly easy to share even the most private impulse, people sometimes tweet before they think. Best to think before you tweet.

5. **Staying invisible:** Some people are afraid that if they stick their necks out (metaphorically speaking), they'll get their heads chopped off. This might be a fine survival tactic in toxic organizational cultures, but in general, it's a recipe for remaining, year after year, in that same small cubicle on the far side of the office.

6. **Sending mixed messages:** Don't tell colleagues you value their time and then show up late for meetings. Don't tell clients you value their business and then not return their calls. Don't tell people you care and then behave in a careless manner.

7. **Not practicing what you preach/not walking the talk:** This is similar to the previous point, aimed at your own behavior. How many moral values politicians and religious leaders have been busted for "walking the Appalachian Trail," as it were? Former South Carolina governor and devout family man Mark Sanford was once mentioned as a possible Republican presidential candidate before he took his alleged hike on that trail; in fact, he was traveling to Argentina to consort with his mistress. So much for that run at the White House. Don't tell others about the importance of family as you destroy yours.

8. **Bad associations:** In some ways, this is obvious. If you want to be seen as an upright person, you shouldn't hang out with criminals. But it's about more than simply avoiding crooks. Are you planning to run for public office? Then perhaps you should quit the men-only private club. Do you tout your record as a responsible steward of the environment? Then why are you sitting on the board of a corporation that routinely pays fines for illegal dumping? A friend of animals? Don't get your pet at a puppy mill! You see my point: avoid entanglements and actions that cast doubt on your message and character.

9. **Competing in the same category where others may be superior:** You've heard the term "he's fighting above his weight class"? The idea is that someone is outmatched by his opponent; not only can he not keep up, but he might get hurt as a result. Having ambition is great; having that ambition run ahead of your ability is not. Stake your claim to an area you can legitimately dominate.

10. **Not being able to differentiate yourself from your competitors:** You're smart, energetic, competent, ambitious—congratulations, so are millions of other people. Credentials, education, accomplishments, privilege, and connections can

all mean a leg up on the competition. But most often, they are just your admission ticket to join the game. What really counts is what you do with your advantages once you're given the chance to prove your mettle. If you pull even with everyone else, you won't be influencing much, let alone in any direction you wish. Take inventory and find a unique angle that can set you apart from the pack and you'll increase your chances of influencing those you wish to sway.

Stealing Thunder

What happens if you ignore the preceding list and mess up? 'Fess up, and as soon as possible. Professor Shelley Wigley of the University of Texas at Arlington looked at the phenomenon of "stealing thunder," whereby an individual breaks his own bad news. She looked at the contrasting strategies of those who respond only after a story breaks and those who initiate the story. Except for a short statement of apology read after the prostitution story hit the news, Eliot Spitzer embargoed the media for two days, at which point he resigned. His replacement, David Paterson, on the other hand, sat down with his wife and gave interviews in which both admitted to extramarital affairs. Wigley quoted *Daily News* reporter Juan Gonzalez: "Like any smart politician, he knows the best way to handle difficult news is to confront it squarely and rapidly." Similarly, Tiger Woods avoided the press about his then-alleged extramarital affairs, while David Letterman made the announcement of his own affair in the intro to his late-night talk show.

Wigley observed that the stealing thunder strategy has a mixed history. Initiators of bad information build credibility for themselves, but they may prompt further investigation. It's also possible that by getting ahead of the story, they can take the air out of it, deflating its value as a "gotcha" item. The results of her study

243

confirmed the latter thesis: in terms of media coverage, "sources who stole thunder were associated with more positive frames in both the headlines and articles."

There are a few wrinkles to the story of each man we used as an example earlier. Spitzer was a governor charged with executing the laws of New York, laws that he broke; Paterson simply admitted to stepping out on his wife. Woods presented himself as a family man, a doting husband and father; Letterman, except for occasional mentions of his son, had no particular public reputation regarding his private life. Perhaps it's easier to own up to your dirt when you've never presented yourself as squeaky clean.

Nonetheless, stealing thunder does seem to work and thus highlights the importance of monitoring the grapevine. If there are murmurs of scandal, better to address them before they develop into a roar. And if you can't get ahead of the bad news, don't stonewall. You've heard of the term *feeding frenzy*? That's what happens when people are hungry for information. Give them the information—all of it—and there's a good chance they'll calm down.

Stealing thunder doesn't mean that you schedule a news conference to discuss the innocent flirtation you engaged in with a colleague or the time you fibbed your way out of a speeding ticket. But if you know there's potentially harmful information about you floating around, think hard about what it would mean if that information got out. If revelation would hurt you, consider how much bigger the hurt would be if you're not the one doing the revealing.

Finally, even if—no, when—you do err, remember that you can recover. You may be lucky and only have to smooth over a rough patch to your reputation, or you may have to rebuild your personal brand from scratch, and it's entirely possible that some aspects of your life will never be the same. But keep in mind this bit of wisdom from Yogi Berra: It ain't over till it's over. And I'll add that only *you* decide when that is.

Summing It Up

Having influence in virtually every direction is more than a skill. It's a lifestyle and a mind-set based on a foundation of critical principles that every modern professional needs to master in order to reach the top of his or her field and achieve personal and career goals, as well as larger objectives that can make a difference in the world.

Virtually none of the insights and skills in this book are taught at even the most elite business schools. However, they're fundamental and essential career skills that, once learned, will profoundly change your life for the better.

As you've seen, you don't have to be a CEO to learn and master these new skills. Whether you're an administrative assistant looking to build your influence in an organization from the ground up, a recent business school graduate seeking an edge over the competition for a corporate job, a sales professional promoting the benefits of your organization's product or service, an entrepreneur aiming to develop interest in a new product, a new manager trying to find effective ways to motivate a diverse team, a project manager who needs to garner support for a counterintuitive course of action, or an innovator who has the courage and drive to become a thought leader, you can apply the techniques I've presented to become a person of influence and consequence in your field and beyond.

NOTES

Chapter 1 Swayed, Nudged, and Driven: Influence Is Constant

1 A *New Zealand bank helpfully nudges customers:* "NZ's Impulse Spending at $16 Million Per Day," TVNZ.co.nz, February 1, 2011.

1 *School cafeterias across the United States:* "What Would the Nudge Cafeteria Look Like?" Nudge.org, February 13, 2009; "The Nudge Cafeteria Part II," Nudge.org, March 9, 2009; "Nudging in New York Cafeterias," Nudge.org, June 9, 2010; and "Nudge Cafeteria Design, Part III," Nudge.org, July 10, 2011.

1 *New York taxicabs have a touchscreen:* I culled this from my vast experience riding in New York taxis.

2 *This exposure to influence begins with our earliest sense of self:* Justin D. Call, Eleanor Galenson, and Robert L. Tyson, eds., *Frontiers of Infant Psychiatry,* vol. 2 (New York: Basic Books, 1983), 40.

2 *With that first infantile desire; Just as instinctual; According to a 1968 study on this interaction:* M. Virginia Wyly, *Infant Assessment* (Boulder, CO: Westview Press, 1997), 144–146.

3 *A recent explosive article in* Rolling Stone: Michael Hastings, "Another Runaway General: Army Deploys Psy-Ops on U.S. Senators," *Rolling Stone,* February 23, 2011.

3 *Competition for resources is intrinsic to the evolution of any surviving species:* Competition, Wikipedia.org; for a couple of specific examples, see David A. Puts, "Beauty and the Beast: Mechanisms of Sexual Selection in Humans," *Evolution and Human Behavior* 31 (3): 157–175, May 2010; and "When Young Men Are Scarce, They're More Likely to Play the Field Than to Propose," ScienceDaily.com, June 10, 2009.

4 *As our species has evolved, our brains:* David Geary and Drew Bailey, as cited in "Social Competition May Be Reason for Bigger Brain," ScienceDaily.com, June 23, 2009.

5 *According to Shalom H. Schwartz, Ph.D., of the Hebrew University:* Shalom H. Schwartz, "Basic Human Values: An Overview," The Hebrew University of Jerusalem, http://segr-did2.fmag.unict.it/Allegati/convegno%207-8-10-05/Schwartzpaper.pdf.

247

7 *A number of esteemed scholars have aligned behind seven basis phases:* As discussed in Patrick F. Bassett, "Effecting Change," *Montessori Life* 16 (3):16–17, Summer 2004.

8 *Employees who demonstrate repeated self-defeating behavior:* Robert Kegan and Lisa Laskow Lahey, "The Real Reason People Won't Change," *Harvard Business Review* 79 (10):51–58, November 2001.

9 *In the growing field of behavioral economics:* Arnerich Massena & Associates, Inc., Tony Arnerich, Howard Biggs, Vincent Galindo, Dane Grouell, Jillian Perkins, Jacob O'Shaughnessy, contributors, "Ain't Misbehavin'! Behavioral Economics Helps Explain the Reality of Participant Behavior," March 2010. [free e-book; multiple download options]

10 *Our brains dictate our choices:* "Roots of Gamblers' Fallacies and Other Superstitions: Causes of Seemingly Irrational Human Decisions," ScienceDaily.com, August 31, 2010; for more on the "gambler's fallacy" see also the work of Alex Piquero, as cited, for example, by Cathy Keen in "UF Study: 'Gamblers Fallacy' Not Criminal Label Results in More Crime," *University of Florida News*, April 15, 2003.

10 *The early research of Amos Tversky and Daniel Kahneman:* Amos Tversky and Daniel Kahneman, "Availability: A Heuristic for Judging Frequency and Probability," *Cognitive Psychology* 5 (2): 207–232, September 1973.

10 *In a nutshell:* Ibid.; see also their work as described in Bruce G. S. Hardie, Eric J. Johnson, and Peter S. Fader, "Modeling Loss Aversion and Reference Dependence Effects on Brand Choice," *Marketing Science* 12 (4): 378–394, fall 1993.

11 *Leavey School of Business's Meir Statman:* Cited in James J. Choi, David Laibson, Brigitte C. Madrian, and Andrew Metrick, "Optimal Defaults and Active Decisions," National Bureau of Economic Research, January 2005.

12 *Today's advertisers use neuroscience-based techniques:* Robert Dooley, "Revealed: How Steve Jobs Turns Customers Into Fanatics," Neuroscience marketing.com, August 25, 2010.

12 *America's favorite fried chicken haunt KFC:* "Smells Can Make You or Break You," Human Behavior Fun Facts, BestFunFacts.com, 2009.

12 Advertising Age *estimated that Procter & Gamble:* "P&G," adbrands.net, http://www.adbrands.net/us/pg_us.htm.

13 *Apple's brand capitalizes:* Dooley, op. cit.

13 *Studies prove that when feedback is imminent:* Keri L. Kettle and Gerald Häubl, "Motivation by Anticipation: Expecting Rapid Feedback Enhances Performance," *Psychological Science* 10 (4): 545–547, April 2010.

13 *One German study proved that the type:* Daniel Oberfeld, Heiko Hecht, Ulrich Allendorf, and Florian Wickelmaier, "Ambient Lighting Modifies

the Flavor of Wine," *Journal of Sensory Studies* 24 (6): 797, 2009. DOI: 10.1111/j.1745-459X.2009.00239.x.

14 *For restaurant owners:* Vladas Griskevicius, Michelle N. Shiota, and Stephen M. Nowlis, "The Many Shades of Rose-Colored Glasses: An Evolutionary Approach to the Influence of Different Positive Emotions," *Journal of Consumer Research* 37: 238–250, August 2010.

14 *Cornell researchers conducted a study:* Cornell University, "Men Overcompensate When Masculinity Is Threatened," ScienceDaily.com, August, 3, 2005.

14 *Voters evaluate the competence of a candidate:* Christopher Y. Olivola and Alexander Todorov, "Elected in 100 Milliseconds: Appearance-Based Trait Inferences and Voting," *Journal of Nonverbal Behavior* 34 (2): 83–110, 2010.

14 *Apparently, it's more of a myth:* "Underdogs Have More Motivation? Not So Fast, Study Says," ScienceDaily.com, February 11, 2010.

15 *New findings published in* Psychological Science: Justin M. Carré, Cheryl M. McCormick, and Catherine J. Mondloch, "Angry Faces: Facial Structure Linked to Aggressive Tendencies, Study Suggests," ScienceDaily.com, November 2, 2009.

16 *Asking for a raise? Buying a car?; The same study aimed to evaluate:* "Tactile Sensations Influence Social Judgments and Decisions," ScienceDaily.com, June 25, 2010.

16 *Two Yale University psychologists tested to see if an open:* John A. Bargh and Lawrence E. Williams, "Keeping One's Distance: The Influence of Spatial Distance Cues on Affect and Evaluation," *Psychological Science* 19 (3): 302–308, March 2008.

17 *One study found that reading newspaper articles; Doron Kliger, Ph.D., who carried out:* "Reading Reports Involving Risk-Taking Affects Financial Decision Making," ScienceDaily.com, April 28, 2009.

18 *Women have traditionally proved to be more democratic; On the other side of this politically sensitive coin:* Linda L. Carli, "Gender Issues in Workplace Groups: Effects of Gender and Communication Style on Social Influence," in Mary Barret and Marilyn J. Davidson, eds., *Gender and Communication at Work* (Burlington, VT: Ashgate Publishing Company, 2006), 69–83.

One study showed that a male presenter: Kathleen M. Propp, "An Experimental Examination of Biological Sex as a Status Cue in Decision-Making Groups and Its Influence on Information Use," *Small Group Research* 26 (4): 451–474.

19 *Jim Moran, a professor of management:* "Narcissistic Bosses Destroy Morale, Drive Down Bottom Line," *FSU News*, 2009, http://www.fsu.edu/news/2009/08/07/narcissistic.bosses/.

19 *One experiment showed that people who felt excluded:* Nicole L. Mead, Roy F. Baumeister, Tyler F. Stillman, Catherine D. Rawn, and Kathleen D. Vohs,

"Social Exclusion Causes People to Spend and Consume in the Service of Affiliation," *Journal of Consumer Research* 37 (5): 902–919, February 2011.

20 *Researchers at the universities of Florida and Illinois; "Certain individuals, those with close-minded":* "People Sometimes Seek the Truth, but Most Prefer Like-Minded Views," ScienceDaily.com, July 2, 2009.

20 *Researchers at the University of Colorado at Boulder discovered that people who spent time; "The mistake we can sometimes make":* Leaf Van Boven and Greg Swenson. "Materialistic People Are Liked Less Than 'Experiential' People, Says University of Colorado Professor," Office of News Service, University of Colorado, April 14, 2010.

21 *In terms of influence, studies have shown that people with high emotional intelligence:* Ken McGuffin, "Leaders of the Pack Display High 'Emotional Intelligence,'" University of Toronto, Rotman School of Management, September 21, 2010.

21 *Nancy Carter and Mark Weber of the Rotman School of Management:* "People Who Are Trusting Are Better at Detecting Liars," *Medical News Today,* August 6, 2010.

22 *Edward M. Hallowell, M.D., an instructor of psychiatry:* Edward M. Hallowell, "The Human Moment at Work," *Harvard Business Review* 77 (1): 58–66.

Chapter 2 360-Degree Influence Starts with You

26 *As far back as 1920:* John F. Kihlstrom and Nancy Cantor, "Social Intelligence," http://socrates.berkeley.edu/~kihlstrm/social_intelligence.htm, 2000.

26 *Howard Gardner is widely known:* Amy C. Brualdi, "Multiple Intelligences: Gardner's Theory," ERICDigest.org, September 1996.

26 *As researcher Mark Smith notes:* Mark K. Smith, "Howard Gardner and Multiple Intelligences," *The Encyclopedia of Informal Education,* infed.org, 2002, 2008.

27 *Goleman and his colleagues Richard Boyatzis and Kenneth Rhee:* Richard Boyatzis, Daniel Goleman, and Kenneth Rhee, "Clustering Competence in Emotional Intelligence: Insights from the Emotional Competence Inventory," Consortium for Research on Emotional Intelligence in Organizations, December 8, 1999; see also Goleman's website, danielgoleman.info.

27 *In a 2004 article with David Caruso:* John D. Mayer, Peter Salovey, and David R. Caruso, "Emotional Intelligence: Theory, Findings, and Implication," *Psychological Inquiry* 15, 3 (2004): 197–215.

28 *. . . used to develop the Mayer-Salovey-Caruso Emotional Intelligence Test:* Mayer-Salovey-Caruso Emotional Intelligence Test (MSCEIT), Consortium for Research on Emotional Intelligence in Organizations, eiconsortium.org.

28 *Stéphane Côté and his colleagues, for example:* Stéphane Côté, Paulo N. Lopes, Peter Salovey, and Christopher T. H. Miners, "Emotional Intelligence and Leadership Emergence in Small Groups," *Leadership Quarterly* 21 (2): 496–508, June 2010; and Stéphane Côté and Christopher T. H. Miners, "Emotional Intelligence, Cognitive Intelligence, and Job Performance," University of Toronto, http://www.rotman.utoronto.ca/~scote/C%C3%B4t%C3%A9andMiners ASQ.pdf.

28 *Similarly, Joshua Freedman and Marvin Smith:* Joshua Freedman and Marvin Smith, "Emotional Intelligence for Athletes' Life Success," Six Seconds, 6seconds.org, May 1, 2008.

28 *Social intelligence (SI) has had some of the same conceptual:* Susan Dunn, "Emotional Intelligence Versus Cognitive Intelligence," teach-nology.com; http://www.teach-nology.com/tutorials/teaching/iq/; Kihlstrom and Cantor, op. cit.

28 *Still, as psychologist Nicholas Humphrey points out:* Nicholas Humphrey, "The Uses of Consciousness," James Arthur Memorial Lecture, American Museum of Natural History, New York, 1987.

29 *Consultant Karl Albrecht, for example, has created:* Karl Albrecht, "Social Intelligence: The New Science of Success," KarlAlbrecht.com.

29 *For example, in a 2004 report, the National Scientific Council on the Developing Child:* National Scientific Council on the Developing Child (NSCDC), *Children's Emotional Development Is Built into the Architecture of Their Brains:* Working Paper No. 2, 2004; see also the NSCDC, *The Science of Early Childhood Development: Closing the Gap Between What We Know and What We Do* (Cambridge, MA: Harvard University, 2007). Both papers available at The Center on the Developing Child, Harvard University.

29 *Whatever the difficulties scholars have in pinning down:* Raymond H. Hartjen. "The Preeminent Intelligence—Social IQ," EducationFutures.org; "High Emotional Intelligence = Best Workers," UPI.com, September 17, 2010; Ernest H. O'Boyle, Ronald H. Humphrey, Jeffrey M. Pollack, Thomas H. Hawver, and Paul A. Story, "The Relation Between Emotional Intelligence and Job Performance: A Meta-Analysis," *Journal of Organizational Behavior* 32 (5): 788–818, July 2010; "High Level of Practical Intelligence a Factor in Entrepreneurial Success," ScienceDaily.com, October 30, 2010; "Leaders of the Pack Display High 'Emotional Intelligence,'" ScienceDaily.com, September 21, 2010; "Emotional Intelligence Predicts Job Performance," ScienceDaily.com, October 27, 2010.

30 *The website Psychometric Success:* "Emotional Intelligence: Assessing Emotional Intelligence," www.psychometric-success.com/emotional-intelligence/assessing-emotional-intellingence.htm.

30 *The latter, for example, asks you more than 100:* Mayer-Salovey-Caruso Emotional Intelligence Test (MSCEIT), op. cit.

32, 33 *Psychology professor Timothy Pychyl says; Was the problem that the plan was too ambitious?:* Timothy A. Pychyl. "Self-Regulation Failure (Part 1): Goal Setting and Monitoring," *PsychologyToday.com*, February 16, 2009.

33 *That's why self-regulation matters:* C. Nathan DeWall, Roy F. Baumeister, Nicole L. Mead, and Kathleen D. Vohs, "How Leaders Self-Regulate Their Task Performance: Evidence That Power Promotes Diligence, Depletion, and Disdain," *Journal of Personality and Social Psychology* 100 (1): 47–65, January 2011.

34 *Tips to Master Self-Regulation:* Information from this section is collected from DeWall et. al., op. cit.; Bruce Duncan Perry, "Self-Regulation: The Second Core Strength," in Teachers, Scholastic.com; Pychyl, op. cit.; and Anna Steidle, "The Influence of Power on Self-Regulation," Dissertation (vorgelegt der Human- und Sozialwissenschaftlichen Fakultät der Technischen Universität Chemnitz, May 2010).

36 *Ten Skills for Becoming More Influential:* Information from this section collected from David Hakala, "The Top 10 Leadership Qualities," HRWorld. com, March 19, 2008; Dan McCarthy, "The Leader of the Future: Ten Skills to Begin Developing Now," GreatLeadershipbyDan.com, May 7, 2009; as well as my own experiences.

Chapter 3 Breaking Through Resistance: The Major Barriers to Influencing Others

43 *The 28th president of the United States; In fact, we have such a strong bias toward keeping things; "I wouldn't have seen it if I hadn't believed it":* All quotes from BrainyQuote.com.

44, 45 *Notable skeptic and author Michael Shermer; Shermer continues in* Scientific American: Michael Shermer, "Patternicity," *Scientific American*, December 2008; see also Shermer's "Why Smart People Believe Weird Things," *Skeptic* 10 (2), 2003, and "On Strange Beliefs," TED, filmed February 2006, posted November 2006.

46 *He calls our brain and nervous system; To help distinguish between:* James Alcock, "The Belief Engine," *Skeptical Inquirer* 19 (3), May/June 1995.

49 *Amos Tversky and Daniel Kahneman—behavioral economists—identified a number of "heuristics":* Amos Tversky and Daniel Kahneman, "Judgment Under Uncertainty: Heuristics and Biases," *Science* 185 (4157): 1124–1131, September 27, 1974; "Choices, Values, and Frames," in Kahneman and Tversky, eds. *Choices, Values, and Frames* (Cambridge: Cambridge University Press, 1984).

49 *In* Scientific American, *writer Christine Nicholson highlights a recent study:* Christine Nicholson, "We Only Trust Experts If They Agree with Us," *Scientific American*, September 18, 2010.

49 *The political science research website The Monkey Cage:* John Sides, "You Want More Epistemic Closure? Global Warming (Again) and Evolution," TheMonkeyCage.org, March 10, 2011; see also Mike Millikin, "Study Presents Evidence for Cultural Cognition of Scientific Evidence," GreenCarCongress.com, September 14, 2010; and "Thaler's Question," Edge.org, November 23, 2010.

50 *Yale Law School operates the Cultural Cognition Project:* Cultural Cognition Project, Yale Law School.

51 *Barry Marshall and his fellow researcher:* Kathryn Schulz, "Stress Doesn't Cause Ulcers! Or, How to Win a Nobel Prize in One Easy Lesson: Barry Marshall on Being . . . Right," *Slate*, September 9, 2010.

53 *What about the rest of us?:* Ken Broda-Bahm, "Adapt Your Scientific Testimony to Jurors' Skeptical Ears," *Litigation Postscript*, February 7, 2011.

55 *To help you on your path toward greater influence:* Information for the following table was drawn from Ron Ashkenas, "Let's Talk About Culture Change," *Harvard Business Review* blogs, March 22, 2011; Randi S. Brenowitz and Marilyn Manning, "How Leaders Get Buy-In," *Innovative Leader* 12 (2), February 2003; "Managing Resistance: Employee Resistance to Change— Why?" BusinessPerformance.com; Joseph Grenny, David Maxfield, and Andrew Shimberg, "Leadership and Organizational Studies: How to Have Influence," MIT *Sloan Management Review* 50 (1): 47–52, fall 2008; Jeff Kehoe and John Kotter, "How to Save Good Ideas," *Harvard Business Review* 88 (10): 129–132, October 2010; Nilofer Merchant, "Culture Trumps Strategy Every Time," *Harvard Business Review* blogs, March 22, 2011; A. J. Schuler, "Overcoming Resistance to Change: Top Ten Reasons for Change Resistance," SchulerSolutions.com; and my own observations and experiences.

Chapter 4 Know What Really Motivates People
and What People Really Care About

60 *Derived from the Greek* pathos *and the German:* Jennifer Block-Lerner, Carrie Adair, Jennifer C. Plumb, Deborah L. Rhatigan, and Susan M. Orsillo, "The Case for Mindfulness-Based Approaches in the Cultivation of Empathy: Does Nonjudgmental, Present-Moment Awareness Increase Capacity for Perspective-Taking and Empathic Concern?" *Journal of Marital and Family Therapy* 33 (4): 501–516, October 2007.

60 *Common social myth holds:* Simon Ross, "Empathic Accuracy," *Psychlopedia*, psych-it.com.au, October 18, 2008.

61 *One Columbia University experiment attempted to measure:* Jamil Zaki, Niall Bolger, and Kevin Ochsner, "Unpacking the Informational Bases of Empathic Accuracy," *Emotion* 9 (4): 478–487, August 2009.

61 *One skill that astute influencers practice:* Block-Lerner, et al., op. cit.

62 *According to Allene Grognet and Carol Van Duzer at the Center:* Allene Grognet and Carol Van Duzer, "Listening Skills in the Workplace," Center for Applied Linguistics, 2002–2003.

64 *First,* pay attention: "The Big 6: An Active Listening Skill Set," Center for Leadership, ccl.org.

67, *The product of this social evolution is what he calls; Using what he calls* reality
68 mining; *Charisma is:* Alex Pentland, "Honest Signaling," *American Scientist* 98 (3): 204–211, May–June 2010; see also Mark Buchanan, "Secret Signals," *Nature* 457 (29): 528–530, January 2009.

70 *If you're in the business; Facebook, too, offers influencers;* Beth Snyder Bulik, "What Your Favorite Social Network Says About You," AdAge.com, July 8, 2009.

Chapter 5 How Our Decisions Define Our Ability to Influence

73 *His predecessor at the top job at HP:* "Portfolio's Worst CEOs of All Time," posted at CNBC.com, April 30, 2009.

74 *Sure, for many people working in large organizations:* See, for example, Jeffrey Pfeffer and Robert I. Sutton, "The Smart Talk Trap," *Harvard Business Review* 77 (3): 134–142, May/June 1999; and Ram Charan, "Conquering a Culture of Indecision," *Harvard Business Review* 79 (4): 74–82, April 2001.

76 *The former Treasury secretary and Wall Street financier Robert Rubin:* Robert Rubin, Commencement Day Address, June 7, 2001, Harvard.edu.

76 *The management consultant Graham Jeffery:* Graham Jeffery, "Tony Blair: Judged on His Outcomes, Not His Decisions?" grahamjeffery.com, October 30, 2009.

76 *Seymour Hersh interviewed intelligence and foreign-policy officials:* Seymour Hersh, *Chain of Command* (New York: Harper Collins, 2004).

77 *Rubin cautions against such certainty:* Rubin, op. cit.

77 *David Weinberger, writing in the* Harvard Business Review: David Weinberger, "Garbage In, Great Stuff Out," *Harvard Business Review* 79 (8): 30–32, September 2001.

78 *Economics professor Dan Ariely observes:* Dan Ariely, "Good Decisions. Bad Outcomes," *Harvard Business Review* 88 (12): 40, December 2010.

78 *Business professors David Garvin and Michael Roberto:* David Garvin and Michael Roberto, "What You Don't Know About Making Decisions," *Harvard Business Review* 79 (8): 108–116, September 2001.

79 *The* New York Times *business columnist Joe Nocera:* Joe Nocera, "Madoff Had Accomplices: His Victims," *New York Times,* B1, March 13, 2009; see also Nocera's blog post, "When Smart People Do Dumb Things," NewYorkTimes. com, March 13, 2009.

80 *Elie Wiesel, whose foundation lost more than $15 million:* "The Madoff Panel Transcript," Portfolio.com, February 26, 2009.

81 *. . . but, as Nocera observes:* Nocera, "Madoff," op. cit.

81 *Jim Chanos, another member of the* Portfolio *panel:* Madoff Panel Transcript, op. cit.

81 *Warren Buffet concurs, observing that:* Warren Buffet, as quoted in William C. Taylor, "Why Do Smart People Do Such Dumb Things?" *Harvard Business Review* blog, January 11, 2011.

82 *John Hammond, Ralph Keeney, and Howard Raiffa, authors of:* John Hammond, Ralph Keeney, and Howard Raiffa, "Thinking About . . . The Hidden Traps in Decision Making," *Harvard Business Review* 76 (5): 47–58, September/October 1998; see also "Cognitive biases," Wikipedia.org.

84, *Psychologists Stephen Garcia, Hyunjin Song, and Abraham Tesser have*
85 *identified; The Social Comparison Bias; Representativeness and Availability; Illusion of Control and Optimism:* Stephen M. Garcia, Hyunjin Song, and Abraham Tesser, "Tainted Recommendations: The Social Comparison Bias," *Organizational Behavior and Human Decision Processes* 113 (2): 97–101, November 2010; see also Suzanne C. Thompson, "Illusions of Control: How We Overestimate Our Personal Influence," *Current Directions in Psychological Science* 8 (6): 187–190, December 1999; Amos Tversky and Daniel Kahneman, "Judgment Under Uncertainty: Heuristics and Biases," *Science* 185 (4157): 1124–1131, September 27, 1974; Daniel Kahneman, Jack L. Knetsch, and Richard Thaler, "Anomalies: The Endowment Effect, Loss Aversion, and Status Quo Bias," *The Journal of Economic Perspectives* 5 (1): 193–206, Winter 1991; and Dan Lovallo and Daniel Kahneman, "Delusions of Success: How Optimism Undermines Executives' Decisions," *Harvard Business Review* 81 (7): 56–63, July 2003.

86 *Reference-class forecasting is designed to eliminate:* Lovallo and Kahneman, op. cit.; see also "JAPA Article Calls on Planners to Help End Inaccuracies in Public Project Revenue Forecasting," American Planning Association news release, April 7, 2005; B. Flyvbjerg, "From Nobel Prize to Project Management: Getting Risks Right," *Project Management Journal* 37 (3): 5–15, August 2006, and Flyvbjerg, "Curbing Optimism Bias and Strategic Misrepresentation in Planning: Reference Class Forecasting in Practice," *European Planning Studies,* 16 (1): 3–21, January 2008; and "Reference class forecasting," Wikipedia.org.

87 *The psychologist Barry Dunn studied the notion:* As quoted in Keri Chiodo, "Trust Your Gut . . . but Only Sometimes," PsychologicalScience.org, January 4, 2011.

87 *Scientist Andrew McAfee is similarly dubious:* Andrew McAfee, "The Future of Decision Making: Less Intuition, More Evidence," *Harvard Business Review* blog, January 7, 2010.

88 *Jeff Stibel, Chairman and CEO of Dun & Bradstreet:* Jeff Stibel, "How Forethought (Not Intuition) Separates the Good from the Great," *Harvard Business Review* blog, October 20, 2010.

88 *The psychology professor William Grove and his colleagues:* William M. Grove, David H. Zald, Boyd S. Lebow, Beth E. Snitz, and Chad Nelson, "Clinical Versus Mechanical Prediction: A Meta-Analysis," *Psychological Assessment,* 12 (1): 18–30, March 2000.

88 *This conclusion concurs with an earlier study:* Lewis Goldberg, "Man Versus Model of Man," *Psychological Bulletin* 73 (6): 422–432, June 1970.

89 *Gary Klein, who advocates in favor of* naturalistic decision making: Daniel Kahneman and Gary Klein, "Conditions for Intuitive Expertise," *American Psychologist* 64 (6): 515–526, September 2009.

90 *I like the observation of one of pundit:* Andrew Sullivan, "A Really Expensive Way to Win a Game Show, Ctd.," The Daily Dish, February 17, 2011.

92 *Shirley Wang at the* Wall Street Journal *interviewed; The social psychologist Frenk van Harreveld:* Shirley S. Wang, "Why So Many People Can't Make Decisions," *Wall Street Journal,* wsj.com, September 27, 2010.

93 *John Hammond, Ralph Keeney, and Howard Raiffa have come up with:* John Hammond, Ralph Keeney, and Howard Raiffa, "Even Swaps," *Harvard Business Review* 76 (2): 137–150, March/April 1998.

95 *List the relevant variables:* Tom Davenport, "The Year Ahead: Make Better Decisions," *Harvard Business Review* blog, January 5, 2009.

96 *Question the process:* John Baldoni, "How to Make Better Decisions," CIO.com, July 21, 2008.

Chapter 6 Setting the Stage: Strategically Influencing People's Decisions

102 *Professor Jeffrey Pfeffer considers perception; "People whose praises are sung":* Jeffrey Pfeffer, "Shape Perceptions of Your Work, Early and Often," *Harvard Business Review* blog, October 21, 2010; see also Pfeffer, Christina T. Fong, Robert B. Cialdini, and Rebecca R. Portnoy, "Overcoming the Self-Promotion Dilemma: Interpersonal Attraction and Extra Help as a Consequence of Who Sings One's Praises," *Personality and Social Psychology Bulletin,* 32 (10): 1362–1374, 2006.

103 *The marketing professor Lars Perner stresses:* Lars Perner, "Consumer Behavior: The Psychology of Marketing," consumerpsychologist.com, ND.

104 *Google's own management culture has created a flexible work:* Adam Lashinsky, "Chaos by design," *Fortune,* October 2, 2006.

105 *When male CEOs in Denmark have daughters:* Christopher Shea, "Male CEOs with Daughters Treat Women Better," *Wall Street Journal,* wsj.com, March 3, 2011.

105 *Seeing someone yawn, hearing someone yawn:* This is widely reported; among the popularizers of the idea is Malcolm Gladwell in *The Tipping Point* (Boston: Little, Brown and Company, 2000).

105 *Customers primed with images of money before they shop:* Yuping Liu-114Thompkins, "The Hidden Power of Context," yupingliu.com, July 13, 2009.

105 *Architects discussing government building structures:* For a general discussion of this phenomenon, see Jon Gertner, "Why Isn't the Brain Green," *New York Times* magazine, MM36, April 16, 2009.

105 *Then there's the less-is-more approach:* Barry Schwartz, as quoted in Beth Kowitt, "Inside the Secret World of Trader Joe's," CNN.com, August 23, 2010; see also Sheena Iyengar and Kanika Agrawal, "A Better Choosing Experience," strategy-business.com, November 23, 2010.

106 *Malcolm Gladwell has made a career exploring how apparently:* Gladwell, op. cit.; see also his website (which displays excerpts of *The Tipping Point*), gladwell.com.

106 *Journalist William Whyte first coined the term* groupthink: Groupthink, Wikipedia.org; see also Noni Richardson Ahlfinger and James K. Esser, "Testing the Groupthink Model: Effects of Promotional Leadership and Conformity Predisposition," *Social Behavior and Personality: An International Journal* 29 (1): 31–41, 2001.

107 *The scholar Robert Baron reviewed groupthink research:* Robert Baron, "So Right It's Wrong: Groupthink and the Ubiquitous Nature of Polarized Group Decision-Making," http://ourcomments.org/psych/GroupthinkII-realFinalADvances-1.pdf, ND.

107 *Professors David Garvin and Michael Roberto suggest:* David Garvin and Michael Roberto, "What You Don't Know About Making Decisions," *Harvard Business Review* 79 (8): 108–116, September 2001.

108 *Hollywood likes architects:* J. Sebastian, "Fictional Architects in Movies," arch-daily.com, March 30, 2009; "Fictional Architects in Movies," MirageStudio7.com; and Ruthe Stein, "And Now Let Us Praise Hot Architects. Hollywood Can't Get Enough of Them," mail to: rstein@sfchronicle.com; A.M. *San Francisco Chronicle,* E1, August 30, 2006.

108, *According to professors Richard Thaler, Cass Sunstein, and John Balz; What*
109, *counts as the default can be controversial; The checklists recommended by the*
110 *doctor and New Yorker writer; What about more complex decisions; Choice architects should also pay attention; One way to cut through this type of muddle:*

Richard Thaler, Cass Sunstein, and John Balz, "Choice Architecture," ssrn. com, April 2, 2010.

111 *Garvin and Roberto don't use the term* choice architecture: Garvin and Roberto, op. cit.

111 *Some thin rationalists despair of the apparent inability*: Will Wilkinson might not call himself a thin rationalists, but he is skeptical of choice architecture—especially of its paternalist potential; see his Wilkinson, "Choice Architecture and Paternalism," willwilkinson.net, April 20, 2008.

115 *Take anything that's complex and turn it into a story*: I discuss stories and narrative at length in Chapter 11.

116 *Research has been shown that many of us like to surround ourselves*: Stephen M. Garcia, Hyunjin Song, and Abraham Tesser, "Tainted Recommendations: The Social Comparison Bias," *Organizational Behavior and Human Decision Processes* 113 (2): 97–101, November 2010.

117 *Many of us are guilty of judging decisions not by their merit*: Dan Ariely, "Good Decisions. Bad Outcomes," *Harvard Business Review* 88 (12): 40, December 2010; Garvin and Roberto, op. cit.; David Weinberger, "Garbage In, Great Stuff Out," *Harvard Business Review* 79 (8): 30–32, September 2001.

117 *Language is used to create understanding*: I discuss the role of language in influencing at greater length in Chapter 11.

Chapter 7 Mastering Organizational Politics

120 *Rex C. Mitchell, Ph.D., professor at the Department*: Rex C. Mitchell, *Introduction to Organizational Politics*, csun.edu, ND, and Andrew Dubrin, *Leadership*, 3rd ed. (New York: Houghton Mifflin, 2001).

122 *"Politics are an organizational fact of life"*: Gill Corkindale, "Reinventing Office Politics," *Harvard Business Review* blog, October 3, 2007.

123, *. . . organizational politics is "a process through which people"; So what's an*
124 *overly political organization to do*: Ben Dattner, and Allison Dunn, "The Causes and Consequences of Organizational Politics," Dattnerconsulting. com, 2002.

124 *Evidence suggests that gossip has a potency*: "Gossip in the Workplace: A Weapon or Gift?" ScienceDaily.com, October 30, 2009; Tim Hallett, Brent Harger, and Donna Eder, "Gossip at Work: Unsanctioned Evaluative Talk in Formal School Meetings," *Journal of Contemporary Ethnography* 38 (5): 584–618, October 2009.

127 *Laura Sabattini, writing for Catalyst, the organization*: Laura Sabattini, "Unwritten Rules: What You Don't Know Can Hurt Your Career," Catalyst. org, June 2008.

128 *Fifty years ago, the social psychologists John French and Bertram Raven*: "French and Raven's Five Forms of Power," MindTools.com, ND.

130 *Jeffrey Pfeffer, who teaches business at Stanford University, concurs; "Stop waiting for things to get better":* Rick Nobles, "Pfeffer Book Explains Acquiring and Maintaining Power, *Stanford Business Magazine Online,* August 2010.

131 *Perhaps most easily spotted is the* enforcer: Mark Teich, "Field Guide to the Enforcer," PsychologyToday.com, March 1, 2009.

132 *All this leads to some predictable hot buttons:* Michael Maccoby, *The Productive Narcissist: The Promise and Peril of Visionary Leadership* (New York: Broadway Books, 2003).

132 *Gladeana McMahon and Adrienne Rosen, writing in a recent issue:* Gladeana McMahon and Adrienne Rosen, "Narcissism at Work," Trainingjournal .com, June 1, 2009.

133 *Bullying is an epidemic:* Jeana Bryner, "Workplace Bullying 'Epidemic' Worse Than Sexual Harassment," Livescience.com, March 8, 2008.

133 *The bully's position insulates him:* Cheryl Dolan and Faith Oliver, "Is Your Boss a Bully? Stop Being a Target," *Harvard Business Review* blog, November 19, 2009.

134, *Working off the insights of Andrew Durbin; Once again Durbin, (via Mitchell),*
135 *is useful:* Mitchell, op. cit.

136 *When you do this continually:* Jim Sellner, "Strategic Management Skill 4: Forming Relationships, Alliances, and Partnerships," ezinearticle.com, December 28, 2010.

136 *Gill Corkindale, whom I mentioned earlier:* Corkindale, op. cit.

Chapter 8 Influencing Up: Bring Your Bosses Around to Your Way of Thinking

140 *It's called* executive presence, *and I wrote an entire book:* Harrison Monarth, *Executive Presence* (New York: McGraw-Hill, 2009).

142 *According to Glenn Llopis, author of* Earning Serendipity: Glenn Llopis, "Executive Presence in the New Normal Workplace," Forbes.com, December 27, 2010.

143 *And you are just as effective when things get serious:* Paul Aldo, "What Is Executive Presence? . . . and How Do I Get It Again?" ajc.com, ND.

144 *In a 2009 survey of 444 global CEOs:* Linda Barrington, "CEO Challenge 2010: Top 10 Challenges," TheConference-Board.org, 2010.

145 *Wharton management professor Adam Grant:* As discussed in "Analyzing Effective Leaders: Why Extraverts Are Not Always the Most Effective Bosses," Knowledge@Wharton, November 23, 2010.

146 *Another study illuminates the true source of response:* Joseph Grenny, "Want More Influence? Just Ask," Businessweek.com, January 11, 2011.

147 *This, too, has been the subject of much research:* "'The Art of Woo': Selling Your Ideas to the Entire Organization, One Person at a Time," Knowledge@ Wharton, October 17, 2007.

147 *Executive Coach Marshall Goldsmith, in an article; All of them, by the way, work even better:* Marshall Goldsmith, "Effectively Influencing Decision Makers: Ensuring That Your Knowledge Makes a Difference," Linkageinc. com, 2009.

150 *If you know you're about to rub elbows:* John Baldoni, "Tips for Making Small Talk with Bigwigs," *Harvard Business Review* blog, March 22, 2010.

151 *In their book,* Buy-In: Saving Your Good Idea: John Kotter and Lorne Whitehead, *Buy-In: Saving Your Good Idea from Getting Shot Down,* excerpted at BusinessWeek.com, October 8, 2010.

152 *Labels like* suck-up, brownnoser, sycophant: Beth Weissenberger, "How to Win at Office Politics," Businessweek.com, February 23, 2010.

152 *Allowing your loyalty to shine through, even:* Randall Hansen, "Seven Strategies to Recession-Proof Your Career: Build Your Future Regardless of Health of the Economy," QuintCareers.com. ND.

153 *A study by Ithai Stern of Northwestern University's:* Aaron Mays, "Flattery Will Get You Far," Kellogg School of Management, kellogg.northwestern .edu, August 16, 2010.

Chapter 9 Influencing the Opposite Gender for Mutual Success

156 *"All sex differences result from the imbalance"; Sometimes genetic and hormonal differences:* Diana E. Pankevich, Theresa Wizemann, and Bruce M. Altevogt, *Sex Differences and Implications for Translational Neuroscience Research: Workshop Summary,* Institute of Medicine (Washington, DC: National Academies Press, 2011).

156 *Christiana Leonard of McKnight Brain Institute:* Christiana M. Leonard, Stephen Towler, Suzanne Welcome, Laura K. Halderman, Ron Otto, Mark A. Eckert, and Christine Chiarello. "Size Matters: Cerebral Volume Influences Sex Differences in Neuroanatomy," *Cerebral Cortex* 18 (12): 2920–2931, December 2008.

157 *Hannah Hoag, writing in* New Scientist: Hannah Hoag, "Brains Apart: The Real Difference Between the Sexes," *New Scientist* 199 (2665): 28–31, July 19, 2008.

157 *Larry Cahill, Ph.D., University of California, Irvine, observing that:* Larry Cahill, "Why Sex Matters for Neuroscience," *Nature Reviews Neuroscience* 7 (6): 477–484, June 2006.

157 *. . . a conclusion backed up by the IOM:* Pankevich, et al., op. cit.

157 *Consider the issue of directions:* Hoag, op. cit.; Cahill, op. cit.; for a general discussion, see Geert J. De Vries, "Minireview: Sex Differences in Adult and Developing Brains: Compensation, Compensation, Compensation," *Endocrinology* 145 (3): 1063–1068, March 2004; and Iris E. C. Sommer, André Aleman, Anke Bouma, and René S. Kahn, "Do Women Really Have

More Bilateral Language Representation Than Men? A Meta-Analysis of Functional Imaging Studies," *Brain* 127(8): 1845–1852, August 2004.

158 *The takeaway from this emergent area:* This is a highly fluid area of research in which results often lead to changes in previous understandings of the brain. Unfortunately, as Cordelia Fine points out in *Delusions of Gender* (New York: W.W. Norton & Company, 2010), careful research is often distorted in the rush to pop culture judgments; see also Diane F. Halpern, "How Neuromythologies Support Sex Role Stereotypes," *Science* 330 (6609): 1320–1321, December 3, 2010.

158 *An article in the* Economist *noted, for example, that "these differences":* "The Mismeasure of Woman," *Economist*, August 3, 3006.

158 *As one study put it, "In employment settings":* Alice H. Eagly and Mary C. Johannesen-Schmidt, "The Leadership Styles of Women and Men," *Journal of Social Issues* 57 (4): 781–797, December 2001.

159 *Yael Hellman, professor of organizational leadership at Woodbury University:* "Leadership Styles," *Smart Business Online*, July 31, 2006.

159 *Anne Cummings, a professor of business administration at the University of Minnesota at Duluth:* "The 'Masculine' and 'Feminine' Sides of Leadership and Culture: Perception vs. Reality," Knowledge@Wharton, October 5, 2005.

159 *Relying too heavily on these generalities, however:* The study of male and female leadership styles is a rich area of research for both social scientists and those in the corporate world; see, for example, Linda L. Carli, "Gender and Social Influence," *Journal of Social Issues*, 57(4): 725–741, December; Alice H. Eagley and Linda L. Carli, "The Female Leadership Advantage: An Evaluation of the Evidence," *The Leadership Quarterly* 14 (6): 807–834, December 2003; Robin J. Ely and Deborah L. Rhode, "Women and Leadership: Defining the Challenges," in Nitin Nohria and Rakesh Khurana, eds., *Handbook of Leadership Theory and Practice* (Boston: Harvard Business Press, 2010); Patterson McGrath & Associates, "Leadership—Being a Woman, What Difference Does it Make?" Paper 2, Women in Leadership Research Project Series 1, September 2010; Cecilia L. Ridgeway, "Gender, Status, and Leadership," *Journal of Social Issues* 57 (4): 637–655, December 2001; and Janice D. Yoder, "Making Leadership Work More Effectively for Women," *Journal of Social Issues* 57 (4): 815–828, December 2001.

159 *Hellman says this can have the devastating effect:* "Leadership styles," op. cit.

159 *Consider military officers:* Still, the stereotypes about military leadership persist; see, for example, Jennifer Boldry and Wendy Wood, "Gender Stereotypes and the Evaluation of Men and Women in Military Training," *Journal of Social Issues* 57 (4): 689–705, December 2001.

160 *Similarly, men and women who don't wear combat boots to work:* Jan O'Daniel, "With More Women in Work Force, Office Cultures Getting a Shakeup," Bizjournals.com, May 4, 2009.

161 *Simma Lieberman, coauthor of* Putting Diversity to Work, *cautions; Conflict in one area may affect the whole of a relationship; . . . the sexes are also unique in how we signal agreement:* Simma Lieberman, "Differences in Male and Female Communication Styles," simmalieberman.com, ND.

162 *True, it's best not to burst into tears:* Joanna L. Krotz, "Six Tips for Bridging the Communication Gap," Microsoft Business, ND.

162 *Nicholas Kristof, writing in the* New York Times: Nicholas Kristof, "When Women Rule," *New York Times,* February 10, 2008; see also Monica Biernat and Kathleen Fuegen, "Shifting Standards and the Evaluation of Competence: Complexity in Gender-Based Judgment and Decision Making," *Journal of Social Issues* 57 (4): 707–724, December 2001; Alice H. Eagly and Steven J. Karau, "Role Congruity Theory of Prejudice Toward Female Leaders," *Psychological Review,* 109 (3): 573–578, July 2002; "Men or Women: Who's the Better Leader?" Pew Research Center, August 25, 2008; and Linda Perriton, "'We Don't Want Complaining Women!' A Critical Analysis of the Business Case for Diversity," *Management Communication Quarterly* 23 (2): 218–243, November 2009.

163 *More than 30 years ago, Robert Altemeyer and Keith Jones:* Robert A. Altemeyer and Keith Jones, "Sexual Identity, Physical Attractiveness and Seating Position as Determinants of Influence in Discussion Groups," *Canadian Journal of Behavioural Sciences,* 6 (4): 357–375, 1974.

163 *As New York University professors Madeline Heilman and Michelle Haynes put it:* Madeline E. Heilman and Michelle C. Haynes, "No Credit Where Credit Is Due: Attributional Rationalization of Women's Success in Male-Female Teams," *Journal of Applied Psychology,* 90 (5): 905–916, September 2005.

163 *A Harvard Business Review study found that even when women leaders:* Herminia Ibarra and Otilia Obodaru, "Women and the Vision Thing," *Harvard Business Review* 87 (1): 62–70, January 2009.

163 *A Catalyst study on women and leadership showed:* "Women 'Take Care,' Men 'Take Charge,' Stereotyping of U.S. Business Leaders Exposed," Catalyst.org, 2005.

164 *Another challenge is the "niceness" problem:* Kristof, op. cit.

164 *Laurie Rudman, professor of psychology at Rutgers, the State University of New Jersey:* Laurie A. Rudman, and Peter Glick, "Prescriptive Gender Stereotypes and Backlash Toward Agentic Women." *Journal of Social Issues* 57 (4): 743–762, December 2001.

164 *Men may engage an autocratic style without repercussion:* Hilary Lips, "Women and Leadership: A Delicate Balance," WomensMedia.com, April 2, 2009.

164 *An informal* Forbes *survey of female bosses:* Meghan Casserly, "The Conversation: Male vs. Female Bosses." Forbes.com, April 23, 2010.

165 *If, however, a woman wants to break through in a "man's" field*: "Women 'Take Care,'" op. cit.

166 *Shaunti Feldhahn, author of* The Male Factor: Shaunti Feldhahn, "Cracking the Male Code of Office Behavior," *New York Times*, February 5, 2011.

166 *. . . if they're not supposed to be emotional at work*: Christopher Shea, "Sexualized Anchors, Uninformed Male Viewers," *Wall Street Journal*, February 3, 2011.

166 *There is zero evidence that men are less verbal than women*: Yvonne K. Fulbright, "Male-Female Communication: Debunking the Mars-Venus Myth," Huffington Post, February 13, 2011.

166 *. . . but this notion of men as verbal kindergartners*: Anne M. Koenig and Alice H. Eagly, "Stereotype Threat in Men on a Test of Social Sensitivity," *Sex Roles* 52 (7/8): 489–496, April 2005.

166 *These are effects of* priming: See, for example, S. Christian Wheeler and Jonah Berger, "When the Same Prime Leads to Different Effects," *Journal of Consumer Research* 34 (3): 357–368, October 2007.

167 *This is one of the dangers of* tokenism: Kelly Danaher and Nyla R. Branscombe, "Maintaining the System with Tokenism: Bolstering Individual Mobility Beliefs and Identification with a Discriminatory Organization," *British Journal of Social Psychology* 49 (2): 343–362, June 2010.

167 *As Deborah Cameron, writing on* The Myth of Mars and Venus, *notes*: Deborah Cameron, "What Language Barrier?" *The Guardian*, October 1, 2007.

167 *Men can also be tripped up if they don't exhibit*: Madeline E. Heilman and Aaron S. Wallen, "Wimpy and Undeserving of Respect: Penalties for Men's Gender-Inconsistent Success," *Journal of Experimental Social Psychology* 46 (4): 664–667, July 2010.

168 *For example, on the topic of mixed teams, one study found*: "Mixed Teams Outperform Single-Sex Teams. Right?" efinancialcareers.com., November 1, 2007; for a somewhat different view, see Lucy Ward and John Carvel, "Best Ideas Come from Work Teams Mixing Men and Women," *The Guardian*, November 1, 2007, who report on a study cited by Lydia Gratton at the London School of Business.

168 *. . . one commenter suggested that this was due to communication problems*: Heilman and Hayes, op. cit.

169 *Professors Nilanjana Dasgupta of University of Massachusetts, Amherst, and Shaki Asgari*: Nilanjana Dasgupta and Shaki Asgari, "Seeing Is Believing: Exposure to Counterstereotypic Women Leaders and Its Effect on the Malleability of Automatic Gender Stereotyping," *Journal of Experimental Social Psychology* 40 (5): 642–658, September 2004.

169 *Joanna Krotz, a contributing columnist at MSN*: Krotz, op. cit.

171 *Research suggests that mixed-gender groups can lead to worse:* "Mixed Teams,"
op. cit.; Ward and Carvel, op. cit.

171. *Note that part of the problem may be due to the extent of the minority sta-*
172 *tus; Gratton and her team also studied; To create better conditions: Innovative*
Potential: Men and Women in Teams (Lehman Brothers Center for Women
in Business, London School of Business, 2007).

Chapter 10 Influencing the Public's Impressions of Your Organization

176 *Companies that rely heavily on their sales force, such as Mary Kay Cosmetics*
or Amway: Michael J. Pratt, "The Good, the Bad, and the Ambivalent:
Managing Identification Among Amway Distributors," *Administrative Science
Quarterly* 45 (3): 456–493, September 2000.

176 *In his* Harvard Business Review *article, writer Paul Hemp reported:* Paul
Hemp, "My Week as a Room-Service Waiter at the Ritz," *Harvard Business
Review,* 80 (6): 50–62, June 2002.

177 *Groupon, for example, is a highly successful:* Utpal Dholakia, "Why
Employees Can Wreck Promotional Offers," *Harvard Business Review* 89
(1/2): 28, January–February 2011.

177 *And for those who dismiss the relevance of employee satisfaction:* Martin
Sprouse, ed. *Sabotage in the American Workplace* (San Francisco: Pressure
Drop Press, 1992).

178. *Bank of America holds more than a million bad mortgages; . . . buying up*
179 *domain names:* David Streitfeld and Louise Story, "Bank of America to Reduce
Mortgage Balances," *New York Times,* B1, March 24, 2010; "Bank of America
Buys Up Nasty Domain Names in Defensive Move," HuffingtonPost.com,
December 23, 2010.

179 *Perhaps Bank of America is entirely innocent of all wrongdoing; Maybe former
Medtronic CEO Bill George hits closer:* Mina Kimes, "The Three-Minute
Manager," *Fortune* 159(5): 30, March 16, 2009.

179 *The year 2010 was not a good one for the energy:* Kirsten Korosec, "Gulf Oil
Spill: BP CEO Hayward Just Can't Help Blaming Someone Else," bNet,
April 29, 2010; Clifford Krauss, "Oil Spill's Blow to BP's Image May Eclipse
Costs," *New York Times,* B1, April 29, 2010; Kirsten Korosec, "BP's History of
Oil Spills and Accidents: Same Strategy, Different Day," bNet, May 7, 2010;
Frank Furedi, "Why BP Is Not Very Slick in an Emergency," FrankFuredi.
com, June 21, 2010.

180 *Are strollers necessary:* Farzad Rastegar, "How I Did It . . . Maclaren's CEO
on Learning from a Recall," *Harvard Business Review* 89 (1): 41–45, January–
February 2011.

182 *Toyota initiated a recall in response to complaints:* "2009–2010 Toyota Vehicle
Recalls," Wikipedia.org.

182 *Andy Beal, an online reputation management consultant*: Andy Beal, "The 11 Unwritten Laws of Reputation Management," Forbes.com, January 4, 2011.

182 *. . . but a little over a year later, the National Highway Transportation Agency*: Matthew L. Wald, "Electronic Flaws Did Not Cause Toyota Problems, U.S. Says," *New York Times*, February 8, 2011, B1.

183 *I could offer you a list of ways to manage*: I compiled this list based on both what should be common sense and the following authors: Ron Ashkenas, "Who's Responsible for Your Company's Reputation?" *Harvard Business Review* blog, April 28, 2010; David Kiley and Burt Helm, "The Great Trust Offensive," Businessweek.com, September 17, 2009; Colin Mitchell, "Selling the Brand Inside," *Harvard Business Review* 80 (1): 99–105, January 2002; ReputationInstitute.com; Sprouse, op. cit.

184 *. . . nothing can destroy it quicker than responding badly to a crisis*: "Bank of America," op. cit.; Beal, op. cit.; Furedi, op. cit.; Korosec, op. cit.; Rastegar, op. cit.

185 *Andy Beal, coauthor of* Radically Transparent: Beal, op. cit.

185 *President and CEO Carlos Ghosn highlighted the importance of strategy*: Carlos Ghosn, "Saving the Business Without Losing the Company," *Harvard Business Review* 80 (1): 47–45, January 2002.

186 *Stories of how the CEO persisted in using the duck*: See, for example, Adam Armbruster, "The Advertising Duck That Roared," TVWeek.com, 2006. http://www.tvweek.com/news/2006/11/the_advertising_duck_that_roar.php.

186 *And, as Andy Beal points out, "Companies rarely rebrand"*: Beal, op. cit.

187 *In the book* Differentiate or Die: Steven Rivkin, *Differentiate or Die*, Executive Summaries, part 2,22 (9): 1–8, September 2000.

187, *A. A. Mohammed, professor of management at Indiana University; Indirect*
188 *tactics follow*: A. A. Mohamed, "A Taxonomy of Organizational Impression Management Tactics. Advances in Competitiveness Research," FindArticles.com, 1999.

188 *Massey Energy (now part of Alpha Natural resources)*: Ian Urbina, "Wealthy Coal Executive Hopes to Turn Democratic West Virginia Republican," *New York Times*, October 22, 2006; Trefis Team, "Someone Will End Up Overpaying for Massey Energy," Forbes.com, January 19, 2011.

189 *Yet despite Southwest Airlines CEO Gary Kelly's blunt; Inder Sidhu, a senior*: Inder Sidhu, "Profiles in Doing Both: The Secret Behind the LUV at Southwest," Forbes.com, January 11, 2010.

189 *Kevin Lane Keller, professor of marketing*: Kevin Lane Keller, "The Brand Report Card," *Harvard Business Review* 78 (1): 147–157, January–February 2000.

190 *According to a survey by Reputation Institute; Such attentiveness to status matters*: ReputationInstitute.com.

191 Forbes *reporter Laurie Burkitt says:* Laurie Burkitt, "America's Most Reputable Companies," Forbes.com, April 20, 2010.

191 *Another survey, focusing on U.S. "thought leaders":* 2010–2011 International Index of Thought Leaders: Executive Summary, November 2010, http://www.tlg-ltd.com/index2010/.

192 *Sometimes actions themselves can tell the story:* Spencer E. Ante, "At Amazon, Marketing Is for Dummies," Businessweek.com, September 17, 2009.

192 *Similarly, Zappos built its business on inventory:* Bill Taylor, "Why Zappos Pays New Workers to Quit—And You Should Too," *Harvard Business Review* blog, May 19, 2008.

193 *Randall Beard, former global chief marketing officer:* Kiley and Helm, op. cit.

193 *The L.L. Bean customer service web page:* Customer Service, LL Bean.com.

193 *The Ritz-Carlton allots every employee:* Hemp, op. cit.; see also Courtney Dillard, Larry D. Browning, Sim B. Sitkin, and Kathleen M. Sutcliffe, "Impression Management and the Use of Procedures at the Ritz-Carlton: Moral Standards and Dramaturgical Discipline," *Communication Studies* 51 (4): 404–414, Winter 2000.

Chapter 11 Using Your Words to Influence and Change Minds

196 *The skill of framing is critical in the tool:* Jay A. Conger, "Inspiring Others: The Language of Leadership," *Academy of Management Executive* 5 (1): 31–45, 1991.

196 *When we attempt to frame an issue:* Steve Woolgar and Dorothy Pawluch, "Ontological Gerrymandering: The Anatomy of Social Problems Explanations," *Social Problems* 32 (3): 214–227, February 1985.

200 *Complicated campaigns—a new venture, renovations of a damaged:* Although not directly examining framing, the following study is nonetheless relevant: R. A. Yaros, "Is It the Medium or the Message? Structuring Complex News to Enhance Engagement and Situational Understanding by Nonexperts," *Communication Research*, 33: 285–309, 2006.

203 *Why do stories work? Simple:* Baesler and Burgoon, op. cit.; Michael Dahlstrom, "The Role of Causality in Information Acceptance in Narratives: An Example from Scientific Communication," *Communication Research* 37 (6): 857–875, 2010; Elizabeth J. Marsh, Michelle L. Meade, and Henry L. Roediger, "Learning Facts from Fiction," *Journal of Memory and Language*, 49 (4): 519–536, November 2003; and, for a more esoteric analysis, see Martin Kreiswirth, "Merely Telling Stories? Narrative and Knowledge in the Human Sciences," *Poetics Today* 21 (2): 293–318, Summer 2000.

203 *Fellow consultant and organizational storytelling expert Stephen Denning:* "Learn the Language of Leadership: Where to Use Storytelling," SteveDenning.com.

206 *The words we use with our clients:* Conger, op. cit.

207 *Famed writer Rudyard Kipling once said:* Rudyard Kipling, BrainyQuote.com.

208 *Concrete is the key word here:* Eugene Borgida and Richard E. Nisbett, "The Differential Impact of Abstract vs. Concrete Information on Decisions," *Journal of Applied Social Psychology* 7(3), 258–271, September 1977.

209 *Metaphors are powerful as they immediately connect:* Conger, op. cit.

209 *Frank Luntz, the pollster and message-strategist to the Republican:* Frank Luntz, "The 11 Words for 2011," *Huffington Post*, March 1, 2011.

211 *Generally speaking, to get someone's attention:* See, for example, Bonnie Erickson, E.Allen Lind, Bruce C. Johnson, and William M. O'Barr, "Speech Style and Impression Formation in a Court Setting; The Effects of 'Powerful' and 'Powerless' Speech," *Journal of Experimental Social Psychology* 14 (3): 266–279, May 1978.

212 *There will be resistance:* Resistance and persuasion are much-studied issue in both the social sciences and in business. One who crosses both fields, Howard Gardner, has written about mind-change in *Changing Minds* (Cambridge: Harvard University Press, 2004); see also E. J. Baesler and J. K. Burgoon, "The Temporal Effects of Story and Statistical Evidence on Belief Change," *Communication Research* 21: 582–602, 1994; H. B. Brosius and A. Bathelt, "The Utility of Exemplars in Persuasive Communications," *Communication Research*, 21(1): 48–78, 1994; John B. F. de Wit, Enny Das, and Raymond Vet, "What Works Best: Objective Statistics or a Personal Testimonial? An Assessment of the Persuasive Effects of Different Types of Message Evidence on Risk Perception," *Health Psychology* 27(1): 110–115, January 2008; Dave Hakala, "Eight Ways to Get Buy In from Company Executives," Itmanagement.com, ND; John P. Kotter and Lorne A. Whitehead, *Buy In* (Boston: Harvard Business Press, 2010); Linda Simon, Jeff Greenberg, and Jack Brehm, "Trivialization—The Forgotten Mode of Dissonance Reduction," *Journal of Personality and Social Psychology* 68 (2): 247–260, February 1995; Gary A.Williams and Robert B. Miller, "Change the Way You Persuade," *Harvard Business Review* 80 (2): 65–73, May 2002; Joseph Yeager and Linda Sommer, "Linguistic Mechanisms Cause Rapid Behavior Change, Part Two: How Linguistic Frames Affect Motivation," *The Qualitative Report* 12 (3): 467–483, September 2007; as well as the general discussion of framing.

216 *One instance is the influence exerted by the work and writings of the late Saul Alinsky; and is often quoted or referenced by modern media pundits:* Saul Alinsky, Wikipedia.org.

216 *He was called a "Prophet of Power"; He was controversial:* "Radical Saul Alinsky: Prophet of Power to the People," *Time*, March 2, 1970.

217 *Paine's fiery pamphlet,* Common Sense: Jill Lepore, "The Sharpened Quill," *New Yorker*, October 16, 2006.

218 *The great secret weapon of influential writing:* Conger, op. cit.

218 *In general, bloggers are known for taking a stand:* Farhad Manjoo, "How to Blog," Slate.com, December 18, 2008.

220 *Like a blog, an op-ed has a tight window of opportunity:* David Jarmul, "15 Ways to Get an Op-Ed Article Published," bnet (originally published at *The Masthead*, Summer 1993).

220 *The challenge is embodied by certain question-based criteria:* "Questions for Op-Ed Writers," The Op-Ed Project.org, ND.

221 *White papers are unique in that:* "Ten Secrets of Effective White Paper Writing," Write2Market.com, ND.

Chapter 12 Managing the Influencing Power of Your Personal Brand

225 *At first glance, John Millard, M.D., seems like:* author's personal anecdote.

226 *Lipo, as it's often called, is, according to various studies:* from interview with John Millard, M.D., March 14, 2011.

227 *Legendary U.S. journalist and newscaster Tom Brokaw:* Tom Brokaw, BrainyQuote.com.

228 *Don't forget, however, that Oprah wasn't always "Oprah":* Oprah Winfrey, Wikipedia.org.

231 *. . . is the story of the would-be Cisco employee:* Helen A. S. Popkin, "Twitter Gets You Fired in 140 Characters or Less," MSNBC.com, March 23, 2009.

232 *"When an individual enters the presence of others":* Erving Goffman. *The Presentation of Self in Everyday Life* (New York: Doubleday, 1959).

233 *Other social scientists have extended his work:* Among them: Adam Arvidson, "Brands: A Critical Perspective," *Journal of Consumer Culture* 5 (2): 325–358, July 2005; William L. Gardner and Mark J. Martinko, "Impression Management in Organizations," *Journal of Management* 14 (2): 321–338, 1988; Alison Hearn, "'John, a 20-year-old Boston Native with a Great Sense of Humour': On the Spectacularization of the 'Self ' and the Incorporation of Identity in the Age of Reality Television," *International Journal of Media and Cultural Politics* 2 (2): 131–147, 2006; Douglas Holt, "Toward a Sociology of Branding," *Journal of Consumer Culture* 6 (3): 299–302, November 2006; Daniel J. Lair, Katie Sullivan, and George Cheney, "Marketization and the Recasting of the Professional Self," *Management Communication Quarterly* 18 (3): 307–343, February 2005; Mark R. Leary and Robin M. Kowalski, "Impression Management: A Literature Review and Two-Component Model," *Psychological Bulletin* 107 (1): 34–47, January 1990; and Ernest Sternberg, "Phantasmagoric Labor: The New Economics of Self-Presentation," *Futures* 30 (1): 3–21, January 1998.

233 *Billie King, Jr., founder of the Bow Tie Cigar Company; Jill Donenfeld, founder of The Dish's Dish; As the wine expert Gary Vaynerchuk:* Lydia

Dishman, "10 Ways to Build Your Personal Brand," BusinessInsider.com, April 9, 2010.

233 *A quick online search of "personal branding" will quickly:* See, for example, WilliamArruda.com; Rancatore; Ryan at PersonalBranding101.com; and Dan Schawbel at PersonalBrandingblog.com, among just a few of the very many.

234 *Which brings me to the first step:* Tom Peters, "The Brand Called You," FastCompany.com, August 31, 1997.

240 *Still, each of us is human:* Peter Gruber, "Apple, Gabrielle Giffords, Toyota: When Good Stories Go Bad," *Huffington Post*, February 8, 2011.

241 *Here's one: the designer Kenneth Cole thought he'd be clever and tie:* Mark Pasetsky, "Kenneth Cole Apologizes for 'Absolutely Inappropriate' Egypt Tweet," Forbes.com, February 3, 2011.

243 *'Fess up, and as soon as possible:* Shelley Wigley, "Telling Your Own Bad News: Eliot Spitzer and a Test of the Stealing Thunder Strategy," *Public Relations Review* 37 (2011): 50–56.

INDEX

Acceptance, 7
Achievement, 5
Activity, 67
Adaptation, 155, 158, 162
Advertising, 12, 186
    money spent on, 12
    neuro-based techniques, 12
Advertising Age, 12
Advocacy models of decision
        making, 111
Aflec, 186
Agendas, 62, 135, 137
Aggression, 15
AIG, 191
Albarracín, Dolores, 20
Albrecht, Karl, 29
Alcock, James, 46, 47
Alinsky, Saul, 216
Allies, 135–36
Altemeyer, Robert, 163
Amazon, 191
Ambivalence, 91–93
Amway, 176
Anchoring, 82–83
Anger
    customers, 179
    proclivity to, 15
Apple (computers), 13, 175, 176, 191
Architects, 108
Argument, 37–38
Ariely, Dan, 9, 78
Aristotle, 31
Aroma dispensers, 12
Asgari, Shaki, 169
Ash, Mary Kay, 175–76

Assessment tools, 101
Association learning, 45
Associations, 242
Attitude, 57, 135
Audience, 211–14
Auto industry, 178
Availability, 85

Bad news, 243–44
Bakker, Jim, 176
Bakker, Tammy Faye, 176
Balz, John, 108, 109
Bank of America, 178–79
Banks, 1, 71, 178–79
Baron, Robert, 107
Baylor University, 53
Beal, Andy, 182, 185, 186
Beaver, The, 240
Beck, Glenn, 216
Behavioral economics, 9, 10–12
Behaviors, 69–72
Belief systems, 6, 20, 44–46, 50.
        See also Values
    critical thinking unit, 46–47
    emotional response unit, 46, 48
    environmental feedback unit,
        46, 48
    input unit, 46–48
    leadership and, 103–5
    learning unit, 46–47
    memory unit, 46, 48
    yearning unit, 46–47
Belittling, 188
Benefits, 149
Benevolence, 6

Berra, Yogi, 244
Biases, 36, 84–86, 89
  smart people, 116
Bill and Melinda Gates Foundation,
  191
Blair, Tony, 76
Blankenship, Don, 188
Blaring, 188
Blasting, 188
Blink (Gladwell), 87
Bloggers, 218–19
Bluring, 188
Body instincts, 87
Boosting, 188
Bosses, influencing, 139–54
  executive presence, 139–43
  managing perceptions of peers,
    152–54
  neutralizing critics, 151–52
  selling ideas, 147–48
  small talk, 150–51
  techniques, 148–50
Boyatzis, Richard, 27, 92
Brain, 4
  belief and, 44
  choice and, 10
  conceptual structures, 197
  gender and, 156–58
  patterns and, 44–45
Braman, Donald, 49
Branding, 119–20, 186–87,
    189–94
  accidental, 228–32
  brand inventory, 190
  brand support, 190
  competition, 236–39, 242–43
  consistency, 190, 237, 240
  influential brands, 234–36
  marketing tactics, 190
  online, 231–32
  personal brands, 225–45, 236–39
  positioning, 190, 236–39
  relevance, 190
  sabotaging, 239–44
  self-branding, 232–34

uniqueness, 236–37
  value and, 238
  visibility, 238–39, 241
Branson, Richard, 229–30
British Petroleum, 179–80
Brock University, 15
Broda-Bahm, Ken, 53–54
Brown, Shona, 104–5
Buckley, William F., 38
Bullying, 19, 133–34
Burke, Warner, 148
Burkitt, Laurie, 191
Burnishing, 188
Burying, 188
Bush, George W., 200
Business as usual, 7
Buy-in, 147
*Buy-In: Saving Your Good Idea
    from Getting Shot Down*
    (Kotter), 151

Cahill, Larry, 157
California State University, 120
Cantor, Nancy, 26, 28
Carter, Nancy, 21
Caruso, David, 27
Catalyst, 127, 163
Caterpillar, 191
Center of Applied Linguistics,
  62
CEOs, 73–74, 175, 179, 245
Chairs, 16
Chance, 90
Change, 55
  cycle of, 7
  versus status quo, 43–44
Changing jobs, 91–92, 93–95
Chanos, Jim, 80–81
Character
  first impressions, 21
  judge of character, 15–16, 21
  trust, 21
Charismatic connector, 68
Checklists, 109
Chiodo, Keri, 87

Choices, 10, 37–38, 62, 75. *See also* Decision making; Leadership
  choice architects, 108–12
  default options, 109
  health insurance, 110
  limited options, 105–6
  structuring, 108–12
Christian Science Monitor, 219
Cicero, 195
Cider House Rules (Irving), 218
Cisco, 189
Clarification, 65
Climate change, 49
Clinton, Hilary, 216, 230
Clipboards, 16
Coalitions, 135–36
Coca-Cola, 191
Coercive power, 129
Cognitive intelligence, 21
Cognitive structures, 197–98
Cole, Kenneth, 241
Coleman, Daniel, 27
Collaboration, 18
Collectivism, 103
Columbia University, 61, 148
Common Sense (Paine), 216–17
Communication, 195–223. *See also* Speaking skills; Writing skills
  blind spots, 101
  gender and, 160–62
Company profiles, 186. *See* Organizations, reputations
Compaq, 74
Competition
  branding, 236–39, 242–43
  for resources, 3–4
Complaining, 194
Computers, 90–91
Confidence, 143, 144–46
Conflict, 107
  gender and, 160–62
Conformity, 5
Consensus, 107
Consistency, 67, 237, 240

Consumer Product Safety Commission (CPSC), 180
Consumers, 173–94
Control, 85–86
Corkindale, Gill, 122, 136
Corporations, cultures of, 104
Cost analysis, 149
Côté, Stéphane, 28, 29
Courage, 149
Credibility, 56, 235
Crisis management, 179, 182
Critical thinking, 38–39, 46, 47
Critics, neutralizing, 151–52
Crowd thinking, 11
Cultural Cognition Project, 50
Culture, 6–7, 103
  fitting into, 119–20
  individualism *versus* collectivism, 103
  masculinity *versus* femininity, 104
  political culture, 125–28
  power distance, 103
  uncertainty avoidance, 104
Cummings, Anne, 159
Customer satisfaction, 189, 190
Cynicism, 139–40

Dallas Cowboys, 175
Dartmouth College's Tuck School of Business, 189
Dasgupta, Nilanjana, 169
Dattner, Ben, 123
Dean Foods, 191
Decision making, 37, 73–97. *See also* Leadership
  advocacy models of, 111
  belief and, 49–50, 103–5
  choice architects, 108–12
  conflict and, 107
  consequences of decisions, 74–75
  default options, 109
  dumb decisions, 79–81
  heuristics and biases, 89
  information and, 77–78, 96

inquiry model of, 111
mistakes, 109
natural decision making, 89
outcomes of decisions, 78–79
process, 75–78
regrets and, 93, 95
saying no, 97
tools, 95–97
traps, 81–85
uncertainty and, 49–50
values and, 103–5
Default options, 109
Demosthenes, 195
Denial, 7
Denning, Stephen, 203
Dezenhall, Eric, 179
Dickey-Wicker Amendment, 200
*Differentiate or Die: Survival in
Our Era of Killer Competition*
(Trout and Rivkin), 187
Differentiation, 242
Digital footprints, 69–72
Directions, 157
Discipline. *See* Self-regulation
Discrimination, 171
Disengagement at meetings,
114–15
Dolan, Cheryl, 133
Donenfeld, Jill, 233
Drucker, Peter, 148
Dun & Bradstreet Credibility Corp.,
88
Dunn, Allison, 123
Dunn, Barry, 87
Durbin, Andrew, 134

*Earning Serendipity: 4 Skills for
Creating and Sustaining Good
Fortune in Your Work* (Llopis),
142
Economics, understanding of, 40
Economist, 158
Educational level, 50
Embryonic stem cell research,
200–202

Emergent concerns, 194
Emotional Competency Inventory
(EIC), 27
Emotional intelligence, 21, 27–31,
39, 165
Empathic accuracy, 60–62
Empathy, 27, 60–62
Enforcers, 131–32
Environmental design, 105
Environmental feedback, 46, 48
Environmental responsibility, 13
Error acknowledgment, 193
Error correction, 194
Evidence, 53
confirming, 83–84
Executive presence, 139–43
Executive Presence (Monarth), 30
Expectations, 241
Experimentation, 35
Experts, 49, 50, 143–44, 235
expert power, 129
Explaining, 194
External threat, 7
Extroverts, 145–46

Face-to-face meetings. *See* In-person
meetings
Facebook, 69–70, 175, 176, 191,
232
Facial expressions, 15–16
Facial-width-to-height ratio, 15
Falwell, Jerry, 176
Fear of failure, 13
Federer, Roger, 31
Feedback, 34
assessment tools, 101
environmental feedback, 46, 48
timing, 13
Feldhahn, Shaunti, 166
Feng shui, 17
Films
architects in, 108
Fiorina, Carly, 73–74
Firefighting, 89
First impressions, 21

Fisher College of Business, 15
Flattery, 153
Florida State University, 19
Focus, 35
Forbes, 191
Fordham University, 169
Forethought, 88
Foster, Jodie, 240
Fox, Michael J., 201
Framing, 84, 196–202
Freedman, Joshua, 28
French, John, 128, 129
Furrowed brow, 16

Galbraith, John Kenneth, 43
Gambler's fallacy, 10
Garcia, Stephen, 84
Gardner, Howard, 26–27
Garvin, David, 78, 107
Gates, Bill, 176
Gawande, Atul, 109
GE, 175
Geary, David, 4
Geico, 186
Gender issues. *See also* Men;
    Women
  brain, 156–58
  communication, 160–62
  conflict, 160–62
  continuums, 160–62
  influencing opposite gender,
      155–72
  leadership styles, 158–60
  mixed-gender teams, 168–72
  stereotypes, 164–65, 166
  tokenism, 167
General Electric corporation, 104,
    206
General Motors, 107–8
George, Bill, 179
Ghosn, Carlos, 185
Gibson, Mel, 240
Gladwell, Malcolm, 87, 106
Glick, Peter, 164
Global warming, 50

Goals, 32–33, 34, 56–57, 186
  organizational, 56
  progress, 33, 35
  size of, 35
Goffman, Erving, 232–33
Goldberg, Lewis, 88
Goldsmith, Marshall, 147
Gonzalez, Juan, 243
Google corporation, 104–5, 191
Googling, 70
Gossip, 124
Graham, David, 53
Grant, Adam, 145
Grapevine, 124, 244
Graphics, 110
Gratton, Lynda, 171–72
Grenny, Joseph, 146
Grocery stores, 105–6
Grognet, Allene, 62
Group exclusion, 19–20
Group inclusion, 19–20
Groupon, 177
Groupthink, 106–8, 112–13
Grove, William, 88
Gut check, 96

H. J. Heinz, 191
Habits, 69–72
Hallett, Tim, 124
Hallowell, Edward M., 22
Hammond, John, 82, 93
Hansen, Randall S., 152
Harger, Brent, 124
Harvard Business Review, 77, 88, 163,
    176, 192
Harvard Medical School, 22
Haynes, Michelle, 163
Hayward, Tony, 179–80
Health insurance, 110
Hedonism, 5
Heilman, Madeline, 163
Helicobacter pylori, 51–53
Hellman, Yael, 159
Hemingway, Ernest, 38
Hemp, Paul, 176–77

Herd mentality, 11
Hersh, Seymour, 76–77
Heuristics, 49
  decision making, 89
High-validity environment, 89
Hiring decisions, 21
Hitchens, Christopher, 38
Hoag, Hannah, 157
Hofstede, Gert, 103
Homeostasis, 32
Huffington Post, 179
Humphrey, Nicholas, 28–29
Hurd, Mark, 73
Hussein, Saddam, 76
Hyatt, Joel, 175

Iacocca, Lee, 175
Ibarra, Herminia, 163
Ideas, selling, 147–48
Illusion of control, 85–86
Illusion of optimism, 85–86
Illusions, 84–86
Image restoration, 179, 180, 187
In-person meetings, 22
Incentives, 110
Indecision, 91–93
Individualism, 103
Influence, 67
  context and, 105–8, 112–18
  demographics, 18–22
  exposure to, 2–3
  industry examples, 1
  influence challenges of women,
    162–65
  influencing bosses, 139–54
  influencing the opposite gender,
    155–72
  irrational behavior and, 8–10
  language of, 196–202
  leveraging, 136–37
  mixed-gender teams, 168–72
  organizational politics, 133–37
  power and, 2–3
  public relations, 173–94
  scenarios, 12–18
  skills for, 36–42

strategy, 22–23
traits, 18–22
values and, 5–8 (*see also* Values)
*Influencer: The Power to Change
  Anything* (Grenny), 146
Information, 77–78, 96
  complex, 115–16
  detailed, 115–16
  options and, 110
  relevance, 96
Inner dialogue, 36
Innovation, 68, 235
Inquiry model of decision making,
  111
Instinct, influence and, 2–3
Institute of Medicine (IOM), 156, 157
Intel, 191
Intelligence quotient, 21, 26–31
  gender, 158
Introverts, 145–46
Intuition, 87–91
  versus actuarial tables, 88
  skilled intuition, 89–91
Irrational behavior, 8–12
  stock market, 10–12
Irrational escalation, 113–14
Irving, John, 218

Janis, Irving, 106
Jeffery, Graham, 76
Jenkins-Smith, Hank, 49
Job performance, 28
Jobs, Steve, 175, 176
Johndrow, Anthony, 191
Johnson & Johnson, 190
Jones, Jerry, 175
Jones, Keith, 163
Journal of Contemporary Ethnography,
  124
Judge of character, 15–16, 21
Judgment suspension, 65

Kahan, Dan, 49
Kahneman, Daniel, 9, 10, 49, 84,
  86, 89
Keeney, Ralph, 82, 93

Keller, Kevin Lane, 189
Kellogg, 191
Kelly, Gary, 189
Kentucky Fried Chicken, 12
Kihlstrom, John, 26, 28
King, Billie, Jr., 233
Kingsolver, Barbara, 38
Kipling, Rudyard, 207
Klein, Gary, 89
Kliger, Doron, 17–18
Kotter, John, 151
Kraft Foods, 191
Kristof, Nicholas, 162, 164
Krotz, Joanna, 169

LaHood, Ray, 182
Lakoff, George, 197
Language, 206–11
    abstract words, 208
    adjectives, 207
    concrete words, 208
    metaphors, 197, 209
    power words, 210
    tactful, 117–18
    verbs, 207
Lawrence University, 164
Leadership, 18–19, 21, 28, 40–41,
        235
    agentic, 158
    assessment tools, 101
    blind spots, 101
    bullying, 133–34
    communal, 158–59
    enforcers, 131–32
    flawed, 74
    gender issues, 158–60
    influence challenges of women,
        162–65
    narcissism, 132
    skills, 168–69
    teaching, 101–2
    thought leaders, 191, 218, 221–23
Learning, 46–47
Leavey School of Business, 11
Legitimate power, 128
Leonard, Christiana, 156, 157

Letterman, David, 243–44
Lieberman, Simma, 161
Lighting, ambient, 13
Likeability, 20–21
Linkage, 147
LinkedIn, 70
Liposuction, 225–27
Lips, Hilary, 164
Listening
    active, 64–66
    with all senses, 62–66
Llopis, Glenn, 142
London School of Business, 171
Losses, cutting, 11
Lount, Robert, 15
Lovallo, Dan, 84, 86
Loyalty, 135, 152
Luntz, Frank, 209–10

Maclaren strollers, 180–82, 192
Madoff, Bernie, 79, 80–81
Male Factor, The (Feldhahn), 166
Mapping, 110
Marshall, Barry, 51–53
Mary Kay Cosmetics, 176
Masculinity, 14
Mass opinion, 50
Massachusetts Institute of
        Technology, 104
Massey Energy, 188–89
Material possessions, 20–21
Matthews, Chris, 216
Mayer, John, 27
Mayer-Salvey-Caruso
        Emotional Intelligence Test
        (MSCEIT), 28
McAfee, Andrew, 87, 88
McCain, John, 230
McLuhan, Marshall, 44
Medical field, 119–20
Medicine, 89
Medtronic, 179
Meeting management, 137
Meetings, disengagement at meetings,
        114–15
Memory, 46, 48

Men. *See also* Gender issues
  brains of, 156–58
  communication issues, 160–62
  conflict and, 160–62
  influence challenges, 165–67
  influencing opposite gender,
    155–72
  male leadership, 18–19
  masculinity *versus* femininity,
    104
  stereotypes, 166
  verbal skills, 166
Mercedes Benz, 13
Message
  core, 205–6
  mixed, 241
Metaphors, 197, 209
Microsoft, 191
Military, 159–60
Millard, John, 225–27
Miller, Arthur, 38
Mimicry, 67
Mind reading, 60–62
Mining, 188–89
Minority Report, 60
Mistakes, built-in corrections to,
    109
Mitchell, Rex C., 119, 134
Mixed-gender teams, 168–72
  working relations tips, 169–70
Moment awareness, 61
Morality, 149
Moran, Jim, 19
Motivation, 14–15, 27, 59–72
Mourning, 7
Moussa, Mario, 147
Moynihan, Brian, 179
Muhammed, A. A., 187

Namie, Gary, 133
Namie, Ruth, 133
Narcissism, 19, 132
NASA survey, 148
National Highway Transportation
    Agency, 182

National Scientific Council on the
    Developing Child, 29
Nature and Origins of Mass Opinion
    (Zaller), 50
Negotiations, 16, 137
Networking, 127
Neuromarketing, 12
New Scientist, 157
New structure (change), 7
New York Daily News, 180
New York Times, 79, 162, 219
New York University, 163
New Yorker, 109
Nicholson, Christie, 49
Nicklaus, Jack, 31
Nissan Motor Company, 185–86
No, importance of, 97
Nocero, Joe, 79
Northwestern University's Kellogg
    School of Management, 153
Notre Dame, 104
Nuclear waste disposal, 49

Obama, Barack, 216, 230
Oberholzer-Gee, Felix, 146
Obodaru, Otilia, 163
Ohio State University, 15
Oliver, Faith, 133
Op-Ed articles, 218–21
Optimism, 85–86
Organ donation, 109
  Illinois, 109
Organizational politics, 119–37
  definition, 120–21, 123
  management skill, 121–25
  strategies, 133–37
  tactics, 133–37
  trust and, 123
Organizations, 6
  base of, 192
  family-friendly policies, 172
  mixed-gender teams, 168–72
  organizational politics, 119–37
  reputations, 173–94
  service-oriented, 176

Outcomes *versus* process, 95, 117
Outside view, 86, 96
Overwork, 56

Paine, Thomas, 216–17
Palin, Sarah, 230–31
Paradox of Choice, The (Schwartz), 105
Parent-child exchange, 2
Pasteur, Louis, 90
Paterson, David, 243–44
Paying attention, 64–65
Peer interaction, 100–101
Peer perception, 152–54
Pentland, Alex, 66–68
PepsiCo, 191
Perceptions
    executive presence, 139–43
    organizational politics, 120–21
    others of you, 99–102
    peer, 152–54
    product safety, 182
    self-branding, 232–34
    strategies for influencing, 185–90
    tactics for influencing, 185–90
Perner, Lars, 103
Persona, 230
Personal intelligence, 27
Pfeffer, Jeffrey, 101–2, 130
Philanthropy, 191
Physical attractiveness, 14
Political culture, 125–28
    participation in, 126
    unwritten rules, 127–28
Political elites, 50
Portfolio, 74, 80–81
Power, 2–3, 5
    assessment, 128–31
    coercive, 129
    expert, 129
    legitimate, 128
    power distance, 103
    referent, 129
    reward power, 128–29
Predictably Irrational (Ariely), 9

Preferences, 69–72
    ordering structures, 103
Presentation of Self in Everyday Life, The (Goffman), 232–33
Pricing, 190
Priming, 17–18, 166, 170
Prince, The (Machiavelli), 216
Priorities
    conflicting, 35–36
Process questioning, 96
Process *versus* outcome, 95, 117
Proctor & Gamble, 12
Progress, 33, 35
Promises, 240–41
Proposals, 56–57
Prospect theory, 10
Psychological operations, 3
Psychological Science, 15
Psychometric Success, 30
Public relations, 173–94
Putting Diversity to Work (Lieberman), 161
Pychyl, Timothy, 32–33

Questioning information, 96
Questioning process, 96

Radford University, 164
Radically Transparent: Monitoring and Managing Reputations Online (Beal), 182, 185
Raiffa, Howard, 82, 93
Randomness, 10
Rastegar, Farzad, 180–82
Rationality
    thick rationality, 103
    thin rationality, 103, 111
Raven, Bertram, 128, 129
Reading between lines, 66–69
Reality mining, 67–68
Reeve, Christopher, 201
Reference-class forecasting, 86
Referent power, 129
Reflection, 65
Regret, 93, 95

Rejections, 99–101
Relational strategy, 217
Reliability, 235
Renewal, 7
Representativeness, 85
Reputation Insatiate, 190
Reputation management, 173–94
    passim. See also Crisis
    management
Reputations, 173–94 *passim. See also*
    Perceptions
  crisis, 184
  day-to-day operations, 183
  importance of, 191
Resistance, 6, 43–57, 55
  change and, 43–44
  overcoming, 54–58
Resources, 3–4, 34
Reward power, 128–29
Rewards, 3–4
Rhee, Kenneth, 27
RIM, 191
Risk, 17–18
  avoiding losses, 11
  capturing gains, 11
Ritz-Carlton, 177, 192
Rivkin, Steve, 187
Roberto, Michael, 78, 107
Rolling Stone, 3
Rooney family, 175
Rotman School of Management, 21
Rubin, Robert, 76–77
Rudman, Laurie, 164
Rules for Radicals (Alinsky), 216
Rutgers University, 164

Sabattini, Laura, 127
Sabotage in the American Workplace
  (Sprouse), 177
Salience meter, 110–11
Salovey, Peter, 28
Sanford, Mark, 242
Sara Lee, 191
Schmooze factor, 141
School food, 1

Schwartz, Barry, 105
Science, 16
Scientific American, 44–45, 49
Security, 5
Self-awareness, 27, 92
Self-direction, 5
Self-image, 19
Self-regulation, 27, 31–36
Sharing, 66
Shell, G. Richard, 147
Shermer, Michael, 44–45, 103
Sides, John, 50
Sidhu, Inder, 189
Six Seconds Emotional Intelligence
  Assessment, 28
Skepticism, 95
Sloan, Alfred, 107–8, 111
Slogans, 203
Small talk, 150–51
Smart Choices: A Practical Guide
  to Making Better Decisions
  (Hammond *et al*), 82
Smith, Mark, 26–27
Smith, Marvin, 28
Snyder, Dan, 175
Social comparison bias, 84–85
Social identity, 13
Social intelligence, 21, 27–31,
  39
Social media, 69–72, 185, 241
Social skills, 27
Socialization, 19
Song, Hyunjin, 84
Southwest Airlines, 189, 191
Space, 16–17
Speaking skills, 39–40, 195–223
  passim
Spitzer, Eliot, 230, 243–44
Sprouse, Martin, 177
Stakeholders, 193
Stanford University, 130
Statman, Meir, 11
Status quo, 43–44, 83
Stealing thunder, 243–44
Steelers football team, 175

Stereotypes, 164
  confronting, 170
Stern, Ithai, 153
Stibel, Jeff, 88
Stimulation, 5
Stock market, 10–12, 17
Storytelling, 38, 192, 202–5
Studies
  acceptance of ideas, 163
  belief systems, 20
  brain, 4, 10
  empathic accuracy, 61
  extroverts, 145
  flattery, 153
  gossip, 124
  group exclusion, 19–20
  lighting, 13
  likeability, 20–21
  narcissism, 19
  parent-child, 2
  reality mining, 68
  risk, 17–18, 49, 50
  space, 16–17
  tactile environment, 16
  underdog, 14–15
  weight and seriousness, 16
  women in leadership, 164
Success, 154
Sullivan, Andrew, 90
Summarizing, 65–66
Sunk costs, 83
Sunstein, Cass, 108, 109
Superstitions, 80
Sutton, Robert, 133

Taco Bell, 186
Tactile environment, 16
Taxicabs, 1
Taylor, Bill, 192
Teaching, 101–2
Team leaders, 18
Team meetings, 213
Teams, mixed-gender, 168–72
Technical language, 110
Technology, understanding, 41

Tesser, Abraham, 84
Thaler, Richard, 9, 108, 109
Thermometers, cost-disclosing,
  110–11
Thompson, Suzanne, 84
Thorndike, E. L., 26
Thought leaders, 191, 218, 221–23
3M, 191
Time magazine, 216
Tokenism, 167
Toyota, 13, 182
Trader Joe's, 105–6
Tradition, 6
Training, 56–57
Transparency, 71–72
Trends, 106
Trout, Jack, 187
Trust, 21, 22, 56
  organizational politics and, 123
Tversky, Amos, 9, 10, 49, 84
Twitter, 70, 231–32, 241

Ulcers, peptic, 51–53
Uncertainty, 49–50
  uncertainty avoidance, 104
Underdog, 14–15
Universalism, 6
Universities, cultures of, 104
University of California at Berkeley,
  104, 197
University of Colorado (Boulder),
  20
University of Florida's McKnight
  Brain Institute, 156
University of Haifa, 17
University of Manitoba, 163
University of Massachusetts, 169
University of Michigan's Ross School
  of Business, 153
University of Minnesota, 10, 159
University of Texas at Arlington, 243
University of Toronto, 21
UPS, 191
URLs, 179
U.S. Army, 3

U.S. Military Academy at West Point, 104
U.S. Senate, 3
U.S. universities, 104
USA Today, 219

Values, 50, 57
  cool and hip, 13
  decision making and, 103–5
  environmental responsibility, 13
  status, 13
  as targets for influence, 5–8
Van Boven, Leaf, 20
Van Duzer, Carol, 62
van Harreveld, Frank, 92
Variables, 95–96
Visibility, 238–39, 241
Vision, 163
Vonn, Lindsay, 31

Wall Street Journal, 92, 219
Walt Disney Company, 191
Wang, Shirley, 92
Warren, Robin, 51–53
Washington Post, 219
Washington Redskins, 175
Watson (computer), 90
Weapons, concealed, 49
Weber, Mark, 21
Websites
  Monkey Cage, 49
  Psychometric Success, 29
Weinberger, David, 77
Welch, Jack, 104, 175, 206
Westphal, James, 153
Wharton, 145, 147
White papers, 221

Whitehead, Lorne, 151
Whole Foods, 191
Whyte, William, 106
Wiesel, Elie, 80
Wigley, Shelley, 243–44
WIIFM, 211
Wilson, Woodrwo, 43
Winfrey, Oprah, 227–28
Women, 18. *See also* Gender issues
  brains of, 156–58
  Catalyst, 127
  communication issues, 160–62
  conflict and, 160–62
  female leadership, 18–19
  influence challenges, 162–65
  influencing opposite gender, 155–72
  masculinity *versus* femininity, 104
  "niceness" problem, 164
Woodbury University, 159
Woods, Tiger, 243–44
Writing skills, 38–39, 195–223 *passim*
  empathy, 216
  relational strategy, 217
  rhetoric, 215
Wynn, Steve, 210

Yale University, 16
Yale University Law School, 50
Yamada, Tachi, 53
York University, 46

Zaki, Jamil, 61
Zaller, John, 50
Zappos, 192
Zuckerberg, Mark, 175

ABOUT THE AUTHOR

New York Times bestselling author Harrison Monarth is a leader in the field of message development, personal branding, and speaker coaching. He is the founder of GuruMaker School of Professional Speaking and one of the most sought-after speech and presentation coaches and communication consultants in the United States. Harrison regularly advises Fortune 500 companies and prepares CEOs, executives, political candidates, and other leading professionals for high-stakes presentations, speaking opportunities, and other communication challenges.

Harrison has personally coached leaders from major organizations in the financial services, technology, medical, legal, hospitality, and consumer industries, as well as real estate, nonprofit, and politics. His client list includes IBM, Merrill Lynch, US Bank, PepsiCo, Intel, Cisco Systems, DHL, Prudential, American Heart Association, Abraham Lincoln Presidential Library and Museum, Haas School of Business, Cardinal Health, Northrop Grumman, Coldwell Banker, Hertz, and many other leading corporations, as well as political candidates and members of Congress.

Harrison's *New York Times* bestselling book *The Confident Speaker* (McGraw-Hill 2007) is based on years of research and practice in the field of persuasive communication and high-impact speaking. His 2009 book *Executive Presence—The Art of Commanding Respect like a CEO* (McGraw-Hill) is considered a key resource by leading executives in executive leadership development.

Harrison resides in New York City.